The Living Voice
of the Gospel

The Living Voice of the Gospel

The Gospels Today

Francis J. Moloney, SDB

PAULIST PRESS
New York/Mahwah

First published in the United States by
PAULIST PRESS
997 Macarthur Boulevard, Mahwah, NJ 07430

Original publication by Collins Dove, Melbourne, Australia

Cover design by Mary Goodburn
Typeset in Australia in 11/12½ Vladimir by
ProComp Productions Pty Ltd, South Australia
Printed in Australia by Globe Press Pty Ltd, Victoria

ISBN 0-8091-2887-X

Contents

Preface   vii
Acknowledgements   xii
Note on Quotations   xii
List of Abbreviations   xii

I. Reading a Gospel

1. Reading a Gospel Today   3

II. The Gospel of Mark

2. Reading the Gospel of Mark   27
3. Reading Mark 8:22-10:52:
   The Way of the Son of Man   43

III. The Gospel of Luke

4. Reading the Gospel of Luke   67
5. Reading Luke 1-2: The Infancy Narrative   93

IV. The Gospel of Matthew

6. Reading the Gospel of Matthew   117
7. Reading Matthew 27:32-28:20: The Cross
   and Resurrection   145

V. The Gospel of John

8. Reading the Gospel of John   161
9. Reading John 1:19-4:54: A Question of
   Faith   203

VI. A Living Gospel

10. "The Living Voice of the Gospel"   223
    (*Dei Verbum* 8). Some Reflections on the
    Dynamism of the Christian Tradition

Index of Gospel References   245

For Oakleigh 1976–1985
With Thanks

Preface

I have always been impressed by the fact that the gospels resonate deeply in the hearts and minds of people who have followed lectures, courses, seminars or days of reflection dedicated to some form of gospel study. Some say that they had never realised that the gospel story, which is very familiar to us in many ways, was so inspiring. This reaction is always comforting and encouraging, but there is another side to the story.

I am increasingly concerned over the widespread lack of knowledge and the indifference towards these privileged sources for the revelation of the Word of God. There is a readiness to speak enthusiastically about the Word of God and its central importance in our lives, but we fall short when it comes to doing the hard work necessary to make an important (but not the only) source of that Word of God come alive: to read a text written nearly two thousand years ago as a 'word of life' can be a difficult task indeed.

Sunday masses go by week after week without congregations being aware that the church offers us a continuous reading of the three Synoptic Gospels over a three-year cycle. This lack of awareness, of course, does not always arise from a lack of good will on the part of either pastor or congregation. A rarefied atmosphere surrounds much biblical exegesis, and biblical scholars tend to lose themselves in the niceties of their very specialised trade. Thus the pastor does not feel confident enough to lead his congregation through a continuous reading of the gospels, and falls back on the system of "looking for a point to make".

This is not what the church wants. We are given our renewed lectionary for a purpose. If we are using our cele-brations of the liturgy of the word well, we would soon have whole communities aware that there are four gospels, and that each of these gospels is a remarkable and inspired contact with the person and the message of Jesus of Nazareth.

I am well aware that it is easy for a highly trained specialist to point the finger at the "man on the shop floor". The task of the contemporary Christian to integrate his Christian values with the ever-increasing pace of contemporary life and of the clergyman to speak relevantly into that situation is becoming more and more difficult. The fact that we are still tied to a "parochial system", which worked marvellously in the stability of the European villages for centuries, but which trails sadly behind the demands of the highly mobile urban situations of today, does not make the task any easier.

I have no intention of standing on the sidelines, raising a questioning finger at the people who are caught in the pell-mell of the play on the field. Much less do I want to be a referee, judging the value, importance or rightness of how the play is going. On the contrary, I am anxious to be in the centre of the play, doing what I can to contribute to a better and more widespread understanding and appreciation of the basic rules of the game: to point out the relevance of the life-style of Jesus of Nazareth, as it is communicated to us through those first-century documents, declared "inspired" by the church, which we call "gospels".

The reflections that follow are the result of many hours devoted to the study and teaching of the gospels. I have attempted to write in a direct and simple fashion, continually addressing myself to my reader, trying to avoid all the byways into which a purely scholarly approach could lead us. However, the suggestions contained in this book, both in terms of the overall structure and theologies of the gospels, are the fruit of my endeavours to keep in touch with contemporary scholarship.

The specialist who reads this book will be able to put authors' names and titles of books to various suggestions I make. However, there will also be occasions where he or she will find that I am striking out on a line peculiar to me. In both my use of the work of other scholars and my personal contributions to the following reflections, my aim is to reach a better understanding of the texts themselves. So this book is best read with the gospels open alongside you. However, as this is not always possible, I report the text and try to "tell the story" throughout my analysis. Ultimately, what matters is not what scholars say to you, but what the gospels themselves say to you.

A few chapters in this book have appeared elsewhere, but nothing here is simply a reprint of an earlier publication. Every word has been rethought and retyped in the last months of 1985 into an Olivetti M24 Personal Computer belonging to the Faculty of Theology at the Salesian Pontifical University, Rome.

As I have been known to say *ad nauseam*, it is my conviction that we have everything to gain and nothing to lose from a serious and critical approach to our sources. I feel deeply hurt when I read and hear a biased and uncritical use of gospel material to prove points or to resolve issues it was never intended to address. In my experience the growing sophistication of believers today gives many people an ability to make public their innate intuitions that such an uncritical use of the Scriptures rings false. In my own Catholic tradition this is a particularly important issue, which will have to be resolved, no matter how long it takes and how much hard work must be devoted to it. We look to our church leaders, especially our bishops—an *essential* part of the structure of the Catholic Church—as the authoritative interpreters of the Word of God. It is vitally important that they be just that.

This work is offered in order to give some direction as to how one should read a gospel, with one eye on the origin and purpose of the documents themselves, and another on the all-important questions of Christian life and practice today. Its structure is simple. After a general introduction to the reading of a gospel, I have devoted two chapters to each of the four gospels. The first of each of these pairs of chapters introduces the argument and major theological issues found within the gospel under consideration. Then there is a reflection on the specifically Marcan, Lucan, Matthean or Johannine point of view in a given section of the gospel texts themselves. The passages for more detailed consideration were selected to demonstrate the different "forms" of literature that one can find in the gospels. We shall analyse the teaching of Jesus, an infancy story, a passion and resurrection account and the uniquely theological use of narrative found in the fourth gospel.

There are now many good books on the gospels, and I shall indicate some of the best of these in my footnotes. I shall keep such notes to essentials, to avoid the confusion that can be created by the trappings of a complete documentation of every issue. This book on the gospels is intended for the many people who are still looking for a key to unlock the treasures of this part of our tradition.

The conclusion to this book is a reflection on the dynamism that has always been a part of the revelation of the Word of God in the Scriptures and in the Tradition. Rather than theorise on the issue, I have taken some examples that indicate this dynamic presence of the Spirit in God's revelation of himself, his Son and his ways. Basing myself on the principles that I hope become clear through a reading of the book itself, I consider a brief section of the Second Vatican Council's document on Divine Revelation, and some christological and mariological themes from the gospels. I offer these as examples of what the Fathers of the Second Vatican Council described as "the living voice of the Gospel" (*Dei Verbum* 8). Despite what the council may have said, the suggestion that traditions grow and develop is not always a welcome one. In its various shapes and forms, this claim stands at the centre of many of the ideological conflicts that exist in Christian churches today. I have tried to deal with this matter in an objective and caring way. Sometimes the discussion of these issues generates great heat—and very little light.

The dedication of this book may puzzle some readers. I have spent the last ten years working among and for the students of Theology at Salesian Theological College, Oakleigh, Victoria, Australia. They have been intensely busy and happy years. Naturally, I have had to work hard to challenge superficiality, to ensure that it was the Word of God that we were listening to and not the words of men and women. Anyone who has worked in the area of priestly and religious formation will be aware of these tasks. My success or failure has been directly related to my own personal living of the values that I have been trying to communicate. That, too, almost goes without saying. However, no matter what the difficulties and conflicts may have been over these years, I have learnt more about the way of the Gospel from the men whom I was supposed to have been forming than from any scholarship. As I celebrate my own twenty-fifth anniversary of religious profession, I am able to acknowledge gratefully that it is life, love and death that ultimately teach us the way of the Lord.

To all the Salesians who have been a part of my journey at Oakleigh, this book is gratefully dedicated.

Oakleigh   Francis J. Moloney, SDB
31 January 1986
Feast of Saint John Bosco

Acknowledgements

Some of the chapters of this book have appeared, in an earlier form, in the following collections:

Chapter 3, "Reading Mark 8:22-10:52: The Way of the Son of Man", first appeared as "The Way of the Son of Man (Mark 8:22-10:52)", in H. McGinlay (ed.), *The Year of Mark* (Melbourne, Desbooks/JBCE, 1984), pp. 50-63.

Chapter 5, "Reading Luke 1-2: The Infancy Narrative", first appeared as "The infancy narrative of Luke", in H. McGinlay (ed.), *The Year of Luke* (Melbourne, Desbooks/JBCE, 1982), pp. 1-10.

Chapter 9, "Reading John 1:19-4:54: A Question of Faith", first appeared as "The first days . . . from Cana to Cana (John 1:19-4:54", in H. McGinlay (ed.), *The Years of John* (Melbourne, Desbooks/JBCE, 1985), pp. 9-17.

Note on Quotations

Unless otherwise stated, Scripture quotations are taken from the Revised Standard Version of the Bible, copyright 1952 and 1971 by the division of Christian Education of the National Council of the Churches of Christ in the USA. On a few occasions the author provides his own translation. This will be indicated by the abbreviation AT. Quotations from the Second Vatican Council are taken from A. Flannery (ed.), *Vatican Council II. The Conciliar and Post Conciliar Documents* (Dublin, Dominican Publication, 1975).

List of Abbreviations

AT	Author's translation
JBCE	Joint Board of Christian Education
JSNT	Journal for the Study of the New Testament
JSOT	Journal for the Study of the Old Testament
SCM	Student Christian Movement
SPCK	Society for the Propagation of Christian Knowledge

PART I
Reading
a Gospel

1.
Reading
a Gospel Today

One of the most important contributions that modern biblical research has made to the interpretation of the New Testament, and especially of the gospels, is to emphasise theological, rather than historical, questions.[1] Yet the historical origins of the Christian message must never be lost in the subjective search of the contemporary reader for an "existential" understanding of the text. Such interpretations are often based on their relevance for an interpreter and his or her particular situation and religious point of view. Nevertheless, modern Gospel study is surely correct when it insists that the documents are *primarily* theological. What exactly is meant

1. See especially R. A. Spivey and D. M. Smith, *Anatomy of the New Testament. A Guide to Its Structure and Meaning* (London, Macmillan, 1982), pp. 59–206, and E.Charpentier, *How to Read the New Testament* (London, SCM Press, 1982), pp. 8–41, 57–104. My familiarity with these two excellent introductions guided me to adopt the approach used in this book. These authors provide the usual general discussions of the authors, the historical setting and major thrust of each of the New Testament works. However, they also analyse a section of the gospel or epistle under discussion to show that particular New Testament author at work. Concentrating only on the gospels, I have been able to broaden both aspects.

by this claim needs further explanation, as it is the key to the issue we are considering: reading a gospel today.

The Gospels and the Life of Jesus

If one reads the gospels carefully, one finds that it is impossible to trace a simple historical account of the life of Jesus, to summarise what he said, or to trace his movements with any certainty. We talk about "the Gospel", but it soon becomes apparent that even though the four gospels have a great amount of material that is similar and even identical (and thus we call three of them Synoptic Gospels[2]), there are many passages that at first sight appear to be identical, but which, on closer reading, are reported in confusingly different ways.

Matthew 5:1-7:28, for example, contains what is commonly called the Sermon on the Mount. Matthew sets the scene for the discourse by telling his readers: 'Seeing the crowds, he *went up on the mountain*, and when he sat down *his disciples* came to him. And he opened his mouth and taught *them*, saying . . ." (Matthew 5:1-2). The sermon then proceeds, uninterrupted, until 7:28, where Matthew concludes: "And when Jesus finished these sayings, *the crowds* were astonished at his teaching." Was he speaking to his disciples, after leaving the crowds (as in 5:1-2), or were the crowds present all the time (as in 7:28)?

In the Gospel of Matthew three chapters are devoted to the sermon, which contains a Matthean synthesis of the moral injunctions of Jesus. His disciples and/or the crowds are told

2. The use of the word "synoptic" indicates that the reader can place Matthew, Mark and Luke side by side and compare the three different accounts with one glance (Greek: sun-opsis: "with the eye"). There are most useful books that present the three Synoptic Gospels in parallel columns to facilitate a comparative study of the way in which each evangelist has used the same tradition. The most useful English "synopsis" (using the Revised Standard Version text) is B. Throckmorton, *Gospel Parallels. A Synopsis of the First Three Gospels* (London/New York, Nelson, 1979).

clearly what is demanded of them if they are to follow Christ. They are to be perfect, as their heavenly Father is perfect (see 5:48). This significant discourse, given solemnly on the top of a mountain, must have marked a memorable day in the public life of Jesus. However, if we look at the gospels of Mark and John, we find no trace of such a day. So, anyone hoping to find history, in the twentieth-century sense of that word, in the gospels, would remain somewhat perplexed.

At first glance it looks as if there may be some consolation in Luke 6:17-49, where a similar discourse is found. However, a careful reading of Luke's passage within its own context shows even more difficulties. In verse 12 Jesus goes up onto a mountain to pray. After praying through the night, Jesus chooses his twelve apostles (verses 13-16). The Lucan text continues:

> And he *came down* with them and stood on a *level place*, with a great crowd of his disciples and a *great multitude of people* from all Judea and Jerusalem and the seacoast of Tyre and Sidon, who came to hear him and to be healed of their diseases; and those who were troubled with unclean spirits were cured. And all the crowd sought to touch him, for power came forth from him and healed them all.

The discourse then follows for thirty-two verses, in a version that abbreviates what Matthew's Gospel had reported. However, everything in Luke 6:17-49 can be found, often in a slightly different form, in the much longer Matthew 5:1-7:28.

Was it on a mountain? Or on a level place? Was it to his disciples? To an unspecified crowd? Or to a great multitude of people, including non-Jews (Tyre and Sidon), who sought to hear his word and be cured? Did he say all that we find in the three chapters of Matthew? Or only the thirty-two verses of Luke? Why is there no trace of the discourse in Mark and John? If we are determined to understand the gospels as a "Life of Jesus", as we of the twentieth century understand the life-story of any great person, these are insurmountable difficulties.

The Gospel
as Good News

We can begin to find some sort of solution to the problem, however, in what was probably the very first line of the first gospel to be written: Mark 1:1. This verse runs: "The beginning of the *gospel* of Jesus Christ, the Son of God." We are not told that the book that this verse prefaces is going to be a life story, but a "gospel". The Greek word for gospel is *evangelion*, but this word does not mean "life-story". It has a long history in the Greek language, and it is associated with the joyful proclamation of good news: victory in battle, the arrival of the king and similar great and joyful events for the people.[3] The evangelists had no intention of writing a twentieth-century "Life of Jesus"; they had something quite different to do, and Mark is careful in his choice of words to let his readers know this fact. The "gospels" (the English word comes from the Old English translation of "good news": god-spel) were written to proclaim the good news that Jesus of Nazareth was the Christ, the Son of God, and to tell the further good news of the salvation that he had wrought by his death and resurrection.

How they did this was conditioned, in many ways, by the particular needs of the ecclesial community in which the evangelist lived, and for whom he wrote, but here we must also remember another important fact, too often neglected by modern scholars. In compiling their various versions of the "good news" about Jesus, who was the Christ, the Son of God, the evangelists went back to words and events from the life of Jesus himself. Jesus' words and deeds had been passed on by word of mouth (called oral tradition); they were recalled in the community's liturgical celebrations, and some of them may have been written down in documents that we no longer possess. These are just some of the more important places where the evangelists found the "traditions" that stand behind

3. See W. Marxsen, *Mark the Evangelist. Studies on the Redaction History of the Gospel* (Nashville, Abingdon, 1969), pp. 117–50.

their written gospels. Each one of them used these traditions in his own particular way, but each took them from the memory of the life and teaching of Jesus, a memory still very much alive in the earliest churches, for whom the evangelists wrote. The gospels *do* tell us about the life, the person and the activity of Jesus of Nazareth, but they were never intended to be *the* life of Jesus.

Once we are prepared to accept that the gospels are primarily theological documents, using words and events from the life of Jesus for their own particular purposes, then the problem of the Sermon on the Mount or the Plain vanishes. Many years of study of the Gospel of Matthew have led contemporary scholars to the almost unanimous conclusion that the gospel is very concerned with Israel and the Old Testament people of God. The Evangelist Matthew was anxious to show that Jesus had not broken with the chosen people of God. There could be no denying that the Christian community, of which Matthew was a member, was "different" from the synagogue, which they all used to attend in their pre-Christian days.

Yet, for many reasons, Matthew was anxious to show that this new people formed part of the ancient promise made to Israel. In order to make this clear, Jesus, therefore, often appears as the new and perfect Moses. This is already clear in the infancy stories, where the slaying of young children accompanies the birth of Jesus (Matthew 2:13-15; see Exodus 1:15-22; 2:1-10), and a passage from Hosea, originally referring to the Exodus, is applied to Jesus: "Out of Egypt have I called my son" (2:15, quoting from Hosea 11:1). However, Moses' great contribution to the formation of Israel as God's people was the reception of the Covenant on Mount Sinai (Exodus 19:10-20:21). With this background in mind, we are able to read through Matthew 5:1-7:28, a presentation of Jesus as the new Moses giving a new law for the new people of God. It is important to notice, however, that this new law does not abolish the old law. The law given by Jesus (notice that Jesus does not receive the law, as Moses did, he gives it by virtue of his own word and person) is the *perfection* of the old law (see especially Matthew 5:17-48). Now we can begin to see that the use of the mountain in the famous sermon is more than an indication of some geographical place by the side of the Lake of Galilee. From a new Sinai, Jesus proclaims the new law of God to a new people of God. The mountain is not just a historical note, but a profoundly important theological comment.

Luke's problem was different. New Testament scholarship has indicated that the community behind Luke's Gospel suffered from its own form of the tyranny of distance. It was clearly a Gentile community, a long way from the land, religion, language and religious history and culture that had produced Jesus and the Jesus-movement. As this community lived its Christianity within the context of its own history, and began to be quite settled in its own ways, the question began to be raised: do we really belong to those origins?

The clearest indication (among many) that Luke the Evangelist was writing into such a situation is found in the fact that he wrote two volumes. He wrote a gospel that had its beginnings in the Old Testament (Zechariah, Elizabeth, Anna, Simeon and John the Baptist in the infancy stories; see also Luke 16:16), and which then told the story of Jesus' life, death, resurrection and ascension. In Luke's Gospel (and only in Luke among the Synoptic Gospels) all the paschal events take place in Jerusalem. In The Acts of the Apostles he begins in Jerusalem, where his first volume ended. As this second volume opens, the risen Jesus commands his apostles to be his witnesses to the ends of the earth (Acts 1:8). The story of the first years of the life of the Christian church closes with Paul in the city of Rome ("the end of the earth") fearlessly preaching the kingdom of God and the Lord Jesus Christ (Acts 28:30-31).

For Luke, however, this was only the beginning. His two volumes are a powerful message to a Christian community that the journey of the church through history is never over. There was a danger that they might settle for what they had, but this would have been to misunderstand Jesus. The genius of Luke is found in the fact that, as time passed, he was able to remind the church—through his two volumes—that the Jesus-movement had to face the reality that its task still lay ahead. Jesus was not going to return in the very near future to destroy its opponents, to win over all opposition, and to reward the faithful, as Mark, especially, seemed to believe (see Mark 9:1 and chapter 13). For this reason, the Jesus of Luke's Gospel takes on a very special character. Luke the Evangelist wrote his account to convince his readers that in their task, which was to go on into the unpredictable future, the spirit of Jesus was with them. This spirit would guide them through their future as the witnesses of Jesus of Nazareth. In this role they would bring the good news of Jesus to the whole world. This meant, of course, that the Gospel was to be preached to people from non-Jewish nations. Luke insists, therefore, that Jesus himself preached his new moral code to all who wished to hear his word, and he brought a message of healing, of forgiveness, love and kindness to all who sought to reach out to him and touch him, to all who waited to hear his word (see Luke 6:17-19).

Which is the correct setting for the giving of the new law of Christ? If we claim that the gospels are historical, in the modern sense of the term, then either Luke or Matthew must have their "facts" wrong. But such is not the case. As we have seen from our glance at the theological use both Matthew and Luke make of the same material, which they have from their authentic Jesus-traditions, they are both correct.[4] They are two equally valid presentations of the mystery of Christ, which the church will continue to contemplate until the end of time. We must not try to harmonise them, as we would thus lose a great deal of the authentic revelation of God, given to us authoritatively in the various books of the New Testament. The point should be clear from this simple example.

4. Parts III and IV (chapters 4–7) of the present work will be devoted to the uniquely Matthean and Lucan contributions to the gospel tradition. See below, pp. 65–158. For an excellent and up-to-date study of the theology and purpose of the gospels of Matthew and Luke, see E. A. Laverdiere and W. G. Thompson, "New Testament Communities in Transition: A Study of Matthew and Luke", *Theological Studies* 37 (1976) 567–97.

Unless we are prepared to understand the gospels as theological documents, we both impoverish our understanding of God's revelation to us through the New Testament, and we do an injustice to the theological significance of each single gospel.

The Gospel and Literary Forms

Although these few pages are dedicated to a reading of the gospels, it is important to know that before the first gospel had been written (the Gospel of Mark) there had been the mighty theological synthesis of Paul, who was probably already martyred (about AD 64) by the time Mark's Gospel came to be written (about AD 70). The life, death and resurrection of Jesus unleashed an extraordinarily novel and rich understanding of God's ways with the world. The vision of Paul, completed only thirty years after the death of Jesus, is a remarkable witness to that fact. For our purposes, however, it is important to notice that Paul's writings, possibly written from the late 40s till the early 60s of the first century, show no interest in "telling the story" of Jesus of Nazareth.

I am stressing this because it is important to appreciate that the form of literature called "gospel" was rather late on the scene in the literary activity of the early church. I have just used an expression that is of great importance for the interpretation of literature: "form". We take literary forms for granted, and we read and interpret our modern "forms" of literature without noticing just what we are doing. Some examples may help. Each morning we take a daily paper and glance at the first headline on the first page. Spectacularly, this headline may be an enormous black word that covers the whole of the front page: WAR! That one word is a form of literature, which communicates profoundly to the reader. The reader may then turn the pages to seek out the editorial comment upon that headline. There he or she will find a reasoned analysis of what has happened, why it has happened, and what are the likely consequences: duration, damage, involvement of Australians, etc. Farther on, one may find an analysis of the current stock market, an important "form" of communication for those able to understand the significance of the figures involved. This list of different forms could go on through the newspaper, down to the comic strips and the sports pages. And only an Australian living in the State of Victoria towards the end of the winter of 1985 knows exactly what is meant by "Sheedy shuts gate on Flag!"[5]

These few examples of the different forms of communication and the different approaches that we subconsciously use in reading them is of great importance for the proper appreciation of the literature of the New Testament. There are several "forms" of literature in the New Testament, and it is impossible to list them all here. For our purposes, it is sufficient to indicate that there is the "gospel form" (Matthew, Mark, Luke and John), the "epistle form" (the letters of Paul) and the "apocalyptic form" (Revelation to John). These forms of literature can be found in a variety of places. For example, it can be argued that Mark 13 uses the apocalyptic form on the lips of Jesus, and that Revelation 2:1-3:22 contains a series of documents written in the epistle form.[6]

To the best of our knowledge the earliest form of literature produced in the Christian church was the epistle, as evidenced by the epistles of Paul. As I mentioned above, it is not part of this form of literature to "tell a story". Thus, if all we had from the earliest church were the letters of Paul, we would

5. For the uninitiated, this headline on the sports page of a Melbourne newspaper was commenting on the fact that the Essendon football club, coached by Kevin Sheedy, had won the Grand Final match of the Victorian Football League. A premiership "flag" is awarded to the winning club.

6. For a general presentation of the role the study of forms has had in modern biblical exegesis, see E. V. McNight, *What is Form Criticism?* (Philadelphia, Fortress Press, 1969). For a detailed discussion, with copious examples, of the gospel "forms", see the very clear introduction of W. Barclay, *The Gospels and Acts* (London, SCM Press, 1976), pp. 33–41. Perhaps the best introduction to the "forms" of the gospels is still V. Taylor, *The Formation of the Gospel Tradition* (London, Macmillan, 1957).

learn very little about the "story of Jesus". However, even here, we would learn three all-important facts:

(a) He was born of a woman, a Jewess: "when the time had fully come, God sent forth his Son, born of woman, born under the law" (Galatians 4:4).

(b) He instituted some sort of new passover meal, which was intimately connected with the proclamation of his death: "For I received from the Lord what I also delivered to you, that the Lord Jesus on the night when he was betrayed took bread, and when he had given thanks, he broke it, and said, 'This is my body which is for you. Do this in remembrance of me.' In the same way also the cup, after supper, saying, 'This cup is the new covenant in my blood. Do this, as often as you drink it, in remembrance of me.' For as often as you eat this bread and drink the cup, you proclaim the Lord's death until he comes" (I Corinthians 11:23-26).

(c) He died, was buried, rose and appeared: "For I delivered to you as of first importance what I also received, that Christ died for our sins in accordance with the scriptures, that he was buried, that he was raised on the third day in accordance with the scriptures, and that he appeared to Cephas, then to the twelve" (I Corinthians 15:3-5).

There is one element in these solitary biographical notes from Paul that should be noticed. In both I Corinthians 11 and 15, Paul tells the Corinthians that he is passing on something that he himself received:

For I received from the Lord what I also delivered to you. (I Corinthians 11:23)

For I delivered to you as of first importance what I also received. (I Corinthians 15:3)

This is the earliest indication in the New Testament that what we have about the life, person and teaching of Jesus is a *traditio* — a handing down. From here comes a word that is of enormous importance for an understanding of the gospels:

tradition. The "traditions" about Jesus were already important for Paul.[7] However, they form the very heart of the gospels, which build their stories of Jesus upon their own particular traditions. A brief analysis of a section of the Gospel of Mark should help us to appreciate this fact.

Mark 8:
A Story
Formed from Stories

In our brief analysis of the Sermon on the Mount/Plain we saw that Matthew and Luke used a piece of material common to them: it is not found in Mark. Both Matthew and Luke have used this material for their own theological and pastoral concerns. A study of Mark 8 will show us how various "traditional" elements are also used by this gospel to piece together a powerful, unified theological message.

Mark 8 is the central chapter of the Gospel of Mark. I have chosen to study this passage both because of its importance in Mark's Gospel, and because it is an excellent example of how the evangelist has worked. There are a series of events narrated:

The miracle of the loaves and fishes.

The dispute with the Pharisees, who, after the sign, still ask for a sign.

A journey in a boat, where Jesus discusses the meaning of the bread with his disciples. They are not able to understand, because their hearts are hardened. He asks them if they are blind. (See Mark 8:18.)

The curing of a blind man (in stages) at Bethsaida.

The interrogation on the identity of Jesus, and Peter's confession at Caesarea Philippi.

7. On the issue of Paul and the Jesus-traditions, see D. L. Dungan, *The Sayings of Jesus in the Churches of Paul* (Philadelphia, Fortress Press, 1971). On Paul in general, see the fine recent work of J. Christiaan Beker, *Paul the Apostle. The Triumph of God in Life and Thought* (Philadelphia, Fortress Press, 1980).

The first prediction of the oncoming passion, and Peter's inability to accept a suffering Son of Man.

Jesus teaches all the disciples and the crowd on the necessity of taking up their cross and following him, if they wish to be his disciples.

The transfiguration.

In this bewildering series of events, the only indication of time is that the transfiguration took place "after six days" (9:2). If all the events narrated in 8:1-9:1 took place on the one day, then Jesus and his disciples must have been exhausted by the end of the day! We have already seen enough to understand that to read the gospel in this strictly "historical" way would be to make nonsense of it. Let us attempt to read through the narrative to rediscover the message that Mark was attempting to communicate by means of his hectic and powerful narrative.

After a careful setting of the scene (8:1), we find the miracle of the loaves and fishes. Bread is important, and much of the language sounds eucharistic (see especially verse 6). There can be little doubt that the message is ultimately about Jesus as the unique nourisher of the people of God. Strangely, this spectacular miracle is followed by a dispute between Jesus and the Pharisees, who have come to ask for a sign. In verse 14 Jesus and his disciples set out in their boat. In the discussion that takes place there, the disciples show that, despite a warning from Jesus (verse 15), they are like the Pharisees, unable to understand the presence of the true bread (see especially verses 16-17). Jesus explains their lack of understanding in terms of blindness and deafness (see verse 18).

The boat comes to Bethsaida, and a blind man is brought to Jesus. He leads the blind man out of the village, lays his hands on him and asks him if he can see. The man has sight, but it is an imperfect sight: men look like walking trees (8:24). He has only partially recovered his sight. We find here a progression in the recovery of sight. Finally, Jesus lays his hands on the man's eyes, total sight is restored, and he sees clearly. This blind man has gone through a journey from no sight (verse 22) to partial sight (verse 24) to complete sight (verse 25). Understandably, when the evangelists Matthew and Luke report this section of Mark's Gospel, they leave out this miracle where Jesus appears to need two attempts to bring the man to true sight. In fact, these short verses are a profound theological statement. This man comes progressively to perfect vision.

To understand properly Mark's message, it is important to remember what preceded this account: the miracle of the loaves and fishes, the discussion with the Pharisees and the disciples' obtuseness over the true bread. Mark is telling his readers, as he leads up to the miracle, that all the people in the story so far have not understood anything. Their sight, their recognition of what God is doing for them in and through Jesus, is still insufficient and imperfect. But the miracle story demonstrates a progressive recovery of sight; sight is possible, but it may have to go down a stumbling journey of faith, with mistakes and failure. The journey from no vision to a partial vision into a full vision has probably been the experience of many of the people in Mark's community.

That this is Mark's message is made clear in the very next episode, a central episode in the Gospel of Mark (8:27-29). The disciples journey with Jesus to Caesarea Philippi, and on the way Jesus asks: "Who do men say that I am?" The disciples respond that most people think that he is one of the great messianic precursor figures: John the Baptist, Elijah or one of the prophets (verse 28). He then asks his followers: "But who do *you* say that I am?", and Peter confesses. "You are the Christ" (verse 29).

This has been rightly judged as the central confession of the gospel, and the reader may think that Peter has come to the correct answer. Strangely, Jesus insists that they must not tell anyone (8:30). This is so because they have not really understood the confession of faith that they have just made and heard. Jesus then begins to teach them that the Son of Man must suffer and be rejected by the elders and the chief priests and the scribes (verse 31). Only now, in Jesus' own explanation of his messiahship in terms of a suffering, dying and rising Son of Man is the real truth of the identity of Jesus revealed. This is true sight. To make this doubly clear, the evangelist adds: "And he said this plainly" (verse 32).

As the blind man in the miracle story of 8:22-26 went through a journey from no sight, through partial and incorrect sight into a fullness of vision, so the same journey has been made here, in terms of belief. "People" are blind in their understanding of Jesus as a precursor, and the disciples (personified by Peter) are only partially correct. They are convinced that the Christ must be a kingly, political messiah, and they will hold fast to this false view until, in the end, they fall away from Jesus and he goes to his cross alone (see especially 14:50-52). This is evident in Peter's refusal to accept Jesus' prophecy of the passion, but Jesus tells his disciple to go where all disciples should be: behind him, following him down *his* way.

The discourse that follows (8:34-9:1) enlarges upon what has just happened to Peter, and it is addressed to his disciples and to all the crowd. If they want to follow him, they must be prepared to tread the same path as that trod by Jesus, the way of the cross.

Despite the variety of "stories" that form this account, what a coherent whole this sequence makes! Mark has assembled a miracle story, an encounter with the Pharisees, a discussion in a boat, another miracle story and then the confession of Peter, followed by a discourse of Jesus. It is quite possible that each one of these pieces of tradition came from various stages in the life of Jesus, but Mark has a point to make, and he assembles his pieces in this way to proclaim the good news of authentic Christian discipleship. He shows that the disciples "in the story" had not understood who Jesus was; that their belief in the Christ was not based on a correct understanding of his mission; that they must suffer and follow him. However, this is a difficult and uncompromising message. One can almost hear the members of the Marcan community asking: how is this possible? Who is this man who has called us into this way of suffering?

The answer to these most understandable queries is found in the Marcan account of the transfiguration. Here the story is completed for the readers of this "good news". The glorious transformation of Jesus is really only background, explanation for the words of the voice from heaven: "This is my beloved Son; listen to him" (9:7). What the evangelist has proclaimed through his narrative in chapter 8 makes sense only in light of 9:2-8. Anyone else who might ask his followers to take up their cross, to lose their lives for his sake and for his Gospel, would be asking for the absurd, but because of the indications of the transfiguration scene, it all makes sense: "This is my beloved Son; listen to him" (9:7).

It is possible that the transfiguration was a post-resurrection experience of the community of Christ, an experience of the glorified Christ. To Mark, its exact chronology is unimportant. Mark wants to remind his readers that Jesus, the one who has called them into a life of suffering, is the Son of God. In the Marcan way of telling the story of Jesus, the transfiguration scene and its proclamation of Jesus as the Son of God is needed within the context of the radical demands that that same Jesus, the suffering Son of Man, makes upon all who wish to follow him.

I have devoted a large amount of space to an analysis of this important section of the Gospel of Mark, so that it would become obvious that Mark is reaching back into his traditions, into his sources, taking miracles, discourses, and events, eventually "telling a story" that made sense of the call to a suffering discipleship, to the following of Jesus. Given the limitations of our reflections here, I have looked at only one section of one of the most important parts of Mark's Gospel. In fact, later in this book I will present the central section of the gospel (Mark 8:22-10:52) under the title "The Way of the Son of Man". Many of the points that I have made in this introductory chapter will be remade, but they will be set in a wider context.8

Because Mark has not given us a day-to-day life-story of

8. See below, pp. 43–63.

17

Jesus, that does not make his account any less valid. What Mark has done here and throughout his gospel is to give us a theological statement of what it means to follow Jesus, Son of Man and Son of God. We are at the heart of the Marcan Gospel written in the late 60s or early 70s for a church suffering crucifixion and death in the context of a Roman persecution. Mark's Gospel presents a suffering yet mysteriously victorious Jesus of Nazareth, and he tells the members of his church that they must not wilt in the face of their own suffering. They, too, as followers of Jesus, must "take up their cross" (8:34) — a day-by-day physical possibility under Roman jurisdiction — and they must not be ashamed to follow a suffering Son of Man, because that same Son of Man will have the last word (verses 37-38). His word must be listened to, as he is the Son of God (9:2-8).

Four Stories of Jesus Read in the Church

This example from Mark's Gospel, and the similar examples from Matthew and Luke should be sufficient to show that the evangelists did not write twentieth-century-style biographies. They wrote "gospels" (see Mark 1:1). The gospel "form" is intimately linked with the beginnings — the life, the preaching and especially the cross and resurrection of Jesus himself — but it must always be understood and read as the "good news" proclaimed, in and for the church, in the spirit and faith in which it was written: that Jesus is the Christ, the Son of God, and that he has saved us! That Matthew, Mark and Luke, although at first glance similar, do this in very different ways is a wonderful testimony to the life of the spirit in the earliest church. Each pastoral and theological problem had to be solved by relying on the ultimate source of all light and truth, as the fourth evangelist will say later in the first century (see John 8:12; 9:5; 14:6): the person and teaching of Jesus. However, there can be no "once and for all" *controllable* person and message of Jesus of Nazareth.[9]

The Matterhorn seen from Italy is one mountain; seen from Switzerland it is another; seen from France yet another. Various faces of the same magnificent mountain present themselves, but it is still one and the same mountain. In the gospels we have a variety of inspired reflections on the person of Jesus of Nazareth, each one equally splendid yet different from the others.

Most of us have to admit that we are puzzled by the mystery of ourselves, and the mystery of the people whom we know and love well. How much more will this be so with the mystery of Jesus of Nazareth. We shall go through the whole of the history of the church without fully understanding all that Jesus means to us. It is important that we appreciate the richness that is ours as a result of our having four different portraits of Jesus. We must avoid the temptation to harmonise them, to insist that all four evangelists are saying the same thing. A Jesus who comes to me in one story only is much easier to control, but the mystery of his person and his ways is lost. Our fourfold gospel tradition leads us into a mystery whose depths we can never hope to control, but which will for ever question our absolutes and challenge our comfortable ways.

Nevertheless, while it is true that a correct reading of the gospels will concentrate upon the situation of the community for which a particular gospel was written, this leaves us with

9. This book is concerned with what the gospels tell us, in their own unique way, about Jesus of Nazareth. However, it is also important to study the gospels to rediscover the man Jesus of Nazareth, whose life, death and resurrection is the very cause of the gospel tradition. On this, a classical work is G. Bornkamm, *Jesus of Nazareth* (London, Hodder & Stoughton, 1960). Three further recent and most helpful studies are: D. Senior, *Jesus. A Gospel Portrait* (Dayton, Pflaum, 1975); H. Echegeray, *The Practice of Jesus* (Maryknoll, Orbis Books, 1984); A. Nolan, *Jesus Before Christianity* (London, Darton, Longman & Todd, 1977). Nolan's book is a quite remarkable study. For my own reflections, see F. J. Moloney, *A Life of Promise: Poverty, Chastity, Obedience* (London, Darton, Longman & Todd, 1985), pp. 122–38.

a further problem. Once I have done all my reading and careful analysis of this first-century text, what have I discovered? The danger is that I may limit myself to the rediscovery of a first-century church with its first-century answers. When it is all said and done, do the gospels still have anything to say to women and men today, or are they simply the dusty pages of an ecclesial situation from the distant past, which may be read today because of the interesting stories that they tell? This sort of approach to the gospels is seriously defective, but it is sometimes found.

We are aware that our major use of these texts is "in the church", as we take them up and read them in our services day after day, week after week. The liturgical use of the Scriptures is a privileged place for the reading of the gospels, and it reflects the church's commitment to the efficacy of the Word of the gospels today. The Fathers of the Second Vatican Council spoke strongly on the question of the Word of the gospels in the life of a Christian:

> Among all the inspired writings, even among those of the New Testament, the Gospels have a special place, and rightly so, because they are our principal source of the life and teaching of the Incarnate Word, our Saviour. (*Dei Verbum* 18)

> The Church has always venerated the divine Scriptures as she venerated the Body of the Lord, in so far as she never ceases, particularly in the sacred liturgy, to partake of the bread of life and to offer it to the faithful from the one table of the Word of God and the Body of Christ. (*Dei Verbum* 21)

It is from within this vision of faith that we read these texts that we regard as *sacred* Scripture. We share the faith of the church, which tells us that the Scriptures "are inspired by God and committed to writing once and for all time, they present God's own word in an unalterable form, and they make the voice of the Holy Spirit sound again and again in the words of the prophets and apostles" (*Dei Verbum* 21). The conviction that there was a link between the word of God, committed to writing in the distant past, and that same word addressing men and women in the church through all its history and in all its vicissitudes is something that the church came to appreciate through experience.

It is important to recognise that the church did not dream up the notion of a New Testament to read alongside the Old Testament, nor did it simply want to have a new Holy Book, just as our forefathers, the Jewish people, had their Holy Book. One can sense, very early in the Christian church, an honour and respect for certain Christian books, which eventually came to form the New Testament (see, for example, the reference to Paul's letters in 2 Peter 3:14-18 and the existence of a manuscript tradition from the second century). Nevertheless, the concept of an authoritative Word of God, revealed to the church in a special way in an Old and a New Testament, was defined for the first time at the Second Council of Nicaea in 787. It was further refined at the Council of Florence in 1442 and was an important part of the debates of the Council of Trent in 1546.

There is something very "real" about these facts. We do not have a belief in a set of sacred books simply because we have been told that they are sacred. On the contrary, the church has come to recognise that they are sacred through the inspiring presence of this literature, read, proclaimed and lived through centuries of experience.[10]

Our study of the four gospels should help us to catch, in some way, the uniqueness of insight into the mystery of the person and message of Jesus of Nazareth, which has given these documents their privileged place in the life of the church. They are "the principal source for the life and teaching of the Incarnate Word, our Saviour" (*Dei Verbum* 18).

Conclusion

As we conclude these reflections, it may be useful to see, in summary, the development of the Jesus traditions in the early

10. See, for a thorough presentation of this development, H. von Campenhausen, *The Formation of the Christian Bible* (London, A. & C. Black, 1972). See also H. Y. Gamble, *The New Testament Canon. Its Making and Meaning* (Philadelphia, Fortress Press, 1985).

church. In the beginning was the person of Jesus. After the impact of the resurrection, a belief in the risen Christ was born, and "the story of Jesus" became the precious heritage of the "oral tradition" of the church. However, as we have seen, Paul concentrated on Jesus' death and resurrection and what these paschal events had wrought for us all. He did not "tell the story of Jesus". Nevertheless, the "traditional" stories were preached to the first Christian liturgical celebrations, told in all sorts of settings (oral tradition) and eventually probably written down and, in part, finding their way into documents that we no longer possess. Thus the Jesus tradition grew. In time, people who had had living contact with the man Jesus began to die off, and the church saw the need to preserve its heritage from the past as it addressed the pastoral and theological problems of its present situation. Thus the gospels eventually came to be written. The examples that we have seen from Matthew, Luke and Mark should serve as an indication of how the evangelists looked *backwards* to the Jesus traditions and *forwards* to the present and future needs of their own communities.

It is most important to notice my insistence upon the "traditions", which were the raw material out of which the gospels were fashioned. In the final chapter of this book, I shall devote further attention to the question of Scripture and Tradition.[11] For the moment we must see that the early church and her "traditions" formed our written gospels. Thus the gospels are a product of the church, and not vice versa, as is sometimes imagined.

We must not underestimate the importance of our first gospel, Mark, as a literary event. The Evangelist Mark created a new "form of literature": a gospel. This "literary form" uses the "story" of the life, teaching, death and resurrection of Jesus of Nazareth to communicate the *evangelion*, the "good news" that Jesus is the Christ, the Son of God, and that God has saved us in and through his Son.

And, finally, those of us who look to the New Testament as

11. See below, pp. 221–243.

a Word of God believe that each gospel was written under divine inspiration. This is what gives the gospels their normative value. It is an incredible blessing that Matthew, Mark and Luke used the same material to give us three different pictures of Jesus. John, of course, goes his own way, with his own equally important traditions and his own equally important "story". Each one of these gospels reveals "the Truth". It happened this way because it was part of God's plan to reveal himself to us by speaking the Word of God in the fragile, but living, words of men and women. The gospels are a living witness to the wisdom of God in choosing men and women to talk to men and women in their own limited way. Not only in the incarnation, but also in the gospels, written by mere humans, with all their failings and limitations: "the Word has become flesh and dwells among us" (see John 1:14).

PART II
The Gospel
of Mark

2.
Reading
the Gospel
of Mark

A reading of the Gospel of Mark can be at the same time fascinating and perplexing. It has often been said that the Gospel of Mark is an enigma, full of contradictions and contrasts. It is precisely in the appreciation of these contradictions and contrasts that we will discover the originality of this Gospel.[1]

1. Reliable and readable commentaries are: D. Nineham, *Saint Mark*, The Pelican Gospel Commentaries (Harmondsworth, Penguin Books, 1969); E. Schweizer, *The Good News According to Mark* (London, SPCK, 1971); H. Anderson, *The Gospel of Mark*, New Century Bible (London, Oliphants, 1976); W. Harrington, *Mark*, New Testament Message 4 (Wilmington, Michael Glazier, 1979); G. Montague, *Mark: Good News for Hard Times. A Popular Commentary on the Earliest Gospel* (Ann Arbor, Servant Books, 1981); P. J. Achtemeier, *Invitation to Mark. A Commentary on the Gospel of Mark with the Complete Text from the Jerusalem Bible*, Image Books (New York, Doubleday, 1978). Although not a commentary, a most useful introduction to this gospel can be found in idem, *Mark*, Proclamation Commentaries (Philadelphia, Fortress Press, 1975). See also three further stimulating recent books on this gospel: M. D. Hooker, *The Message of Mark* (London, Epworth Press, 1983); W. Kelber, *Mark's Story of Jesus* (Philadelphia, Fortress Press, 1979); H. McGinlay (ed.), *The Year of Mark* (Melbourne, Desbooks/JBCE, 1984).

The Gospel
of Mark: Good News?

The very first verse of the gospel announces, as we have seen, that the reader is about to be told an incredible story: the "good news" that Jesus of Nazareth is the Christ, the Son of God (Mark 1:1). One of the great enigmas of this gospel is that while there is certainly a great deal of material in it that is "good news", the clear indication that in this man, a Son of God, the reigning presence of God has definitively broken into history, there is also a great deal of material that—to judge by our standards—must be considered as "bad news": and some of it is very bad news indeed!

The gospel opens with an exciting fulfilment of its promise to be "good news" about Jesus of Nazareth. We immediately find a powerful presentation of Jesus as the Son of God, full of the Holy Spirit, and driven by the Holy Spirit to be ultimately victorious over Satan (1:1-13). There may even be an indication in 1:13, where his presence in the desert is marked by the company of wild beasts, that the original order of peace and unity in creation, as portrayed in Genesis 2:18-25, has been restored in him.[2] Jesus then breaks into his public life, proclaiming what in many ways is a synthesis of all his preaching: "The time is fulfilled, and the kingdom of God is at hand; repent, and believe in the gospel" (1:15).

This is indeed good news, and it continues, as he calls his first disciples, who follow him down his way without a word of dissent (1:16-20). Together they set out, and Jesus shows that the reigning presence of a good God is truly present as he heals all sorts of illness (1:29-31, 40-45; 5:21-43), and drives out demons (1:21-28, 32-34; 5:1-20). The evil forces of the demonic and physical illness seem to be helpless against him, even though the demons try to take control of him by calling him by his correct name (see 1:24 and 5:7). In the ancient

2. For an excellent and moving contemporary appreciation of Mark 1:1-13, see H. R. Weber, *Immanuel. The Coming of Jesus in Art and in the Bible* (Geneva, World Council of Churches, 1984), pp. 7–24.

Semitic world, the naming of a person made that person yours (see, for example, Genesis 2:20, 23), but this does not happen with Jesus. Little wonder that people are led to ask, with wonder: "What is this? A new teaching! With authority he commands even the unclean spirits, and they obey him" (1:27). Even his disciples are dumbfounded, after a spectacular victory over nature, as they question: "Who then is this, that even wind and sea obey him?" (4:41).

It is quite clear from this early section of the gospel that the Evangelist Mark wants us to have no doubts about the fact that in Jesus of Nazareth an incredible, new authority has broken into history. In his person, in his word, and in his touch, God's reigning presence among men and women can be seen and experienced. Evil is conquered, broken bodies are healed, and desperate lives are once again given hope and dignity. However, that is not the whole story of these first chapters of the Gospel of Mark.

From 2:1-3:6 Jesus is in continual conflict with the religious authorities of Judaism. At the centre of this conflict Jesus announces ominously: "The days will come, when the bride-groom is taken away from them, and then they will fast in that day" (verse 20).[3] This hint becomes a central part of the story when, as a conclusion to the last of these conflicts (which are taken up again with added ferocity towards the end of the gospel in 11:27-12:43), Mark tells his readers: "The Pharisees went out, and immediately held counsel with the Herodians against him, how to destroy him" (3:6). This is an incredible comment. It would have been impossible for the religiously committed and fiercely patriotic Pharisees to "hold counsel" with the Herodians, who were regarded as being religiously indifferent political opportunists. By closing a

3. It has been attractively suggested that this passage forms the centre of the series of conflicts that run from 2:1-3:6. The suggestion was originally made in J. Dewey, "The Literary Structure of the Controversy Stories in Mark 2:1-3:6", *Journal of Biblical Literature* 92 (1973) 394–401. This has now been developed into a full-scale book (her doctoral thesis) entitled: *Marcan Public Debate. Literary Technique and Concentric Structure and Theology in Mark 2:1-3:6*, Society for Biblical Literature Dissertation Series 48 (Chico, Scholars Press, 1980).

long series of conflicts with this incisive comment, however, Mark informs us that the unique inbreak of the reigning presence of God in Jesus is threatening the worlds of both religious and political absolutists. They are prepared to join to rid themselves of their common enemy. Such is their response to the provocative newness that Jesus has come to bring, so powerfully announced at the centre of these conflicts:

> No one sews a piece of unshrunk cloth on an old garment; if he does, the patch tears away from it, the new from the old, and a worse tear is made. And no one puts new wine into old wineskins; if he does, the wine will burst the skins, and the wine is lost, and so are the skins . . . (2:21-22)

Coming so early in the gospel, these indications of the inevitable collision between the reigning presence of God in Jesus and the powers who oppose him show clearly that the news about Jesus of Nazareth will not always be what we would call "good news".

The Misunderstanding and Opposition Grow

Looking back, of course, it does not come as a great shock to us that the political and religious authorities of his own times opposed Jesus. After all, he was rather strongly opposed to them, it would appear (see especially 12:1-12). It does come as a surprise, however, that quite early in the gospel "his own" do not understand him, and eventually appear to restrict and oppose his activity.

The section of the gospel that runs from 3:20-35 is set within a "frame" (a common literary technique in Mark's Gospel, as we shall see). The first part of this frame is formed by verses 20-22, where we are told that Jesus' own family regard him as "beside himself". That is the euphemistic expression used by the Revised Standard Version to indicate that they thought that he was insane. The second part of this frame, formed by verses 31-35, insists that Jesus now belongs to a new family. His mother and brothers standing outside are only his "blood" family, and their significance fades as he sets up a new family: "Whoever does the will of God is my brother, and sister and mother" (verse 35). Naturally, in these passages where Mark uses his "frames", the material in the middle of the frame is important for determining the meaning of the whole section. In this case (verses 22-30), it is dominated by Jesus' teaching on the unforgivable sin: blasphemy against the Holy Spirit (verse 29). The hint is that both the scribes from Jerusalem (verse 22) and his own family (verses 21 and 31) run that danger.

The major part of Mark 4 is devoted to Jesus the teacher. From a boat he teaches very solemnly and with a unique authority through parables (4:1-34). This section on Jesus the teacher is immediately followed by a long section on Jesus the miracle worker (4:35-5:43). Here Jesus overcomes the elements (the calming of a storm), defeats a legion of demons, cures a woman with a flow of blood, and, finally, incredibly overcomes death itself in the raising of Jairus' daughter. He then proceeds to his own home town, Nazareth (6:1-6a). There his towns-folk ask the right question: "Where did this man get all this?" (verse 2), but they give the wrong answer. Because they know his mother and father, brothers and sisters, they think that they have exhausted all that is to be known about Jesus of Nazareth; and it is precisely here that they err so gravely. Yet, Jesus himself is astounded at the lack of faith in "his own", and is unable to do anything (verses 4-6).

If it is surprising to find that Jesus' own family and kinsfolk are unable to accept him and the unique presence of God that comes in his very person, it is even more surprising to see how Mark draws a bold picture of a group of disciples who fail their master quite miserably. After a most promising start, as they respond unerringly and promptly to the call of Jesus to "follow" him (1:16-20; 2:13-14; 3:13-19), a rift gradually begins to open between Jesus and those whom he called "to be with him" (see 3:14). The list of the names of the twelve ends with Iscariot, "who betrayed him" (3:19). The appearance of Jesus on the waters and the calming of the storm leads only to fear, and a question: "Who then is this . . .?" (4:41). After a successful sharing in the mission of Jesus, the disciples return to tell Jesus all the wonderful things that *they* had achieved (6:30). Notice the "frame" again: in 6:6b-13 Jesus sends out the twelve to drive out demons and heal the sick, exactly the "works" that he has done to show the presence of God as King. They actively share in the mission of Jesus. The central part of the framed section tells of the nature of true discipleship as the Baptist goes uncompromisingly to his death in defence of the ways of God in verses 14-29. In 6:30 the disciples return, full of their own achievements. They have missed the point: they can share in the mission of Jesus only if they are "with him". This point has been made very clear in the vocation and appointment of the twelve in 3:13-14. There is an indication that the twelve have not understood the nature of their discipleship, and they have certainly not understood what it will cost them, if they claim to be the "followers" of Jesus of Nazareth.

Although the dramatic movement towards the death of Jesus and his attempts to draw his disciples into this destiny dominate the gospel from this point onwards, the "good news" is still in evidence. On two occasions (6:31-44; 8:1-10) Jesus miraculously feeds the multitudes with loaves and fishes, and his journey from one feeding to the other shows a movement into the Gentile lands. There he heals the daughter of the Syrophoenician woman and continues his journey outside the sacred territory of Israel (see 7:31) to restore a deaf and dumb man to wholeness (verses 31-37). Indeed, it is outside the land of Israel that we find the first positive recognition of Jesus as the Messiah, the fulfilment of the messianic prophecy of Isaiah: "He has done all things well; he even makes the deaf hear and the dumb speak" (7:37; see Isaiah 35:5-6).

Jesus comes to bring nourishment to Jews (6:31-44) and Gentiles alike (8:1-10), but conflict is still found in these pages. The miracle of the feeding of the Jews meets only with hostility and opposition from religious authorities, because things are not being done in the "proper" way (7:1-5). Jesus' reply is a stinging rejection of the superficiality of a religious practice that is measured by the external observance of law (verses 6-23). The faith of the Syrophoenician woman is an obvious contrast to these self-righteous religious dignitaries insisting on their way to God. She presents herself before Jesus fully aware of her nothingness (see especially verses 27-28), and can thus be filled with the wholeness that Jesus has come to bring. It is not by chance that the miracle of the Syrophoenician woman comes between a gift of bread to Israel (6:31-44) and a gift of bread to the Gentiles (8:1-10). She, in the name of the Gentile world, begs for crumbs from the table of the Lord; and it is given in its fullness.

Yet, despite the wonders that are described, from this point onwards the disciples move farther and farther away from Jesus, and become more and more frightened of what it means "to follow" him down his way.[4] In the next chapter of this book, devoted to a detailed analysis of the central section of the Gospel of Mark (8:22-10:52), we shall see that this point is made very clearly.[5] In the midst of a long list of people who appear to refuse or fail Jesus, in the Marcan story there is one fixed point: Jesus never fails the failing disciple.

As we shall see in some detail, the whole of Mark 8:22-10:52 is devoted to the disciples. The section is also "framed", this time between two miracles where blind men come to sight (8:22-26; 10:46-52). It is also clearly structured around

---

4. J. Delorme has, for many years, suggested that the Gospel of Mark should be structured around two "mysteries". After the prologue (1:1-13), the obvious presence of God as King in the person and message of Jesus of Nazareth raises the question: can this man be the Messiah? Thus 1:14-8:30 can be entitled "The mystery of the Messiah". After Peter's confession that Jesis is the Christ (8:29), the nature of Jesus' messiahship, which is equally mysterious, is revealed: Jesus is the suffering Son of Man. This revelation takes place both in word (especially in 8:22-10:52) and in deed, in the passion and resurrection narrative (chapters 14-16). Thus 8:31-16:8 can be entitled "The mystery of the Son of Man". For a good summary statement of this argument, see A. George and P. Grelot, *Introduction à la Bible* (Paris, Desclée, 1976), vol. III/2, pp. 46–51.

5. See below, pp. 43–63.

three passion predictions, explicitly addressed to the disciples (8:31; 9:31; 10:32-34). At no stage of this part of the gospel do the disciples seem to believe or understand either the mystery of the Son of Man or their own destiny (see 8:32; 9:32; 10:35-37, 41). They are indeed "blind" (see also 8:17, where they are described as such by Jesus himself). Yet the two miracles point to a possible reversal of such a situation in a sight that only Jesus can give. This is acted out in the experience of the disciples as Jesus calls them to himself after each moment of failure, and instructs them once again (8:34; 9:35; 10:38, 42). Again the fascinating and perplexing story of good and bad news, of blessing and failure, is strongly present.

This, I believe, is a most important part of the strange balance between "good news" and "bad news" that one finds in the Gospel of Mark. In many ways, as I hope to indicate, it is the bad news that is, after all, the best news! One of the wonders of this gospel is the extreme realism of the portrait of all those who *should be* closest to Jesus. Then, as now, their lives are marked by failure. This, of course, is a very important indication that there were many people in Mark's own community whose lives were marked by failure and betrayal, even from among those who should have been leaders in the community's following of the way of Jesus.

I have already suggested that this gospel is the fruit of the experience of a Christian community under persecution. It is nowadays widely accepted that the Gospel of Mark has to be located somewhere close to the confused period either just before, during, or just after the Jewish war, amid all the disasters, physical and religious, that this experience brought upon Israel. The power of Rome was making itself felt in no uncertain terms. Fear and a preparedness to compromise one's stance on matters of belief to save one's life would have been an understandable enough position for some of the early Christians to take. In fact, it appears to me that the Gospel of Mark makes it very clear that many of the members of the community were doing just that. Our evangelist, in telling his particular story of Jesus, also tells the story of failed disciples, and he tells the story in this way because it was being listened to and read by failed and failing disciples. We are now beginning to see one of the reasons for the perennial significance of the Gospel of Mark. The message of a discipleship that is heavily marked by failure speaks strongly to all who have set out to "follow Jesus" down his way.[6]

There is no let-up in the miserable failure of those called to be closest to Jesus. Although we portray Jesus' entry into Jerusalem as a moment of glory and recognition, it does not appear as such in the Gospel of Mark. Before he ever enters Jerusalem, "those who followed" hail him as the expected Davidic Messiah (11:9-10). His "followers", his disciples, are still blinded by their own hopes.

Jesus enters Jerusalem alone, ominously goes straight to the Temple, looks around, and then returns to Bethany (11:11). Again "framing" his narrative with the account of a fig tree that does not bear fruit, Mark has Jesus put an end to both the business and cultic affairs of the Temple. He is about to establish a Temple "not made by human hands" (see 14:58 and 15:29), based on faith, prayer and forgiveness (11:12-26).[7] He fiercely attacks the failure of Jewish religious authority through the parable of the vineyard (12:1-12), and then through a further series of conflict stories, silences the Pharisees (12:13-17), the Sadducees (verses 18-27) and one of the scribes (verses 28-34). After finally dismissing any

6. It could be claimed (correctly, in my opinion) that the Gospel of Mark is dominated by two features: christology and ecclesiology, or, as Mark would have said: Jesus and his disciples. Excellent recent studies on these two issues are J. D. Kingsbury, *The Christology of Mark's Gospel* (Philadelphia, Fortress Press, 1984), and E. Best, *Following Jesus. Discipleship in the Gospel of Mark*, JSNT Supplement Series 4 (Sheffield, University Press, 1981). See also, F. J. Moloney, "The Vocation of the Disciples in the Gospel of Mark", *Salesianum* 43 (1981) 487–516, and J. J. H. Neyrey, *Christ is Community. The Christologies of the New Testament*, Good News Studies 13 (Wilmington, Michael Glazier, 1985), pp. 33–64.

7. For an excellent study of the Marcan use of the Temple and the "new Temple" constructed by Jesus, see D. Juel, *Messiah and Temple. The Trial of Jesus in the Gospel of Mark*, Society of Biblical Literature Dissertation Series 31 (Missoula, Scholars Press, 1977).

idea that the Messiah could possibly be the Son of David (verses 35-37), the disciples are again called to witness what true religion is about (see verse 43), as Jesus both condemns the hypocrisy of the scribes, and praises the widow who gives her all (verses 38-44).

In a final discourse, Jesus speaks of the end of Jerusalem (13:1-23), but warns his disciples not to be led astray, as this is not the end of all time, as "the gospel must first be preached to all nations" (verse 10). They are to live through the disasters of the destruction of Jerusalem and "endure to the end" if they wish to be saved (verse 13). The end will come (verses 24-37), but it will come only in God's time, a time unknown to either the angels in heaven or the Son on earth (verse 32). One thing is clear. It will not come until the Gospel has been preached to the four corners of the earth. At the end of time, the Son of Man "will send out the angels, and gather his elect from the four winds, from the ends of the earth to the ends of heaven" (verse 27). In all of this, his disciples are never far away. He instructs them that they must persevere to the end (verse 13) and warns that they must watch (verses 33, 37).

God's Way Revealed in the Way of Jesus

The close blend between "good news" and "bad news" reaches its climax over the last few chapters of the gospel. In his celebration of a last meal together with his now terrified disciples, Jesus sets up a covenant with them, a new union based on a broken body and spilt blood (14:22-26). This is a promise of unfailing faithfulness, set within the context of a passover meal, when the disciples were able to recall the faithfulness of Jahweh to his people. This new covenant, however, does not look *backwards* to the Exodus for its basis, but *forwards* to the cross of the following day. Although written some thirty years after these events, one feels the power of the Johannine understanding of the christology that lies beneath such a covenant: "Greater love has no man than this, that a man lay down his life for his friend" (John 15:13). Yet, surrounding this account of the meal is a further frame: the prophecy of the betrayal of Judas (Mark 14:17-21) and the further prophecy of the betrayal of Peter and the rest of his disciples (verses 27-31). Again the fourth gospel provides an excellent commentary on this scene. In John 13 there is a similar presentation of Jesus' gift of himself in love to failing disciples. At the centre of the Johannine scene one reads the incisive words of Jesus: "I tell you this now, before it takes place, that when it does take place you may believe that I AM HE (John 13:19). It is precisely in this gift of self in love to *failing disciples* that the uniqueness of Jesus, the Son of God, is revealed.[8]

Despite the master's extraordinary gestures of a loving and guiding presence among this group of failing disciples, when danger threatens in Gethsemane, we hear of them as a group for the last time: "And they all forsook him, and fled" (Mark 14:50). The following section of the gospel (verses 51-52) tells of a young man who was also following Jesus, but who, as danger threatened, fled naked, leaving his only covering, a *linen cloth*, in the hands of his pursuers. This is a parable on the situation of the fleeing disciples. As long as they were "following" Jesus, they were a part of his story. Now that they have fled, they are naked in their nothingness. The importance of "being with" Jesus, as indicated in 3:13-14, when the twelve were first called and appointed must not be underestimated. They are no longer "with him", and thus they are "naked".[9]

Peter stays in the story a little longer, only to deny Jesus three times (15:66-72). Again there is a powerful use of contrast and irony as Mark tells his story. During the trials of

8. For this interpretation of John 13, see F. J. Moloney, "The Structure and Message of John 13:1-38", *Australian Biblical Review* 34 (1986), 1–16.

9. See especially H. Fledderman, "The Flight of a Naked Young Man", *Catholic Biblical Quarterly* 41 (1979) 412–18.

Jesus, the truth is ironically proclaimed. Mark uses the accusations of the Jewish judges to proclaim that Jesus is the founder of a new and perfect temple, not made by human hands (14:58), the Christ, the Son of God and the Prophet (verses 61-65). The trial before Pilate proclaims his kingship (15:1-20). Thus, while the *truth* is being proclaimed by Jesus, one of his disciples is out in the courtyard, telling *lies*.[10]

Jesus goes to his death alone, except for a small group of women, who look on from afar (15:40-41). After an ignominious crucifixion, Jesus dies, first asking the question that all careful readers of the Marcan Gospel story must be asking at this stage of the narrative: "My God, my God, why hast thou forsaken me?" (verse 34), and then uttering a loud scream (verse 37). It would appear that the universal opposition to the ways of God as they have been revealed in the story of Jesus of Nazareth has won through. Yet this is only the beginning of a different story. Already at Jesus' death the veil of the Temple is torn asunder: the separation between the privileged place for God in the Temple and the rest of the world (already forecast in Jesus' activity among the Gentiles from 7:21-8:10) is eliminated, and a Gentile centurion confesses: "Truly this man was the Son of God" (verses 38-39). But what of his failed disciples?

As we have just seen, the passion of Jesus closed with an agonised cry from Jesus, and this cry is still ringing in the readers' ears, as we come to the account of the women's journey to the tomb: "My God, my God, why hast thou forsaken me?" (15:34). Abandoned by his disciples (14:50), Jesus faces trial and death alone—and goes to his final moment with a fearful question and a loud scream on his lips. As far as Jesus is concerned, his opponents seem to have won the day. They have done their very worst to him—and this leads him to cry out to his God in terror.[11]

10. On the Marcan version of the trial of Jesus, as well as the commentaries, see the fine study of Juel, *Messiah and Temple*.

11. On this theme, see U. Wilckens, *Resurrection. Biblical Testimony to the Resurrection: An Historical Examination and Explanation* (Edinburgh, The Saint Andrew Press, 1977), pp. 27–44, especially pp. 40–4.

The discovery of an empty tomb, and the message of a young man at the tomb, *dressed in a linen cloth* (remember 14:51-52) reverses everything. The question asked by Jesus on the cross is answered by God in the empty tomb. The opponents of Jesus have not won at all: "they" did their worst—but to no avail: "You are seeking Jesus the Nazarene, the crucified one. He has been raised [by God]. He is not here: look at the place where *they* laid him" (16:6.AT). The incredible journey of the Son of Man through a life of love and service, in a total and radical obedience to God whom he called "Abba" (see especially 14:36), ends with a final reversal of values: resurrection. The story of Jesus, as it is told throughout the Gospel of Mark, is a story of human failure, but it closes with a loud, clear message: in his journey away from the absolutes of a human success story, Jesus of Nazareth has led the way into the only enduring success story: resurrection. The *christology* of the Gospel of Mark is clear: Jesus the Son wins through to life by his preparedness to lay himself open to the ways of God, no matter how much these ways may question the absolutes of history and culture. But, as we have seen, throughout the gospel he has attempted to draw other people into a "following" of this way.

What of the disciples? What of the women? The disciples, whose "following" of Jesus had been marked by fear once Jesus set his face towards Jerusalem (see 9:30-32; 10:32; 14:51-52) have ended in flight: "And they all forsook him, and fled" (14:50). It appears, however, that this will all be resolved, as the women are commanded to take the Easter message to the failed disciples: "But go, tell his disciples and Peter that he is going before you to Galilee; there you will see him, as he told you" (16:7). As we look back from our comfortable position of many centuries of Christian faith, it appears extraordinary that the reaction of the women to this message is one of terror:

And they went out and fled from the tomb; for trembling and astonishment had come upon them; and they said nothing to any one, for they were afraid. (16:8)

Another incredible turn of events in this incredible gospel story! Although the later scribes added more comfortable endings to this gospel (our present 16:9-20 is only *one* of several such endings found in the ancient manuscripts), this is where the Evangelist Mark ended his gospel: a resurrection proclamation in the midst of terror and flight.

Throughout the Gospel of Mark it has been the disciples who have had the "good sense" to oppose Jesus' ridiculous journey to Jerusalem and to death (see especially 8:32-33); to make a few plans about how things should be organised when Jesus finally made his coup and re-established the Davidic kingdom (see especially 9:34 and 10:35-37). Even their eventual flight (14:50), Peter's denials (14:66-72) and the flight of the women from an empty tomb full of strange messages (16:8) are sensible approaches to rather uncomfortable situations. Yet it is the conviction of the Evangelist Mark that the "good news" that Jesus is and which Jesus himself proclaimed shows that it is the disciples and the women who get it wrong! The Marcan resurrection story proclaims that the way of Jesus is the way to victory, and the way of the worldly wise leads only into terror and flight (see 14:50 and 16:8).

The terrible question of the crucified Jesus is resolved by the action of God in his resurrection. What about the terror of the disciples and the women? The gospel ends with flight and terror, yet it also ends with a promise. Even to the worldly wise there is a word of hope in the midst of their failure and terror: "But go, tell his disciples and Peter that he is going before you to Galilee; there you will see him, as he told you" (16:7). Do the terror and flight of the women thwart the promise of an eventual encounter with the risen Lord in Galilee?[12]

12. As the gospel draws to its conclusion, the point made about Jesus and his disciples in note 6 (page 35) becomes very clear. This is the case argued in the final chapter of a fine and most readable recent study of the passion in Mark: D. Senior, *The Passion of Jesus in the Gospel of Mark*, The Passion Series 2 (Wilmington, Michael Glazier, 1984), pp. 139–58.

A Question Answered

The very fact that today, some two thousand years later, we go on celebrating Easter indicates that the Galilee encounter took place in the lives of the failed disciples, and that the church rose from its own failure and flight. This is the message of the Evangelist Mark to his terrified disciples of all times. We proclaim this remarkable gospel at the Easter Vigil in Year B of our liturgical cycle.[13] We live it again and again in Jesus' incredible gift of himself in love at every eucharistic celebration; in the brokenness of our own ambiguous Christian lives. The "story of Jesus", as it is told by the Evangelist Mark is not just a dusty page from the past experience of a remote Christian community. It proclaims an extraordinarily simple yet profound truth. Here we find no illusions about the ambiguity of the human condition, and ultimately about the ambiguity of the church made up of failing and terrified men and women. Yet it proclaims, in the midst of that terror: "I will go before you to Galilee." (14:28; see 16:7). There they would see him.

A reading of this enigmatic gospel challenges us all to a greater hope. As we read the Gospel of Mark our own terror and failure can be given sense and purpose. He "is going before us into Galilee;" There we will see him, as he has "gone before us", summoning us towards our experience of resurrection, as we continually meet him, touch him and are inspired by his living presence in our "Galilees". His never-failing presence to the failed and failing disciples always has and always will make sense out of our nonsense. A careful and contemporary reading of this "story of Jesus" can teach us that no matter how fragile the Christian response to the

13. It is opportune to recall here what I wrote earlier (see above, pp. 20–21) about the church's use of the gospels: "The conviction that there was a link between the Word of God, committed to writing in the distant past, and that same word addressing men and women in the church through all its history and in all its vicissitudes is something that the Church came to appreciate through experience."

41

challenge of Jesus may be, the Easter proclamation of the *Exultet* has rightly interpreted the message of the Gospel of Mark: "Christ has conquered, and darkness has vanished for ever."

3.
Reading
Mark 8:22-10:52:
The Way of
the Son of Man

The immediately obvious feature of Mark 8:22-10:52 is the continual appearance of "passion predictions" at 8:31, 9:31 and 10:32-33. It is very important to notice that all the passion predictions are aimed at the disciples:

> And Jesus went on with his disciples to the villages of Caesarea Philippi ... And he began to teach them that the Son of man must suffer many things, and be rejected by the elders and the chief priests and the scribes, and be killed, and after three days rise again. (8:27, 31)

> They went on from there and passed through Galilee. And he would not have any one know it; for he was teaching his disciples, saying to them, "The Son of man will be delivered into the hands of men, and they will kill him . . ." (9:30-31)

> And taking the twelve again, he began to tell them what was to happen to him, saying "Behold we are going up to Jerusalem; and the Son of man will be delivered to the chief priests and the scribes, and they will condemn him to death, and deliver him to the Gentiles; and they will mock him, and scourge him, and kill him; and after three days he will rise." (10:32-33)

Although there are developments and differences between these three predictions, it is obvious that they are all structurally based on the same elements: a journey to Jerusalem, a violent death and a resurrection. The passion predictions would have originated in Jesus' own prophecies about his destiny, and Mark 9:31 must be very close to Jesus' own words (see also Luke 9:44).[1] Nevertheless, they have been further developed in the tradition, as they have been told and retold in the earliest church, using the actual events as they happened. This is particularly clear in 10:32-33, which is, in many ways, a summary of Mark 14:53-16:8. Here we have a first hint that the Evangelist Mark is using traditional material for his own special purposes, strategically placing the three passion predictions so that he can unfold the argument of the central section of his gospel around them.

However, there are further features that indicate that the evangelist is deliberately constructing this section of his gospel around certain themes, and one of the most important of them is his use of blind men. The passage that we are considering opens with the story of the blind man at Bethsaida (8:22-26) and closes with the curing of blind Bartimaeus (10:46-52). Reaching back farther still into Mark 8, we can find that there was a deliberate association drawn by the evangelist between the disciples and "blindness". Immediately after the multiplication of the bread (8:1-10) and the encounter between Jesus and the Pharisees (8:11-13), we find that the

1. Here we are touching upon one of the central issues in contemporary discussions over Jesus' own knowledge of himself and his destiny. For some biblical reflections on these matters, see R. E. Brown, "Who Do Men Say That I Am? — A Survey of Modern Scholarship on Gospel Christology", in *Biblical Reflections on Crises Facing the Church* (New York, Paulist, 1975), pp. 20–37. A practical survey of gospel christology can be found in J. A. Fitzmyer, *A Christological Catechism. New Testament Answers* (New York, Paulist, 1982), while a more comprehensive and helpful analysis is now provided by W. M. Thompson, *The Jesus Debate. A Survey and Synthesis* (New York, Paulist Press, 1985). See also, F. J. Moloney, "The End of the Son of Man?", *Downside Review* 98 (1980) 280–90, especially pp. 288–90. For an excellent theological reflection on this question, see J. H. P. Wong, "Karl Rahner on the Consciousness of Jesus: Implications and Assessment", *Salesianum* 48 (1986) 225–279.

disciples—now alone with Jesus on the lake—are unable to "perceive or understand" (8:17). Jesus then asks: "Are your hearts hardened? *Having eyes do you not see*, and having ears do you not hear?" (8:17-18). There can be little doubt that this central section of the Gospel of Mark touches upon the themes of discipleship, blindness and suffering, but there may well be others!

Structure and Message

Starting from these indications, one can move closer to the text and discover that we are dealing with a section of Mark's Gospel that begins and ends with the cure of a blind man (8:22-26 and 10:46-52). It is further highlighted by three passion predictions (8:31; 9:31; 10:32-33). They are, in their own turn, followed by further material gathered from a series of sources (especially obvious in 9:38-50), aimed at the instruction of anyone who would pretend to be a disciple of Jesus. We thus have an overall structure of the passage:[2]

8:22-26	The cure of the *blind man* at Bethsaida.
8:27-33	The *first passion prediction* and the failure of Peter.
8:34-9:29	The *first instruction* of the disciples:
8:34-9:1	*The cross* and disciples.
9:2-13	The transfiguration and the cross.
9:14-29	The boy the disciples could not heal.
9:30-34	The *second passion prediction* and the failure of the disciples.
9:35-10:31	The *second instruction* of the disciples:
9:35-50	*Service, humility and receptivity* as marks of a disciple.

2. Most commentators see this section of the Gospel of Mark as central to its structure and theology (especially regarding christology and discipleship). Not all would accept the structure I am presenting. For other opinions, see the commentators mentioned in Chapter 2, note 1, p. 27.

10:1-31	The practice of discipleship:
	(a) 1-12 in marriage,
	(b) 13-16 through *receptivity* (children),
	(c) 17-31 in one's attitude to riches and possessions.
10:32-35	The *third passion prediction.*
10:36-40	The *failure* of James and John and their *instruction*: the *cross.*
10:41-44	The *failure* of "the other ten" and their *instruction*: *service* and *humility.*
	Christological conclusion and motivation for the teaching on cross, service, humility and receptivity as the cost of discipleship (8:27-10:44): "For the Son of man also came not to be served but to serve, and to give his life as a ransom for many" (10:45).
10:46-52	The cure of the *blind man:* Bartimaeus.

You will have noticed that I have gathered all the material in the passage that follows the passion predictions under the general heading of "instruction for disciples" even though different "forms" of material are found there: teaching, transfiguration, a discussion over divorce, a collection of proverbs (9:38-50), etc. I have done this because it appears to me that this is what Mark the Evangelist was attempting to do as he skilfully arranged this section of his book. Aware of the danger of imposing my criteria upon the author, there seem to be clear indications that the overall thrust of Mark's argument can be summarised as follows.

(a) The use of the motif of "blindness" is intimately linked with discipleship. As I have already indicated, this is found in the link that exists between 8:17 and 8:22-26. We can now add the further cure of the blind man in 10:46-52.

(b) Within this overall setting, there is the threefold repetition of Jesus' destiny, as told through the three passion predictions, explicitly addressed to the disciples in each case.

This is the first hint that the way of Jesus is the suffering way of the Son of Man, and that the way of the follower of Jesus must be the same.

(c) The disciples, *in every case*, are either unable or unwilling to accept that it should be so. They fail. This particular theme is always noticed by commentators and scholars.

(d) What is often not noticed, however, is that within the structure that I have just outlined, *Jesus never fails the failing disciples*. No matter how obdurate or ignorant they are in their reactions to the passion predictions, he gathers his disciples around him yet again and instructs them on the demands of Christian discipleship: take up your cross (8:34), be an open, receptive and humble servant (9:35-37), because "the Son of man also came not to be served but to serve, and to give his life as a ransom for many" (10:45). Unless one sees the never-failing presence of Jesus to his failing disciple — in both his teaching and in his very life-style — this section of the gospel, and subsequently one of the major thrusts of the whole gospel, is lost. Some scholars have argued that Mark's Gospel is about the absence of Jesus. I would claim that the *opposite* is the case![3]

---

3. Many contemporary scholars, accentuating the failure of the disciples in this gospel, claim that Mark is using them as the "vehicle" to present the false teachings that his community must reject. This case has been systematically argued by T. J. Weeden, *Mark — Traditions in Conflict* (Philadelphia, Fortress Press, 1971) and is followed (with various nuances) by many American scholars. The most complete work on the positive Marcan use of the discipleship motif is Best, *Following Jesus*. See also, D. Stanley, *The Call to Discipleship. The Spiritual Exercises with the Gospel of Mark*, The Way Supplement 43–44 (London, The Way Publications, 1982) and A. Stock, *Call to Discipleship. A Literary Study of Mark's Gospel*, Good News Studies 1 (Wilmington, Michael Glazier, 1982). For a survey of contemporary opinions on the failure of the disciples in the Gospel of Mark, see Moloney, "The Vocation of the Disciples in the Gospel of Mark", pp. 487–95.

A Journey from
Blindness to Sight (8:22-26)

The former of the two cures of blind men that we meet in this section (8:22-26) is a strange miracle indeed. It appears as if Jesus needs two attempts to bring the man to sight, as he does not quite get it right the first time. In fact, as I have already mentioned, when Matthew and Luke came to tell this section of the life of Jesus (see Matthew 16:5-39; Luke 9:10-27), they simply omit this episode. A careful reading of the text, especially paying close attention to the overall development of Mark's argument, shows that there may be more to it. It appears very important to notice that there are three moments in this man's journey from complete darkness into the light.

We meet this man as he is *led* by other people who speak for him. He is totally incapacitated: unable to walk or even speak for himself. We are in a stage of *complete darkness* (8:22). Jesus then performs a miracle by using spittle (verse 23), a method used commonly enough by the miracle workers of his own time (Tacitus, Suetonius and Dio Cassius all report that even the Emperor Vespasian worked such miracles), and also used both by Aborigines and experienced bushmen in my own Australian outback to treat eye problems. However, the use of the methods of a miracle worker produces only a *partial sight*. "I see men; but they look like trees, walking" (verse 24). Only when all the "tricks of the trade" are abandoned and Jesus simply lays his hands upon his eyes is the man "restored, and he saw everything clearly" (verse 25). In this third moment, the journey to perfect sight comes to an end, but the formerly blind man is immediately dismissed from the story (verse 26) as a longer, but parallel, journey is about to begin; this time on the part of the disciples.

The Way of
the Son of Man:
the Cross (8:27-9:22)

In our general survey of the Gospel of Mark, we noticed that there was already an indication in 3:19 that a disciple could betray Jesus, and that in 6:30, "those sent out" returned from their missionary experience full of "all that they had done and taught". However, up to this stage of the gospel, the disciples have not been directly challenged. Hints have been given that they really have not come to understand all that is happening before their eyes, as even the miracle of the calming of the waters has not led them to a confession of faith. They only wonder, and ask: "Who then is this, that even wind and sea obey him?" (4:41).

The crucial moment for the disciples comes in 8:27-33, where Jesus asks them who it is they think they are following. After all that the disciples have seen, heard and even shared in, Jesus leads them, for the first time, to a correct understanding of who he is. In 8:27, he asks his disciples, "Who do men say that I am?", and they answer in terms of great precursor figures: John the Baptist, Elijah or one of the prophets. Matching the first experience of the blind man in verses 22-26, which we have just examined, they are in total darkness as they have no understanding of just who Jesus is. He then asks his disciples "But who do you say that I am?" (verse 29). Peter, in the name of all the disciples, replies, "You are the Christ."

There is a sense, of course, in which this is correct, but there is also the possibility that the disciples are measuring Jesus' being the Messiah in terms of their expectations of what the Messiah should be: an all-conquering, dominant, political, kingly figure.[4] It is clear from the context that in the faith that is expressed here the "partial" experience of true sight from the blind man's journey is repeated.

Jesus charged them to tell no one about him (8:30). "And he began to teach them that the Son of man must suffer many

---

4. First-century Jewish messianic expectation is a complex phenomenon. For a survey, see F. Hahn, *The Titles of Jesus in Christology. Their History in Early Christianity* (London, Lutterworth Press, 1969), pp. 136–48, and C. Rowland, *Christian Origins. An Account of the Setting and Character of the most Important Messianic Sect of Judaism* (London, SPCK, 1985), pp. 87–108. For a powerful evocation of the royal/military concept of the

things, and be rejected by the elders and the chief priests and the scribes, and be killed, and after three days rise again. *And he said this plainly"* (verses 31-32). Here, for the first time in Mark's Gospel, Jesus speaks clearly of who he is, and he describes his destiny. He is not a powerful, kingly messiah. His messiahship is to be found in his being a suffering Son of Man. This is true sight, a fullness of vision. There is no need to hide this reality. Indeed, it must be openly proclaimed.

This passage contains the first of our three passion predictions (8:31). Through each prediction, we find Jesus trying to lead his disciples first to a correct understanding of who he is and, flowing out of this, to a correct understanding of what it means to be his disciple. It is here that he spells out for them, by first presenting the way which he must tread, the price which they must pay if they wish "to come after him". In this first moment, we will find that Peter is in no way

Messiah, see the first-century Jewish document, *The Psalms of Solomon* 17:21-25:

> See, Lord, and raise up for them their king,
>   the son of David to rule over your servant Israel
>   in the time known to you, O God.
> Undergird with the strength to destroy the unrighteous rulers,
>   to purge Jerusalem from gentiles
>   who trample her to destruction;
>   in wisdom and in righteousness to drive out
>   the sinners from the inheritance;
> to smash the arrogance of sinners
>   like a potter's jar;
> To shatter all their substance with an iron rod;
>   to destroy the unlawful nations with the word of his mouth;
> At his warning the nations will flee from his presence;
>   and he will condemn sinners by the thoughts of their hearts.

The English text is taken from J. H. Charlesworth, *The Old Testament Pseudepigrapha* (London, Darton, Longman & Todd, 1983–85), vol. II, p. 667. For further information on the Psalms of Solomon, see ibid. pp. 639–50 and G. W. Nickelsberg, *Jewish Literature Between the Bible and the Mishnah* (London, SCM Press, 1981), pp. 203–12. On Psalm 17, see pp. 207–9.

prepared to accept Jesus as a suffering messiah. The text is quite strong. Peter was ready to confess that Jesus was *the* Messiah, as he and the culture of his time understood that figure. Jesus' talk of death and resurrection was not a part of these schemes. The text says that Peter "took hold" of Jesus. Peter is attempting to impose his schemes upon Jesus in no uncertain terms.

One must notice Jesus' reaction to Peter's unreported words and significant gestures: "Turning and *seeing his disciples*, he rebuked Peter, and said, 'Get behind me, Satan! For you are not on the side of God, but *of men*'" (8:33).

The correction of Peter is not for Peter alone, but for all the disciples. It is important to know that the Greek word for Satan transcribes the Hebrew/Aramaic, where it originally meant "stumbling block, obstruction" (see Matthew 16:23). Peter, an obstruction to the Son of Man as he goes along his God-given way, must "get behind" Jesus. This is the only place for any disciple. The issue is that the disciples are seeing Jesus from the point of view of their human expectations. They are on the side "of men". God does not work within these categories. Jesus is to be a suffering messiah, and anyone who wishes to follow him must follow him along his way of suffering.

The discourse that follows hardly needs comment. It clearly tells the disciples of all ages that the cost of following Jesus is nothing less than the cross: "If any man would *come after me*, let him deny himself and take up his cross and *follow me*" (8:34). Notice the deliberate use of discipleship language, which one finds in the very first vocation story 1:16-20: "come after me" and "follow me". The rest of the discourse (8:34-9:1) makes crystal clear what Jesus demands from his disciples. Jesus, however, saw himself as coming to his final vindication and glory through suffering (8:31: "and after three days rise again"). So it will be with any disciple who is prepared to lose his life for Jesus and the Gospel, which is the continuing presence of Jesus among us. They will see the kingdom of God come with power (9:1).

Mark's vision of the transfiguration (9:2-8) is marked by two parallel themes:

(1) The ultimate significance of Jesus, and the reason why he can ask his disciples to follow him down the way of the Son of Man: "This is my beloved Son; listen to him" (9:7).

(2) Disciples who are confused, afraid (9:6), desiring to "hold" Jesus in his glory by setting up tabernacles. This cannot be, and "suddenly looking around they no longer saw any one with them but Jesus only" (verse 8).

Thus the journey has begun in all seriousness; the glorious Jesus of 9:2-8 will make sense only in the light of his death and resurrection (verses 9-13). Again the disciples are unable to understand (verse 10), and it is not only Peter, James and John who are of little faith and understanding. The rest of the disciples are unable to cure an epileptic boy because ultimately they are not sufficiently open to God's ways: "This kind cannot be driven out by anything but prayer" (verse 29). Mark deliberately uses the boy's father, with his openness, humility and faith to throw into sharp relief the lack of these traits in the disciples: "I believe; help my unbelief" (verse 24).

The Way of the Son of Man: Service, Openness and Humility (9:30-10:31)

Mark introduces his second passion prediction by again stressing both the "journey" theme: "They went on from there and passed through Galilee" (9:30), and that of the disciples: "for he was teaching his disciples, saying to them, 'The Son of man will be delivered into the hands of men, and they will kill him; and when he is killed, after three days he will rise'" (verse 31). The reaction of the disciples, as usual, is marked by fear and lack of understanding: "But they did not understand the saying, and they were afraid to ask him" (verse 32).

Not only do the disciples not understand, but again they show that they are not prepared to accept the messiahship, the kingdom and the discipleship that these words of Jesus demand. They are on their way to Capernaum, and when they arrive there and are settled for the night, Jesus asks them what they were discussing along the way. Their reaction shows that they have not gone beyond the hopes expressed in Peter's confession (8:27-33). They are still thinking in terms of human achievement: "they were silent; for on the way they had discussed with one another who was the greatest" (9:34). Their interest is in who will have most authority in the human power structure that they imagine Jesus intends to establish. Again Jesus does not leave them in their ignorance. He takes the matter up with them, and tells them that to follow him means to abandon all human ambitions of power and authority: "If anyone would be first, he must be last of all and servant of all" (9:35).

He goes on to explain what this means in practice by taking a child and putting the child in the midst of them. He holds the child in his arms. This gesture, coming through the pages of the gospel as a precious memory of the sort of man Jesus was, is not, however, simply that. Jesus is using the child to show just what it means to be "with him" as his true disciple. We have already seen in our general study of the Gospel of Mark that this characteristic—to be "with Jesus"—was shown to be of fundamental importance in the vocation and institution of the twelve (see especially 3:13-14).

The disciple of Jesus is not one who dictates terms in the kingdom, but one who is *receptive*. Openness, the mark of the humble servant and the innocent child, is reflected in the disciple's openness to all that Jesus asks of him. Ultimately, this means that the disciple will be open to God. Only with such an approach to others is one a disciple of Jesus: "Whoever receives one such child in my name receives me; and whoever receives me, receives not me but him who sent me" (9:37).

The fourfold repetition of the same verb "to receive" clearly indicates the main point of the passage. Jesus points out that he himself is not a man who acts through his own authority and power. He too is "receiving". He is merely serving the one who sent him. As always in the gospel teaching on discipleship, Jesus does not, as a distant legislator, demand the impossible from his disciples. He always asks them to "follow" him, to go along the way which he himself must walk.

The following episodes (9:38-48) have been gathered by Mark to round off this section by giving more practical indications how this service, openness and humility are to be lived.[5] John shows immediately that the lesson has *not* been learnt: "we saw a man casting out demons in *your* name, and we forbade him, because he was not following *us*" (verse 38). Again such an attitude of dictating terms in a kingdom that is not theirs has to be corrected by Jesus (verses 39-41).

This episode is followed by a series of warnings against the causes of sin. "These little ones who believe in me" (9:42) refers not only to the physically young, but also (especially in the light of verses 38-41) to recent believers in Jesus. In Mark's church, therefore, all could be designated "little ones". There are three parallel sayings about the causes of sin, referring to hand, foot and eye, linked together and to verse 42 by the catchwords, "cause to sin" and "it is better". The harshness of these sayings may well be examples of Semitic hyperbole, and are not to be taken literally. Yet while we must be careful to indicate that Christianity is not a call to the literal observance of these practices, there is still a powerful message behind what is being said, which is, in some way, connected with the oddity of these sayings. They have their place in the message of Jesus exactly as they stand.

5. On this difficult collection of passages, see the helpful analysis of Schweizer, *The Good News According to Mark*, pp. 193–200. An excellent, though more scholarly, analysis can be found in H. Fledderman, "The Discipleship Discourse (Mark 9:33-50)", *The Catholic Biblical Quarterly* 43 (1981) 57–75.

Their observance is an appreciation of the seriousness of the message: to stand in the way of the coming of the kingdom of God is to lose everything promised by the good news of Jesus for the sake of something that can be done without, the fruits of our human ambition.

The remaining "instructions" of this section are again very strongly directed to the practical side of being a disciple (10:1-31). The journey motif is continued in 10:1, while the questions of marriage, divorce and possessions are discussed in 10:2-31.

In an attempt to trap Jesus, the Pharisees are presented as trying to have a definite answer from Jesus on divorce, a matter that was hotly disputed among the rabbis in the first century (10:2). Jesus forces them back to the Scriptures, to what Moses taught, and they settle for the prescriptions of Deuteronomy 24:1 (10:3-4). He shows that this is only a concession to weakness, and that the original situation is found in the Torah's description of the union between man and woman (verses 5-8; see Genesis 2:24). The use of Scripture is concluded, as in all rabbinic discussion, with the master's interpretation. "What therefore God has joined together, let not man put asunder" (verse 9).

Thus far the discussion is centred upon divorce, and Jesus has come to the extraordinary conclusion that there should be no divorce! As is to be expected, in this section of the gospel, he next turns to the disciples and drives home this teaching, reaffirming what he has already said in unequivocal language. In this treatment of marriage, the most intimate of human experiences, the suffering and denial of self that was Jesus' own destiny and was to be the destiny of all who claim to be his followers are shown to be more than mere words. Jesus' new law in a new situation of God-man relationships *costs*. Perhaps nowhere in the life of a disciple of Jesus is this felt more keenly than in the continual demand to give oneself unswervingly within the bonds of Christian marriage. The teaching of Jesus on this matter is as idealistic, counter-cultural and difficult today as it was in the time of Jesus and in the time of Mark. It has been said that Jesus was a dreamer.[6] However, the life of Jesus and his ways were no dream, and their challenge remains. As we continue to read the gospels, we continue to dream the dreams of Jesus.

The theme of openness and receptivity, leading to discipleship (the significance of Jesus taking the children in his arms in 10:16), reappears in verses 13-16 before a further urgent problem for the potential disciple is tackled: riches and possessions.

Mark's account of the rich man (10:17-22) begins with a very difficult question: the man, in asking how to inherit eternal life, addresses Jesus as "Good teacher" (10:17). Jesus answers that only God is good (verse 18). This, of course, is an indication that we are dealing with a passage that has its roots in the experience of the historical Jesus of Nazareth, who would have spoken in this way to share his experience of and belief in the goodness of God. In the deepening christological understanding of the early church, such statements from Jesus, where he subordinates himself and his goodness to God, tend to disappear. This is already happening in Matthew's version of the story of the rich young man in Matthew 19:16-22.[7]

Having settled that only God is good, Jesus tests the justice of the man, according to the law of Israel. This is the point of the list of commandments that Jesus asks him to observe (10:19). Jesus does not give a list of all the commandments. Those chosen are what we might call the social commandments, those that deal with his treatment of his neighbour: adultery, theft, false witness, defrauding and respect for parents. These are the commandments that a powerful, rich man would be most prone to offend. It is easy enough to observe (at least externally) one's ritual obligations towards God and church while dealing unjustly and sinfully with one's weaker neighbour.

The man replies that he has always lived a life of love and

6. See, for example, Nolan, *Jesus Before Christianity*, pp. 117–25.

7. For a comparative study of the Marcan and Matthean use of the story of the rich man, see Moloney, *A Life of Promise*, pp. 55–64.

respect for his neighbour. On hearing this reply, "Jesus looking upon him loved him" (10:21). Notice that this is the first indication of a movement from Jesus towards the rich man. Thus far all the initiative has come from the man himself. Quite capable of doing everything that he sets out to do, and having the means to do it, he asks Jesus' advice on the attainment of eternal life. Jesus now sees that the man has a deep desire to go further than he has gone so far through his observance of the commandments, and so, loving him, he attempts to wrest the initiative from the man, and he then calls him to discipleship: "You lack one thing; go, sell what you have, and give to the poor, and you will have treasure in heaven; and come, follow me" (10:21).

This is the radical demand that has inspired many generous and courageous hearts to extraordinary initiatives, but these wonderful examples from the history of Christian life must not be allowed to lead us astray in our attempt to rediscover the real point of this famous story. The use of the technical term "Come, follow me" links this account to a series of other vocation stories in Mark's Gospel, especially 1:16-20; 2:13-17 and 3:13-19.

In each of those stories one of the outstanding features of the vocation to discipleship was the *absolute initiative* of Jesus, and the immediate, wordless obedience of the one called. We have already seen that here the initiative has come from the rich man. In comparison with the other Marcan vocation stories, another feature emerges. Even though the first disciples leave their nets, boats, hired servants and their father (1:16-20) and Levi leaves his tax-house (2:13-15), there is no command that they should sell everything and give it to the poor before they could hope to become disciples of Jesus. Such a command is found *only* in this story. In fact, if there is any historical background to John 21, the disciples returned to the lake and their fishing after the paschal events.[8]

Two closely related problems are emerging. Why is this

8. This is a complex issue, depending upon what one makes of the links that may or may not exist between the fishing miracle of John 21:1-14 and

man (and no other disciple) asked to sell everything and give it to the poor before he can follow Jesus? Is it a universal law of the Gospel that *only* those who follow such a course of action can regard themselves as disciples of Jesus? The solution to the first problem, in fact, will make sense or nonsense of the second. We must look closely at the text itself.

The key to the whole passage is found in all three versions of the account (Mark 10:17; Matthew 19:16; Luke 18:18): "what must *I do* to inherit eternal life?" Here we have a man who is used to deciding his own destiny, because he has the power and the wealth to force the issue. This is not the way of faith. To become a disciple of Jesus, *this man* has to be stripped of all that stands between him and a radical commitment to Jesus. *In the case of this man*, it is his wealth. He is blocked from a total commitment to Jesus because he wants to control his own destiny, as he always has. Even in his enquiries about the best way to come to eternal life, he is simply asking what *he* must do. Thus, the means he has at his disposal to dictate such terms must go. The story is ultimately about the radical nature of true faith. One must have sufficient trust and faith in the person of Jesus of Nazareth to be able to pay the price — and it costs no less than everything. All that stands between the believer and an unconditional surrender of self to Jesus must be stripped away, but this man fails, and sorrowfully loses his chance of discipleship (verse 22).

In exact parallel with the discussion of divorce, Jesus now takes this matter farther with his disciples (10:23). The case is made even more urgent, as the absolute *human* impossibility of a rich man's entering the kingdom of heaven is conveyed through the famous image of the camel and the eye of a

Luke 5:1-11. There may also be links between Peter's confession in John 21:15-19, and the Matthean confession in Matthew 16:13-20, especially verses 16-19. On these issues, see R. Schnackenburg, *The Gospel According to St John* (London/New York, Burns & Oates/Crossroads, 3 vols, 1966–82), vol. III, pp. 341–51.

needle (verse 25). The absolute impossibility of passing a camel through the eye of a needle leads to the disciples' understandable amazement, and their conclusion that— standing by the teaching of Jesus—it appears that no one can be saved. The surprising authority of Jesus, speaking out of his incredible immediacy with God, shows that the disciples are still measuring the ways of God with the wrong criteria: "With men it is impossible, but not with God; for all things are possible with God" (verses 26-27).

Again, the "dream" of Jesus is in evidence. He insists that it is not what you have or do not have that matters: it is your preparedness or lack of preparedness to be open to the strange ways of God—and all who are prepared to risk everything for the sake of Jesus and the Gospel will reap their reward (10:28-30). As with the way a disciple lives his married life, so also in his dealing with his possessions, to follow Jesus means to take up a counter-cultural and in many ways revolutionary position: "many that are first will be last, and the last first" (verse 31).

The Way of the Son of Man: the Cross and Servanthood (10:32-45)

In our consideration of the section of Mark's Gospel devoted especially to Jesus' teaching his disciples the cost of their discipleship, we saw that he has made it clear to them that they are called to share his vocation to a *cross* (8:27-9:1) and to *service* (9:30-37). In the context of the third and final passion prediction (10:32-34), we find that there is no new teaching, but that there is a continuation and a further deepening of these two aspects of discipleship. Like Jesus, the Son of Man, the disciple is called to *the cross and to service*.

The third and final passion prediction is full of all the details of what actually happened to Jesus, and thus his destiny is made crystal clear. However, Mark introduces this prediction by centring his attention, not on Jesus, but on the disciples:

> And they were on the road, going up to Jerusalem, and Jesus was walking ahead of them; and they were amazed, and those who followed were afraid'. (10:32)

Again Mark has set the scene by showing that the message is for Jesus' disciples. They are "on the road". In this way Mark indicates that they are still involved in the "following" of Jesus down his way to Jerusalem. However, they are far from comfortable. To speak of their amazement and fear, the evangelist chooses two Greek words that express a profound emotional experience. They are deeply moved as Jesus strides on ahead of them, but despite all this, they are still called "those who followed". A gap is widening as Jesus strides on, and they struggle along behind, full of commotion and fear, but they are still there "with him".

In this situation, Jesus confirms them in the worst of their fears:

> Behold, we are going up to Jerusalem; and the Son of man will be delivered to the chief priests and the scribes, and they will condemn him to death, and deliver him to the Gentiles; and they will mock him, and spit upon him, and scourge him, and kill him; and after three days he will rise. (10:33-34)

Mark has already shown us, through his indication of their amazement and fear in 10:32, that they were still not prepared for this teaching about a suffering Son of Man. The passage that *immediately* follows shows why such is the case. The disciples are still at the level of the messianic expectations of 8:27-33. The sons of Zebedee step forward and ask: "Grant us to sit, one at your right hand and one at your left, in your glory" (10:37). Again, complete misunderstanding!

Translated into modern terms, one might say that James and John, who were among the very first to respond spontaneously to the call to discipleship (1:16-20), are asking that one might be Prime Minister and the other the Minister of Finance in the powerful kingdom that they believe Jesus is about to set up on his arrival in Jerusalem! How different this is from the attitude of Jesus himself: "Abba, Father, all things are possible to thee; remove this cup from me; yet not what I will, but what thou wilt" (14:36). Yet Jesus does not abandon his failing disciples. He instructs them further, telling them that they must share in the cup of his suffering and the baptism of his death (10:38-9). As in the section of the gospel that surrounded the first passion prediction (8:34-9:1), Jesus tells them, in the face of their failure, that they are called to follow him along the way of the cross. Yet again, Jesus' teaching of his disciples is not accepted, and is met with further misunderstanding.

"And when the ten heard it, they began to be indignant at James and John" (10:41). Their sentiments are understandable, as they are angry with these two "pushy" characters who are trying to jockey themselves into powerful positions by requesting special favours of the Lord (see verse 35-36). In the face of Jesus' continual call to suffering and service, they are still limited to seeing things "in the ways of men" (8:33). Even now Jesus does not abandon them, but taking them to himself, instructs them once more on the price of discipleship. This preaching, like all Jesus' teaching on discipleship, is not a laying down of laws, but an invitation to "follow" the way of the suffering and serving Son of Man, a way that reverses and calls into question all human patterns of authority and service:

> You know that those who are supposed to rule over the Gentiles lord it over them, and their great men exercise authority over them. *But it shall not be so among you*; but whoever would be great among you must be your servant, and whoever would be first among you must be slave of all. (10:42-44)

In this way, Jesus' three moments of intensive preparation of his disciples come to a conclusion. The passion prediction here, even clearer than either of the other two, is simply ignored by his disciples. The sons of Zebedee request positions of earthly power and honour, and Jesus' answer to them is the promise of suffering and the cross. He then has to turn to all of the *disciples* (the other ten) and call them to service. The disciples of Jesus are called to a gift of self in service and suffering. Thus the series of instructions concludes with the presentation of the way of Jesus' own life of service and gift of self unto death as the model for all disciples: "For the Son of man also came not to be served but to serve, and to give his life as a ransom for many" (10:45).

A Journey from Blindness to Sight: Following down the Way (10:46-52)

Mark, our skilful evangelist, now concludes this central section of his Gospel with a second cure of a blind man (10:46-52). While the blind man at Bethsaida stumbled gradually to sight (8:22-26), Bartimaeus leaps from his lowly place in the gutter, crying out to a procession that included Jesus, a crowd, *and his disciples* (verse 46): "Jesus, Son of David, have mercy on me!" (verse 47). He insists, despite the protests of Jesus' more respectable entourage (disciples?), and Jesus *calls* him to himself. "And they *called* the blind man; saying to him, 'Take heart; rise, he is *calling* you'" (verse 49). The language of a vocation to discipleship is found here. Blind Bartimaeus asks that Jesus give him sight, and his radical openness to Jesus' way leads to the gift of sight and to the gift of discipleship.

The earlier description of the disciples as men without sight (8:17) led to a miracle story showing that a journey from blindness to sight was possible if one was prepared to go down the way of Jesus (verses 22-26). Our whole section (8:27-10:45) has shown such a journey in process. The disciples continue to fail, but Jesus never abandons his failing disciples. The passage closes with a message of hope, acted out in the experience of another blind man, Bartimaeus.

Mark closes the central section of his gospel with an

encouraging challenge to disciples of all times: shed all pretension, be prepared to follow the way of the cross, of humility and service, the way of the Son of Man, and sight will be given to you. In this way you will become a true disciple of Jesus. The experience of blind Bartimaeus is a promise made to disciples of all times: "And immediately he received his sight and followed him on the way" (10:52).

PART III
The Gospel
of Luke

4.
Reading
the Gospel
of Luke

The Gospel of Luke has both excited and perplexed serious readers of the gospels for many decades. It is most obviously the work of a sensitive and inspired author. One indication of this fact can be found in the various sub-titles that this work has been given over the ages: the Gospel of the Spirit, the Gospel of Mercy, the Gospel of the Poor, the Gospel of Women. There is an air of gentleness in the Jesus of Luke's Gospel that is difficult to find in the Gospel of Mark.

It is the striking *differences* between the story of Jesus as told by Mark and the story of the same man as told by Luke that have created difficulties for the interpreters. I would hope, however, that at this stage of our reflections on the story of Jesus as told by the four evangelists, the reader sees that it is in the differences in "the story" that the uniqueness of each gospel may be found.

The reader will recall that we devoted a large part of our first chapter to a comparison of the sermon given by Jesus on the mountain in Matthew's Gospel (Matthew 5:1-7:28), but on a plain in Luke's Gospel (Luke 6:17-49). I pointed out that while this discourse is found in both Matthew and Luke, there is not a sign of it in Mark or John. This indicates that there could be a closeness between Matthew and Luke, as they seem to reach back to the same Jesus traditions. The material from the Sermon on the Mountain/Plain is only one piece of a great deal of material that is common to these two Gospel traditions and not found anywhere else.[1]

It is impossible for me to do full justice to the richness of the Gospel according to Luke within these few reflections. However, it is very important for our purposes to single out some central and overarching themes that will help us in our contemporary reading of the Gospel of Luke.[2]

1. This is commonly called "Q" material, taking the letter Q from the German word *Quelle*, which means "source". We are able to reconstruct this source only from the material that is common to Matthew and Luke, but absent from Mark, their other major source. As such, the "Q hypothesis" is very much just that — a hypothesis. However, we do have documents from the second century that indicate that there was a tendency to make collections of the "sayings of Jesus", and the so-called Q document is largely sayings material. For an example of this, see The Gospel of Thomas. A handy English translation is found in J. M. Robinson (ed.), *The Nag Hammadi Library in English* (Leiden, E. J. Brill, 1977), pp. 117–30. Some recent scholarship attempts too much in rediscovering the theology and setting of this hypothetical document. For two studies of Q, see T. W. Manson, *The Sayings of Jesus as Recorded in the Gospels of St Matthew and St Luke* (London, SCM Press, 1949); R. A. Edwards, *A Theology of Q: Eschatology, Prophecy, Wisdom* (Philadelphia, Fortress Press, 1976).

2. There are two important large-scale commentaries on the Gospel of Luke: J. A. Fitzmyer, *The Gospel According to Luke*, The Anchor Bible 28–28b (New York, Doubleday, 1981–84); I. H. Marshall, *The Gospel of Luke. A Commentary on the Greek Text* (Exeter, Paternoster Press, 1978). Simpler, but reliable commentaries are: E. Schweizer, *The Good News According to Luke* (London, SPCK, 1984); E. Laverdiere, *Luke*, New Testament Message 5 (Wilmington, Michael Glazier, 1980); E. E. Ellis, *The Gospel of Luke*, New Century Bible (London, Oliphants, 1974); R. J. Karris, *Invitation to Luke: A Commentary on the Gospel of Luke with the Complete Text from the Jerusalem Bible* (New York, Doubleday, 1977); G. H. P. Thompson, *The Gospel According to Luke in the Revised Standard Version*, New Clarendon Bible (Oxford, Clarendon Press, 1972). Other most helpful general works are: O. C. Edwards, *Luke's Story of Jesus* (Philadelphia, Fortress Press, 1981); R. F. O'Toole, *The Unity of Luke's Theology. An Analysis of Luke-Acts* (Wilmington, Michael Glazier, 1984); D. Juel, *Luke-Acts: The Promise of History* (London, SPCK, 1983); L. Doohan, *Luke. The Perennial Spirituality* (Santa Fe, Bear & Co, 1985); E. Schweizer, *Luke: A Challenge to Present Theology* (Atlanta, John Knox Press, 1982); Neyrey, *Christ is Community*, pp. 105–41.

The Theme of a "Journey" in Luke

It would be easy enough to single out some specifically Lucan themes and to concentrate our attention upon them, but I would prefer to give some indications, not only of themes, but also of the structure of this refined piece of early Christian literature. It appears to me that the best way to do this is through one of the great themes of the Gospel of Luke, which is a major structural and thematic element of this Gospel: the theme of a "journey".[3]

It has long been noticed that the whole of the second part of the gospel presents Jesus and his disciples on a journey to Jerusalem. A brief glance at the text indicates that there are deliberate indications of time and place—inserted by the evangelist as he keeps his story moving—which show that the journey towards Jerusalem is important to him, and that he wants the reader to be aware if its importance.

9:51	When the days drew near for him to be received up, he set his face to go to Jerusalem.
9:57	And as they were going along the road.
10:38	Now as they went on their way he entered a village.
13:22	He went on his way through towns and villages, teaching.
17:11	On the way to Jerusalem he was passing along between Samaria and Galilee.
18:31	"Behold, we are going up to Jerusalem . . ."
19:11	He was near to Jerusalem.
19:28	He went on ahead, going up to Jerusalem.
19:37	As he was now drawing near, at the descent of the Mount of Olives.
19:41	And when he drew near and saw the city.
19:45	And he entered the temple.

3. Although probably not available to most readers of this book, an indication of the richness of the Gospel of Luke can be had from the fine survey of Lucan theology in F. Bovon, *Luc le théologien. Vingt-cinq ans de recherche (1950–1975)* (Neuchatel, Delachaux & Niestlé, 1978). This work runs to 474 pages.

Both Mark and Matthew place most of Jesus' preaching in Galilee, yet the facts of history demanded that he must eventually make a journey to Jerusalem to meet his death, and so both must include an account of a journey to Jerusalem. This journey, however, is not a matter of great literary importance for them, as it appears to be for Luke. For the Gospel of Mark, Jesus' journey to Jerusalem takes only one chapter (Mark 10), and in Matthew this is slightly enlarged, to fill two chapters (Matthew 19-20).

If we presuppose that the Evangelist Luke had the Gospel of Mark before him as one of his sources for his story of Jesus (a theory that most gospel scholars would take for granted), then we are faced with some very clear evidence, which will help us to understand both the structure and the message of the Gospel of Luke. He appears to have taken the theme of the journey to Jerusalem—a geographical necessity in Mark— and to have developed it into a theological motif to such an extent that it dominates almost half of his gospel (Luke 9:51-19:45). The evidence of a uniquely Lucan insistence on a journey to Jerusalem is clearly present, but what does this development of a long journey mean to the evangelist? As we learnt in our earlier study of the gospels in general, it is not enough to discover why an evangelist wrote a gospel. We must ask a further question: why did the evangelist write his gospel *in this way*?

This question becomes even more urgent if one is prepared to notice that the theme of "journey" is not limited to 9:51-19:45. The theme of journey is not limited to a journey "to Jerusalem", either. That geographical journey, although the most obvious journey in the gospel, is only a part of a much larger and deeper journey theme, which permeates the whole gospel, and runs on into Luke's second volume, the Acts of the Apostles. The evangelist has been able to take the tradition of a journey of Jesus from Galilee to Jerusalem and use it as the basic sub-theme for the whole of that section of his gospel where the geographical journey of Jesus from Galilee to Jerusalem was already a part of the traditional story. However, a close reading of the gospel shows that the theme is all-pervading, and cannot be strictly limited to this physical journey of Jesus with his disciples.

The Journey Begins at Birth

As we will see in our following reflection, which is devoted to the infancy stories in Luke's Gospel, the use of the literary form of an infancy story serves as a summary of the whole of the theology of the gospel. One could claim that an infancy narrative is a theological prologue used by an evangelist to introduce the story of Jesus' public life.[4] We have already seen that Mark did this in Mark 1:1-13; and we shall see that the fourth evangelist does the same thing — much more obviously — in the famous prologue of John 1:1-18. The beautifully written accounts of the events surrounding the birth of Jesus (especially as they are told in the Gospel of Luke) are very dear to the whole of Christendom after centuries of artistic, literary and liturgical celebration (especially in our Christmas liturgies and pageantry). Nevertheless, we must not lose sight of their theological relevance for an understanding of the gospel that they preface. If we are to be true to the principles laid down in our first reflection on the reading of a gospel, we must admit that neither Luke nor Matthew wrote these accounts for Christmas celebrations. They had something else in mind.[5]

As this is the case, it will come as no surprise that the birth of Jesus, as it is told in the Gospel of Luke (2:1-7) is marked by the theme of a journey. Because the "great ones" of history

4. See below, pp. 93–98.

5. I am in no way trying to drive a wedge between our traditional Christmas use of the birth stories and the biblical accounts. It is possible to blend both tradition and biblical scholarship. It has been most tastefully done by Weber, *Immanuel.* On Luke 1-2 (see pp. 26–59), Weber's exegesis and reflections are precise, well-informed and movingly linked to his artistic selections.

(Caesar Augustus and his envoy Quirinius) summon a census, some "small ones" (Joseph and his wife, heavy with child) must set out on a journey (verses 1-5). While they are on that journey, the child is born. However, Luke goes to considerable detail to indicate that this child is not born in a home (as Matthew 2:1-12 would presuppose), "because there was no place for them in the *resting place*" (Greek: *kataluma*). We are used to hearing the word "inn", but the word that Luke uses refers to the large, open-sided tents that were used by travellers to rest for the night. This small group of people, specially chosen by God as both the willing instruments (Joseph and Mary) and the incredible reality (Jesus) of his unique presence among men and women, cannot be contained by such resting places. Not even at his birth could Jesus find a resting place. He is born *on* a journey, *for* a journey. Only in Luke is there no "resting place" for the infant Jesus, born while his mother and father are on a journey.

Once this theme is clear, then there are other features of the infancy story that take on a further significance. Now we are in a better position to understand the presence of a whole series of people who virtually represent the Old Testament: Zechariah, Elizabeth, John the Baptist (see also 16:16), Anna, and especially Simeon. This last representative of the Old Testament succinctly expresses a profoundly Lucan point of view as he proclaims:

> Lord, now lettest thou thy servant depart in peace, according to thy word; for mine eyes have seen thy salvation which thou hast prepared in the presence of all peoples, a light for revelation to the Gentiles, and for glory to thy people Israel. (2:29-32)

God's history, begun authoritatively in the Old Testament, but deeply open to a new moment when all its hopes would be fulfilled, has now come to the moment of that fulfilment.[6]

The promises made of old have now been fulfilled, bringing revelation and glory to Jew and Gentile alike. Another journey

6. For a brief and accurate analysis of Luke's use of the Old Testament to make this point throughout the whole of Luke-Acts, see Neyrey, *Christ is Community*, pp. 110–14.

is under way: a journey away from the old dispensation given in the law and the whole of the Old Testament heritage of the religion of the chosen people of Israel into a new, universal promise of revelation and salvation to Jew and Gentile alike. This is a journey indeed, but not only a geographical journey. It will have its geographical consequences, as the Acts of the Apostles will indicate, but behind the journeys of the missionaries of the earliest church (especially, but not exclusively, the journeys of Paul) stands the profounder journey of the gradual unfolding of God's history of salvation, beginning in the Old Testament (Zechariah, Elizabeth, the Baptist, Anna and Simeon), through the central and all-illuminating life, death, resurrection and ascension of Jesus, to the end of the earth (Luke 24:45-49; Acts 1:8; 28:30-31).[7]

I can only indicate some of the rich Lucan ideas in these few reflections. Already in the infancy story we find that the Old Testament is presented as a part of God's history of salvation. Luke, however, reflects the belief of the early church when he tells us that it has been perfectly fulfilled in Jesus. Luke uses these narratives (and he will continue to do the same thing throughout the whole of his gospel) to insist that God has worked *through the history and the events of the lives of men and women.* He has skilfully developed his theme of a journey to communicate this conviction. It is the journey theme of Luke's Gospel, as we shall see, that shows that the story of Jesus does not end with Jesus. A journey begins at Nazareth, which does not end at Calvary. In Jerusalem, through the events of Jesus' resurrection and his ascension, another journey begins. This journey becomes the journey of the church. In theological language it can be correctly said that Luke's Gospel is deeply concerned with a "history of salvation". The words of Simeon also indicate a necessary consequence of such a view: the revelation of God

7. In 1953 Hans Conzelmann published an epoch-making study of the theology of Luke-Acts that saw this clearly. His title for the book in German said it well: *Die Mitte der Zeit:* "The mid-point of time". The English translation has been given a more prosaic title: *The Theology of St Luke* (London, Faber & Faber, 1960).

in Jesus of Nazareth is a message of salvation to both Gentile and Jew.

These themes indicate that Luke's Gospel is a universal gospel. This has led all scholars to agree that it is a gospel written by a Gentile in a Gentile world. At the centre of this story of salvation for the whole of mankind stands the person of Jesus, the centre of all history and the hopes of all mankind. However, Luke's Gentile community apparently lived a long way from that all-important beginning. Here we have one of the important reasons for Luke's use of his journey theme. Despite their distance of both time and space from the beginnings of the Christian movement, he wants to show that his own community belongs to those origins, that they are a part of a movement that had its beginnings in Moses, and which is still unfolding at "the end of the earth" (see Acts 1:8), where they are presumably attempting to live their Christian lives. It appears very obvious to me that such important features of Luke's theology can be gleaned from a careful reading of these few passages from the infancy narrative, if we are aware of the importance of the journey theme in this gospel.

We will see more of the richness of these infancy stories in our next reflection. What we have already seen shows that the journey theme is not just geographical, but deeply embedded in this beautiful gospel. It appears again very clearly in the early description of the public ministry of Jesus. We have already indicated that John the Baptist is an important Old Testament forerunner for Jesus, in the Lucan vision of things. For this reason, the early section of Luke's Gospel covers all the events of the life of Jesus where the Baptist played an important role. It concludes with the Baptist's imprisonment in 3:20. We then read of Jesus' genealogy (3:23-38), reaching back to Adam, the father of the *whole* of the human race (Matthew 1:1-17 traces Jesus' ancestry only back to Abraham, the father of Israel). As the genealogy ends with an indication that Jesus is the Son of God, the following section on the temptation of Jesus (4:1-13) takes up the same theme and shows that this Son of God can be tested, but is ultimately victorious, as he depends entirely upon God, his Father.

The Journey Continues in Galilee

Luke has Jesus begin his public ministry (4:14-15), journeying through the whole of Galilee, full of the spirit, meriting the praise of all. This summary statement is followed by one of the most important sections of the gospel, 4:16-30, a scene found only in this gospel.[8] It is in many ways a summary of Jesus' programme through the whole of the Gospel of Luke. Themes central to our evangelist return. In the synagogue Jesus reads an Old Testament passage (a combination of Isaiah 61:1-2 and 58:6) announcing his messianic mission to bring grace, comfort and forgiveness to the broken ones—and solemnly announces that this very day such prophecies are fulfilled in him (4:17-21). Again, the theme of Jesus as the fulfilment of the Old Testament returns. At first, such a proclamation leads to joy, gradually fading to doubt as the people from Nazareth ask how the son of Joseph, whom they know so well, could dare to say such things (verse 22). Jesus' answer indicates that the failure of his own people to accept such a message will lead to the eventual acceptance and blessing of the Gentiles—just as it did in the days of the prophets Elijah and Elisha—and this leads to an attempt to murder Jesus. However, he escapes their clutches and passes through the crowd (verses 25-30).

I suggest that this is a programme for the life of Jesus. He preached a message of release, forgiveness and love to his own, but they refused to accept such a message. In fact, his story ends as they attempted to kill him through crucifixion, but he "passed through the midst of them" and thus lived.

8. Mark 6:1-6a also reports a description of Jesus' presence in his home town and his eventual rejection. However, the situation and most of the events are quite different.

Even the resurrection is alluded to in these few verses! Obviously 4:16-30, placed strategically at the beginning of the public ministry of Jesus (and at the beginning of an even longer story, which begins in a synagogue in Nazareth and ends with Paul preaching boldly in Rome), is of great importance for a correct understanding of Luke's story of Jesus (and, as I have just hinted, for an understanding of the experiences of his followers).[9]

A perceptive reader who has the Gospel of Luke open may have noticed, however, that I have failed to comment on the most difficult section of this famous passage: 4:23-24. There Jesus tells his people that they will ask him to do the things for them, in his own country, that he did at Capernaum. This is difficult because, at this stage of the gospel, Jesus has not been to Capernaum! It appears to me that the journey theme is again present. The very next episodes (all miracles) take place at Capernaum (verses 31-44). Jesus ends his stay with "his own"—the place of his physical and family origins (4:16)—by "going away" (verse 30), just as he ends his stay in Capernaum by taking on further journeys (verse 44). Ultimately, his own people make the mistake of desiring to *hold him*, to make him their own private magic man. This is to misunderstand Jesus and his task to go farther and farther down the way of God, in his relentless journey to God. There is no way that he will go back on his tracks, after he has left Nazareth (verse 30). His own people will, one day, say to him, "what we have heard you did at Capernaum, do here also in your own country" (verse 23). But such a "return" would be impossible. Jesus begins his public life among his own people, in his home town, but he never again will return to them, to do among his own people the things that he has done in Capernaum. That is what is refused in verses 23-24.

9. Although we are unable to explore this theme here, Luke often uses the pattern of the life of Jesus for the life of the leading characters in the Acts of the Apostles. This foundational experience of Jesus is repeatedly used in the description of Paul's preaching. See, for example, Acts 13:13-52; 17:1-9; 19:8-10. See O'Toole, *The Unity of Luke's Theology*, pp. 62–94.

He will not and cannot *go back on his journey!*[10]

They will also quote him a proverb: "Physician, heal yourself" (verse 24). This is fulfilled towards the end of the journey as they scream out to the crucified Jesus: "He saved others; let him save himself" (23:35).

Luke now reports a great deal of the material from the early chapters of the Gospel of Mark. Using that gospel as one of his major sources, Luke follows that gospel story rather closely. The miracles (Luke 4:31-41), the calling of the first disciples (5:1-11), further miracles (5:12-26), the calling of Levi (5:27-32) and the series of disputes with the Jewish religious authorities (5:33-6:11) can all be found, in that order, in the Gospel of Mark (Mark 1:16-3:6).

However, even here Luke's own special interests emerge, as can be noticed if we were to compare Luke's calling of the first disciples (Luke 5:1-11) and the parallel scene in Mark (Mark 1:16-20). Instead of the sudden inbreak of Jesus into the lives and day-to-day activity of the disciples so typical of Mark, Luke shows a Jesus who is prepared to lead his disciples through their own gradual recognition of who he is and what he can do for them (see 5:4-8). This more gentle, and perhaps more realistic, presentation of the vocation of the disciples shows Luke's skill and care in presenting the ambiguous human response of Peter to the call of the Lord who is his ultimate hope and support (see especially the expression "Do not be afraid" in the commissioning of the disciples in verse 10).[11]

The following section of the gospel turns again to the specifically Lucan way of telling the Jesus story. Luke leaves

10. For a useful survey article, indicating the central importance of this passage for the interpretation of Luke-Acts, see J. Kodell, "Luke's Gospel in a Nutshell (Lk 4:16-30)", *Biblical Theology Bulletin* 13 (1983) 16–18. See further, the fine study of D. L. Tiede, *Prophecy and History in Luke-Acts* (Philadelphia, Fortress, 1980), pp. 19–63.On verses 23–24, see pp. 36–7.

11. For a brief analysis of this passage, see F. J. Moloney, *Disciples and Prophets. A Biblical Model for the Religious Life* (London, Darton, Longman & Todd, 1980), pp. 137.–8.

his Marcan source, as Jesus calls and appoints the twelve on a mountain, after praying the whole night through (another typically Lucan theme). He then comes down *with them all* onto a level place. Now Jesus is totally available, along with the twelve, the future founders of the universal church. As people from "all Judea and Jerusalem and the seacoast of Tyre and Sidon" (6:17) come to touch him, be healed by him and hear his word, he gazes at his disciples, the future bearers of this message (6:20) and lays down a new law of God for a new people of God (6:20-49).

Further miracles follow, showing that he is not just a preacher of the word, but also a doer of the word, bringing God's healing presence to the son of a Gentile centurion (7:1-10) and to the dead son of a widow (verses 11-17). The theme of Jesus' presence to the periphery people comes to the fore here, and it causes a puzzled question from the Baptist. This gives Jesus the chance to praise the greatness of the forerunner, but still to indicate that a new era has begun (verses 24-30). The messianic expectations of Israel are being fulfilled in Jesus (verses 21-23). The new way of Jesus is further indicated as he allows himself to be touched by a sinful woman, exalting the saving significance of her love in contrast to the hypocrisy of the religious authorities (verses 36-50). In fact, Luke adds, as Jesus journeys down his way, he does so in the continual company of such women (8:1-3).

Luke prepares for the central part of his gospel by returning to what is basically the Marcan story, presenting Jesus as the great teacher of parables (8:4-18; see Mark 4:1-25) and the founder of a new family of God who hears the Word of God and lives by it (8:19-21; see Mark 3:31-35). As always, in Luke, Jesus not only speaks the word of God, but he also does the actions of God, and thus a series of miracles (again taken from Mark) now follows (8:22-56; see Mark 5:1-43). Another special interest of Luke can also be seen when, after these words and wonders, the twelve are sent out "to preach the kingdom of God and to heal" (9:1-6; see Mark 6:6b-13).

As the decisive moment approaches, when Jesus will set his face for Jerusalem, Luke deliberately gathers material that raises questions about the person of Jesus. Up to this stage in the gospel he has done and said so many things. He has associated others with him, and now the question must arise: just who is this man? Herod guesses (9:7-9), Jesus feeds the five thousand, and thus, as Jesus prays, the question of his identity is raised. Unlike the Marcan confession, Peter's answer is exact: Jesus is the Christ of God (verse 20). There is no story of a blind man stumbling to sight, and no refusal of Peter to accept the passion prediction, which immediately follows (verses 21-27). The transfiguration illuminates further a series of affirmations about the person of Jesus which dominate this section of the Gospel. We have already seen that he is not a forerunner, but the Christ of God himself. He will exercise this messiahship through his gift of self as the Son of Man. In the transfiguration he speaks with Moses, the giver of the Torah, and Elijah, the founder of the prophetic movement, of his oncoming exodus, his departure, which will be accomplished in Jerusalem. All that has gone before in God's history is now about to be perfected in this Christ, Son of Man, because, as the voice from heaven proclaims: "This is my Son, my Chosen" (verse 35).

Although Luke is generally more gentle with the disciples, the future founders of the universal church (i.e. of Luke's own community), they still have a lot to learn. They are unable to cure a boy who has an unclean spirit because of their lack of faith (9:37-43a). In their ignorance about the full meaning of the future death and resurrection of the Son of Man, they are afraid to ask Jesus about this saying (verses 43b-45). Indeed, picking up important themes from Mark (see Mark 9:30-37), Luke has the disciples arguing about who will be the greatest in the kingdom, which they believe Jesus has come to establish when they take possession of Jerusalem (verses 46-48). They attempt to dictate their terms to those wishing to follow Jesus (verses 49-50).

Luke's message to his community depends heavily upon a direct and unfailing link from the beginnings of the existence of the Christian movement in Jesus of Nazareth himself down to his own far-flung Gentile Christians. Yet he still points to the fragility of the faith of the first disciples. The powerful message of Mark on the never-failing presence of Jesus to an ever-failing group of disciples may not be as strong in Luke, but it is still present. This should not surprise us, as it would have been the experience of disciples in the Lucan community, just as it remains today the experience of all who attempt to join Jesus on his journey.

The Journey to Jerusalem

The reader will remember that the central point of Mark's Gospel was concerned with the mystery of Jesus as the Christ, the Son of Man, as the disciples were questioned about the person of Jesus. That scene has also been used by Luke, but as a preparation of the disciples for the journey that they are now about to take.[12] The turning-point in the Gospel of Luke comes in 9:51. After a long preparation, both in terms of his revelation of himself through word and deed and in the explicit revelation of himself as the Christ and the Son of God to his immediate disciples, Luke now announces:

> When the days drew near for him to be received up, he set his face to go to Jerusalem. (9:51)

From this moment in the Gospel of Luke we are dealing with the most original section of the whole gospel. It has been easy enough to trace a plan and an inner logic in the events of the gospel so far. The so-called "journey section" of this gospel has been the subject of a great deal of study in an attempt to rediscover its particular internal logic. There has been no universal acceptance of any single plan.[13] To give some direction, I would like to suggest a thematic structure to

12. The headings from Fitzmyer's commentary for this section of the gospel are indicative: "The progressive revelation of Jesus' power", "Who is this?", "Further miracles and sayings of Jesus". See Fitzmyer, *The Gospel According to Luke*, pp. 726, 756, 805.

13. For an excellent survey of the problem and the many attempts to explain the literary structure and message of the journey to Jerusalem, see H. L. Egelkraut, *Jesus' Mission to Jerusalem: A Redaction Critical Study of the Travel Narrative in the Gospel of Luke, Lk 9:51-19:48*, Europäische Hochschulschriften XXIII/80 (Frankfurt/Bern, Peter Lang, 1976), pp.

the journey narrative, aware of the tentative nature of my suggestion.

One of the major features of this section of the gospel is the beautifully constructed chapter 15, which seems to form the central piece of the whole narrative. Taking that as a clue, it appears that 9:51-14:35, leading up to the central statement of the narrative, deals in the main with the theme of the qualities that Jesus demands from those who follow him. The central chapter 15 deals with one of the main thrusts of the Lucan Gospel: the message of a God who seeks out the lost one: a message of pardon, peace and reconciliation. From there on the narrative that runs from 16:1-19:44 returns to the theme of the followers of Jesus, and dwells on the overarching theme of the difficulties they will have to face.

Given that tentative suggestion for the structure of the journey narrative, there is much more to be said. This section of the gospel is almost completely taken up with Jesus' teaching. Through all the teaching, as we have already indicated, the theme of a physical journey of Jesus from Galilee to Jerusalem is clearly in evidence, even though, at times, Luke's geography is a little difficult to understand (see, for example, 10:13-15 and 13:31-33, which seem to be situated in Galilee, and 13:34-35, which presupposes that Jesus has already preached in Jerusalem). Of course, it is not so much the geography that interests Luke, but the deeper theological theme of a journey. Luke uses this section to present Jesus as a teacher on a journey, and a part of that teaching—a central part of that teaching—is the journey itself.[14] There is no structure that can encompass this all-pervading Lucan theme.

1-61. My own tentative suggestion, which follows, is based on the centrality of the disciples and their association with Jesus' mission through this section. This, of course, has often been noticed. See the summary in Egelkraut, *op. cit.*, pp. 50-5. It does not, however, give sufficient attention to the rejection of Jesus by Israel, which is also found in the narrative. Egelkraut (*op. cit.* pp. 213-23) stresses this theme in his analysis, but makes too much of it.

14. See Fitzmyer, *The Gospel According to Luke*, pp. 823-7, and the indication of further bibliography on pp. 830-2.

There are, in fact, two journeys emerging. It has often been noticed that the fourth gospel is dominated by a last discourse during which Jesus instructs his disciples on the difficulties they will face and the attitudes they must adopt *once he has returned to his Father* (John 13:1-17:26). It appears to me that exactly the same literary technique is being used here. Although the material that Luke uses for this section of his Gospel comes from Mark, from Q or from his own special sources, and there is little that he has in common with the actual material of John's last discourse, both evangelists are trying to do the same thing. For Luke, the journey of Jesus is not a journey that comes to a conclusion when he reaches Jerusalem. On the contrary, the journey of Jesus is a journey to the Father. Because this is the case, only Luke has an ascension, where Jesus leaves his disciples here on earth, and goes to the Father (see Luke 24:50-52 and Acts 1:6-11). The fourth evangelist, of course, has a similar concept, but there is no description of an ascension, as in Luke (see, for example, John 17:5, 13; 20:17).

But this is only one of the journeys that Luke deals with in his two-volume work. As the journey of Jesus ends in his return to his Father from Jerusalem, the journey of the disciples, *without the physical presence of Jesus*, begins from Jerusalem, and will reach out to the end of the earth:

> Thus it is written, that the Christ should suffer and on the third day rise from the dead, and that repentance and forgiveness of sins should be preached in his name to all nations, beginning from Jerusalem. (24:45-46)

Once again, it is the deeper sense of the journey theme that offers some unity to the teaching of Jesus in Luke 9:51-19:44. Jesus never journeys outside Israel, and he speaks to all those who make up that chosen nation. He has sharp encounters with the scribes and the Pharisees (see 11:37-52), and he calls all the people to conversion (see 12:51-13:9). He has no illusions. He is well aware of his possible rejection by this people of dull hearts, deaf ears and blind eyes (see 13:23-25; 14:16-24, and also Acts 28:27), but he never shuts the door on them. They are a part of the universal mission of salvation for Jew and Gentile alike, a theme central to this gospel.

However, as I have already indicated, Jesus' teaching is especially concerned with the future witnesses to his story (for the ultimate importance of their formation, see Luke 24:44-49 and Acts 1:8). He forms them for that period after his return to his Father, when they must have a clear idea of their mission (see 9:52-10:20). They are to live in union among themselves and with their God, a union that can only be had in prayer (11:1-13) and sacrifice (12:22-34, 51-53; 14:26-33; 16:1-13; 18:28-30). Some of the hardest sayings on discipleship are found in this section of Luke's Gospel. There is every possibility that while Luke was not as critical of the foundational "disciples and apostles" as Mark, the cost of discipleship was something that he needed to stress in all its radicality. We must remember that he was writing for far-flung communities of disciples, in the church's third generation, and they were probably all too ready to become comfortable in their Christianity. Such a stress was essential, because, as we have already seen from our survey of the first part of the gospel, prayer and loss of self in love and service were the characteristics of the life of Jesus.[15] Luke's Jesus, like Mark's Jesus, instructs his disciples to live as he lived, while he was with them. There will come a time, however, when the disciples themselves will have to call on the Holy Spirit (11:13), profess their faith in their Lord before mankind (12:1-12) as they await his return (12:33-40; 17:22-18:8; 19:11-27), not knowing the times and the seasons of such a return (Acts 1:7). In the meantime they are to care for all who belong to the community (12:41-48). In this they are to repeat

15. This is important. It has been claimed, since the middle of the nineteenth century, that the Lucan Gospel was a "compromise" gospel. A school headed by F. C. Bauer at Tübingen claimed that this gospel had been written in an attempt to resolve many of the tensions that had arisen between more extreme positions taken by the preachers of the early church. In various ways Bauer's position has had many followers, as even contemporary scholars argue that the Gospel of Luke is somewhat bourgeois. See, on this, H. Harris, *The Tübingen School* (Oxford, Clarendon Press, 1975), pp. 226–9. In fact, the contrary is the case.

in their life-style, the life-style of Jesus of Nazareth.

Perhaps some of the most beautiful material in all four gospels is found in these instructions of Jesus to his future witnesses: the call to be neighbours as the Good Samaritan was a neighbour (10:25-37); immediately followed, however, by a poignant instruction that such active apostolic love can only be Christian when it is nourished by the word of Jesus himself, as Martha learns from Mary (verses 38-42). Jesus then teaches his disciples how to pray, how to be nourished by his Word and that of his Father (11:1-13). Equally powerful is the whole of chapter 15, devoted entirely to the seeking out and finding of the lost one: the lost sheep (15:1-7), the lost coin (verses 8-10), the two lost sons, both called back to the house of the Father (verses 11-32).[16]

Towards the end of the journey, Luke goes back to his Marcan source (Luke 18:15 picks up Mark 10:13), but he still has his own point to make. He adds the story of Zacchaeus (19:1-10) to indicate that Jesus brings salvation to anyone and everyone, even the most despised of people, as long as they are prepared to take the risk of faith. The opposite point is made through the parable of the talents (verses 11-27). There is a condition to this salvation: make use of the gifts that have been offered you, as the one who gave you those gifts will one day come back and make his reckoning. This, of course, is an ominous warning to an Israel that seems to have refused the God-given opportunity of Jesus of Nazareth. The Lucan scheme of a "history of salvation" is again in evidence: there is a history, a passage of time, set in the plan of God; all must use the time and the talents given to them to ensure their eternal blessing when the king returns. Although Luke never dares to speculate on *when* that will be, he has no doubt about the fact *that* it will eventually take place (see especially 21:25-27).[17]

16. On this, see Schweizer, *Luke: A Challenge to Present Theology*, pp. 78–81.

17. Some scholars (e.g. Conzelmann) have suggested that Luke has betrayed the eschatological element in the teaching of Jesus. This is not true. He certainly draws it away into a future that only God can determine,

Jesus' entry into Jerusalem is then prepared (19:28-34), but ambiguously received (verses 36-40). As the journey comes to an end Jesus weeps over Jerusalem (verses 41-44), and then decisively enters the Temple, cleanses it of all impurity, and takes control of it so that he might preach the Word of God in the House of God (verses 45-48).

Jerusalem:
A Journey Ends and Another Begins

Once Jesus is in Jerusalem, things rush to their conclusion. Unlike Mark's account of Jesus' presence in Jerusalem (see Mark 11:11, 15, 27), Jesus never leaves the Temple. He is preaching there all the time and he enters into conflict with the Jewish authorities (20:1-21:4). He speaks of the end of Jerusalem, and of a final end to history one must wait for, attending God's time, and his signs (21:5-38).

Luke has his own way of narrating the plot to kill Jesus, and the Last Supper, into which he inserts a discourse. He warns his disciples that they must face the future with his attitudes. These attitudes are magnificently synthesised in the eucharistic meal: a body broken and blood spilt for a group of disciples who have shared many meals with Jesus.[18] Yet the table-fellowship will be broken as, in the very near

but eschatology, i.e. a final end and a judgement, is still part of Luke's message. See, on this, O'Toole, *The Unity of Luke's Theology*, pp. 149–59, and A. J. Mattill, *Luke and the Last Things. A Perspective for the Understanding of Lucan Thought* (Dillsboro, Western North Carolina Press, 1979).

18. See E. Laverdiere, "The Eucharist in Luke's Gospel", *Emmanuel* 89 (1983) 446–9, 452–3. See further, R. J. Karris, *Luke: Artist and Theologian. Luke's Passion Account as Literature* (New York, Paulist Press, 1985), pp. 47–78.

future, they will betray him. His discourse at table still insists that their lives must contrast sharply with those of the great ones of this world (see 22:22-30). This is once again met with the obtuseness of the disciples, and the prophecy of their future betrayal (verses 31-38).

At Gethsemane, Jesus prays to his Father in a spirit of profound obedience, and he exhorts the disciples to pray that they too may not enter into temptation (22:39-46). He is betrayed by a friend through a kiss. The bringer of peace and healing is still present at his arrest, but it is the hour of darkness and violence (verses 47-53).

Luke's version of the trials of Jesus is also a little different from that of Mark. Luke places his Jewish trial (more correctly) in the morning after the arrest, while in Mark it took place in the night. He also has two trials before Pilate, broken by a visit to Herod. It is clear that Luke has used these trials to proclaim — ironically — the truth about Jesus.[19]

In the trial before the Jewish authorities he is proclaimed Christ (22:67), Son of Man (verse 69) and Son of God (verse 70). Before Pilate he is again called Christ, but two further dimensions are added before the political authority: he is king (23:3-4) and, most important of all for Luke, he is proclaimed as the innocent one (verse 4). Unable to resolve the question, Pilate tries to pass Jesus off to Herod, but that leads only to further mockery, where the silent dignity of Jesus makes the fumblings of Herod look so foolish (verses 9-11). However,

19. It is especially in the passion narrative that the Gospel of Luke seems to differ most strongly from Mark. This has led to the suggestion that there was an earlier form of the Gospel of Luke, which had had no contact with Mark's Gospel. Scholars have come to call this hypothetical document "Proto-Luke". Only in the last stage of the gospel's development would Luke have inserted some of the Marcan material. This theory was first argued by B. H. Streeter, *The Four Gospels. A Study of Origins* (London, Macmillan, 1924), pp. 233-70. A recent study, which still argues this case for the passion narrative, is V. Taylor, *The Passion Narrative of St Luke. A Critical and Historical Investigation*, Society for New Testament Studies Monography Series 19 (Cambridge, University Press, 1972). I am still presupposing a Marcan source. On this, see Fitzmyer, *The Gospel According to Luke*, pp. 89–91, 104–5.

Luke informs us that as a result of this encounter two evil forces (a corrupt Jewish ruler and a corrupt Roman governor) join in collusion against the innocent and holy one (verse 12). Jesus' return to Pilate leads to a further double proclamation of Jesus as the innocent one (verses 13-16, 22), but between the "frame" of these public proclamations of Jesus' innocence, Barabbas, whose violent life-style is described in some detail, is preferred to Jesus. A choice of violence over against goodness and innocence has been made (verses 17-19). Thus, Jesus is condemned to death (verses 23-25).

Although the traditional story of the cross is told, there is again a beautifully insinuated Lucan message throughout. On his way to the place of the Skull, Jesus is followed by someone carrying his cross, Simon of Cyrene, a model of all future Christians following Jesus on his journey (23:26). Still on the road to his place of death he speaks words of comfort and warning to the women of Jerusalem (verses 27-31).

Jesus, the innocent one, is crucified between two criminals (23:33). From the cross two themes that we have met before through the gospel reappear. Ironically, the truth is proclaimed about Jesus: "the Christ of God" (verse 35, recalling 9:20), "the Chosen One" (verse 37, recalling 9:35) and king (verse 38). The theme of the innocence of Jesus is picked up by one of the crucified criminals (verse 39-41). Jesus forgives all who have worked for this moment of darkness (verse 34), further forgiving and welcoming into his kingdom the one who, no matter what his defects may have been, is prepared to turn from sin, and confess his faith in Jesus (verses 42-43, looking forward to 24:46-47).

The Marcan signs of the end of the old religion, the tearing apart of the veil that separated the holy of holies from the rest of the world, are retained (verses 44-45). The death of Jesus is not marked by anguish and loud screams, but by a more gentle giving up of his spirit into the hands of the Father, for whom he has spent his life in love and service (verse 46). The response of the Gentile centurion to his life is not the Marcan proclamation of Jesus as the Son of God, but one of Luke's very dear themes: "Certainly this man was innocent!" (verse

47). Watched by women, Jesus is taken down and buried (verses 50-56).[20]

As is to be expected, each of the evangelists has his own particular way of approaching the central mystery of our faith: the resurrection of Jesus. They were aware that there was no point in preaching the cross of Jesus—unless it was an empty cross! Luke is no exception in this. Again, I can only point out a few features, singling out the theme of the journey, especially as it is in evidence in the Emmaus story—a beautiful piece of gospel material, which is found only in Luke's Gospel.

All the events of Easter in the Gospel of Luke take place in Jerusalem, *on the same day* (see 24:1, 13, 28-29, 33, 36, 50). Thus oneness of time and place ties all these central moments in Luke's view of salvation history into a tight unity. Already in the Easter proclamation we sense that the journey theme is returning to the centre of the stage. The women are not instructed to tell the disciples to go back to Galilee (as in Mark 16:7). On the contrary, they are reminded of the journey that they have made with Jesus from Galilee (see 8:1-3), where he had already instructed them on the need for the Messiah to suffer at the hands of men, to be crucified and then—after three days—to rise again (verses 4-8). They are not to seek the living among the dead: there is something more to be done.

We have followed Jesus on his journey from Galilee to Jerusalem, and we have seen that all the saving events of the paschal mysteries are happening in Jerusalem. It is in Jerusalem that the turning-point of God's story among women and men is taking place. However, on this very day of Easter, two disciples of Jesus have decided that they have had enough, and so they set out on a journey *away from Jerusalem* (24:13). It is most important to recognise that the two disciples of Emmaus are *walking out of God's salvation history*. In that situation of abandon, the risen Lord sets out after them. Naturally, they do not recognise the Lord whom they are

---

20. On Luke 23, see Karris, *Luke: Artist and Theologian*, pp. 79–119.

abandoning. Notice that these disciples know all the *facts* that are needed for true resurrection faith:

> They know the story of the life of Jesus, "a prophet mighty in deed and word before God and all the people" (verse 19).
> They know of his death and resurrection (verse 20).
> They know that it is now "the third day" (verse 21).
> They know that some women were at the tomb, and found it empty (verses 22-23).
> They even know of angels who have proclaimed the Easter message: "He is alive" (verse 23).

However, despite their knowledge of all these "facts", they have no faith, because "we had hoped that he was the one to redeem Israel" (24:21).

Blinded by their own aspirations, they are unable to see through their ways into the ways of God. Thus Jesus breaks open the word for them, explaining, through all the teachings of Moses and the prophets, that such things had to happen to the Messiah (24:25-27). Finally, he also breaks open the eucharistic bread, and suddenly their eyes are opened. They recognise Jesus in the breaking of the bread, and they recall the explanation of the Word (verses 29-32). "And they rose that same hour and returned to Jerusalem" (verse 33). These men, walking away from Jerusalem, abandoning their Lord and a God-directed salvation history, have been sought, found and led back to Jerusalem — and Luke has used a magnificent piece of literature to tell his readers of a saving encounter between the risen Lord and the sinful disciple in the Eucharist, which did not cease at Emmaus.[21]

This remarkable gospel closes with Jesus' appearance to all the disciples, where it becomes clear that the risen Lord is the same Lord who had shared many meals with them during his

21. Although I have developed my own understanding of the Emmaus account, the link between "the journey" and the encounter between Jesus and these two disciples was first suggested to me by an article of Sr J. d'Arc, "Catechesis on the Road to Emmaus", *Lumen Vitae* 32 (1977) 143-56.

life (24:36-42). Luke has Jesus take up the Old Testament again, as he had with the disciples of Emmaus, and his theme of Jesus as the perfection of all the hopes of Israel is repeated. This time, however, a further dimension is added. Those disciples who have been with him through all his journey, some of whom he has had to call back from waywardness, are to be witnesses of the salvation and forgiveness that they have seen in Jesus — to all nations (verses 44-48). However, they will not be alone, as they are promised a life-giving power from on high which will accompany them on their journey. Another journey is about to begin, and it will begin in earnest from Jerusalem after another central moment in God's salvation history: Pentecost (verse 49). Jesus leaves his disciples (verses 50-51), but this time the separation from him is not marked by the sorrow of the Emmaus disciples. Rather, they go back to the Temple, where this Gospel began (remember Zechariah in 1:5-25), full of joy and praising God.[22]

Conclusion

As Jesus began his geographical journey to Jerusalem, we were told that he was "to be taken up into heaven" (9:51. AT). I have insisted throughout this reflection that his journey did not end in Jerusalem, but in the ascension, as he returned to his Father.

Jesus' departure marked the beginnings of a new journey. Luke was the author of two volumes: the gospel and The Acts of the Apostles. As we have seen so often, this two-volume work began in the Old Testament, it journeyed through the

22. The nature of this book has necessitated my considering one of Luke's overarching themes. There are many other themes that a careful reader may have noticed. As we can see from this closing section of the gospel and the beginnings of The Acts of the Apostles, the city of Jerusalem and its Temple play a very important role. See, on these themes, F. X. Reitzel, "St Luke's Use of the Temple", *Review for Religious* 38 (1979) 520–39; F. D. Weinert, "The Meaning of the Temple in Luke–Acts", *Biblical Theology Bulletin* 11 (1981) 85–9.

life of Jesus as he went towards his Father, but with the completion of one journey, another began. In Acts 1:8 the risen Jesus tells his disciples:

> But you shall receive power when the Holy Spirit has come upon you; and you shall be my witnesses in Jerusalem and in all Judea and Samaria and to the end of the earth.

This is the essentially open-ended journey of the church. Luke has identified this issue and spelt it out with a remarkable and inspired profundity through his gospel. There can be no escaping the centrality of this important Lucan theme. It is a key to a proper understanding of the church and the Christian life. The church was formed around Jesus of Nazareth, as a pilgrim people called to journey on towards God's future. The Lucan Gospel calls upon us to accept a radical openness—following the journey of Jesus—as a central feature of our response to God.

However, the journey of Jesus in the gospel and the journeys of Paul in The Acts of the Apostles ultimately lead into loss of self in suffering. Often the only way to be "open", is to be "broken open", another of Luke's major themes: Jesus as the innocent slain one whose loss of self is gloriously overcome by the faithfulness of a loving and saving God.

Although these reflections are devoted to the reading of the Gospel of Luke, a final word must come from the Acts of the Apostles. As Christians caught up in the same journey of faith as the Lucan church (and Luke wrote his two volumes because he saw the danger of their slipping out of the journey), it is apt for us to listen carefully to the words of the two men to the original disciples as they gazed into the sky after Jesus' ascension; it is a message to the Church of all ages:

> Men of Galilee, why do you stand there looking into heaven? This Jesus, who was taken up from you into heaven, will come in the same way as you saw him go into heaven. (Acts 1:11)

In the meantime, there is a path to be trod, a Jerusalem to be reached, a martyrdom to be endured. The darkness of the road—for which we have no map—is lit up by a loving and faithful God, alive among us as "the power from on high", the promise of the Father who led Jesus through a journey, back to himself. As it was with him, so shall it be with us.[23]

23. Linking my concluding remarks on Luke's journey theme to the dedication of this book, I would like to share a reflection of a young man from my community who has just left the religious life after ten years, and after three careful years of discernment. As he left, we shared the following poem, a final word on this particular stage of his journey:

THE FLAME

The text and titles of a life changed course . . .
  adrift midstream
  these boxed memories in cardboard cartons
  lie charged with life now sleeping.
Yet in these musty muted carriers
  of dreams and visions
  loves grasped and lost
    and more often held to
    seeping warmth of naked chest
    reflecting a deeper, truer truth
these cartons
  crumpled though they be
  hold still the spark
  that in an instant leaps to
  a greater glorious fire
  that sears the flesh
  and in an instant cuts to free the hobbled hearts.
This latent flame
  —though still—
burns with a heat unknown
  and lies not now quenched
  but rather silently simmering
  till life or times
  demand a sign that is myself
    and that which burns within.

(Peter J. Walsh, Christmas 1985)

5.
Reading Luke 1-2:
The Infancy Narrative

The Origin and Function
of an Infancy Narrative

Most of our traditional Christmas folklore comes from the
Lucan infancy stories, which are so full of joy, angels, simple
people and a virgin mother. The only Matthean contributions
to it are the Magi, the star and their gifts (see Matthew 2:1-
12). We hear little of a suspected illegitimate birth (Matthew
1:18-25) or the wicked, lurking Herod, seeking to slay the
child, who has to flee for his life (Matthew 2:13-23). In fact,
the annual celebration of the Feast of the Holy Innocents on
28 December in the Roman Church comes as rather a surprise
in the midst of the Christmas joy and cheer. It would probably
come as a further, more serious surprise to most of our
regular churchgoers that there are *two very different* versions
of the birth of Jesus of Nazareth.

We cannot pause here to delve into the theological and
historical difficulties created by these two very different
narratives (Matthew 1-2 and Luke 1-2), although we would
all do well to read some of the fine recent treatments of these

questions.[1] For the purposes of the reflections that follow, it is sufficient for me to insist that the Lucan infancy stories belong to the whole Lucan contribution to the New Testament (the Gospel of Luke and the Acts of the Apostles): they serve as a theological prelude to his two-volume work. My reflections on the journey of Mary and Joseph at the birth of Jesus and the person and words of Simeon indicate how skilfully Luke uses the narrative of chapters 1-2 to communicate profound theological truths.[2]

Luke is not alone in his use of a prelude to the life and ministry of Jesus. He alone, however, used the first two chapters of his gospel to serve also as a theological prelude for the story of both the life and ministry of Jesus and the life, ministry and missionary activity of the earliest church. Only Luke, of course, wrote both a gospel and a story of the church reaching out from Jerusalem to "the end of the earth".

The fourth evangelist has his obvious and well-known prologue to his gospel (John 1:1-18). It is widely recognised that the same can be said for Mark, even though it is made up of neither the Johannine poetry nor an infancy narrative (see Mark 1:1-13). Matthew 1-2 is as much a theological prelude

---

1. Especially R. E. Brown, *The Birth of the Messiah* (New York, Doubleday, 1977) and Fitzmyer, *The Gospel According to Luke*, pp. 303–448. Most recently R. Laurentin has written a detailed and somewhat hostile commentary on the infancy narratives. Unfortunately, he is generally at odds with many contemporary Catholic scholars (including Brown and Fitzmyer), as the work is a long and complex attempt to show that modern biblical methods are destructive. His own use of semiotics is somewhat misplaced as an attempt to prove the historicity of the narratives. It is not the task of semiotics to prove historicity. As yet the book is unavailable to me in English. The original, French title is: *Les Évangiles de l'Enfance du Christ. Vérité de Noël au-delà des mythes* (Paris, Desclée de Brouwer, 1982). On this book, see R. E. Brown, "Liberals, Ultraconservatives, and the Misinterpretation of Catholic Biblical Exegesis", *Cross Currents* 34 (1985) 311–28, especially pp. 319–25. See also, F. J. Moloney, "The Infancy Narratives. Another View of Raymond Brown's *The Birth of the Messiah*", *Clergy Review* 64 (1979) 161–6.

2. See above, pp. 70–74.

to that particular gospel as Luke 1-2 is to the Lucan works.[3] As the prologue to the fourth gospel is a beautiful synthesis of the whole of Johannine christology, the same must be said for the prologue to Luke's Gospel: Luke 1-2.

How can the *beginnings* of the story of the life of Jesus be a synthesis of the person and role of Jesus of Nazareth in God's salvation history?

Although *we read* the Lucan Gospel story from the birth of Jesus through to his death, resurrection and ascension in Jerusalem, and then on through the various activities of the spreading church into the Mediterranean world until Paul stands boldly preaching Jesus in Rome (see Acts 28:30-31), it was not originally *told* that way. The earliest church did not begin its preaching of Jesus (and "preaching" was the earliest form used to communicate faith in Jesus) by telling his life-story from beginning to end. The greatest difficulty that the earliest church had to face was the fact that Jesus of Nazareth had been humiliatingly and disgracefully put to death on a tree by the Romans, at the instigation of the Jews. As Paul himself, one of the earliest and greatest preachers of Jesus Christ, tells us, this message of Jesus crucified was: "a stumbling block to Jews and folly to Gentiles" (I Corinthians 1:23).

To the best of our knowledge, the letters of Paul are the earliest form of Christian literature that we still have in our possession. We have already seen that the form of literature used by Paul did not give a great deal of attention to telling the story of Jesus.[4] In fact, going by the evidence of Paul's letters, the earliest preaching concentrated its attention, not on the story of the beginnings, but on the end: a death that made sense because of a resurrection (see I Corinthians 15:3b-8; Acts 1:22-24; 3:14-15; 4:10; 10:39-40).

The next elements to grow were the stories from the public

3. See, as well as the large-scale commentaries mentioned in note 1, F. J. Moloney, "The Infancy Narrative in Matthew", in H. McGinlay (ed.), *The Year of Matthew* (Melbourne, Desbooks/JBCE, 1983), pp. 1–9.

4. See above, pp. 10–13.

ministry of Jesus. Once the scandal of the cross was explained, then a further series of questions arose. What sort of life did he live, and what was the message that he preached that necessitated such an end? What sort of man was he? To answer these questions, the preaching, teaching and praying church went back to the traditions of what Jesus said and did. These elements were particularly useful for the further formation of those who had responded to the proclamation (*kerygma*) of the death and resurrection of Jesus, yet now had to be taught (*didachē*) more about him.[5] As we saw in our earlier study of the growth of the gospels, it was within this context that collections of sayings, parables and miracle stories had been gathered over the years to form the primitive oral, liturgical and perhaps even some written traditions about the ministry of Jesus. Not originally told as a coherent narrative (while the passion and resurrection story probably was), they were very much alive in the story-telling of communities looking back to the life and ministry of Jesus for their encouragement, light and direction. The collections were forged into a coherent narrative (as far as we can say with any certainty[6]) as the gospels came to be written.

Our analysis of Mark 8 indicated that the arrangements of the various pieces of traditional material will differ slightly, according to the use that each evangelist made of it when he came to write his particular version of the story. In the synoptic tradition, however, Matthew and Luke were heavily

5. On these two important stages in the gradual formation of the Christian message, see the classical work of C. H. Dodd, *The Apostolic Preaching and Its Developments* (London, Hodder & Stoughton, 1936). It has been reprinted many times since then.

6. It must always be admitted that we only have the evidence of the gospels themselves, and that we cannot be absolutely certain of exactly what was in existence before they were written. It is more than possible that there might have been longer pieces of narrative, where various stories had been assembled, well before the evangelists began their task. However, we have no documents that actually prove this. We have only the gospels.

influenced by Mark's choices in many questions. Mark's Gospel has come only as far as telling the story of the death and resurrection of Jesus, prefaced by the story of his public life. He has no infancy narratives, and no resurrection appearances. The Gospel of Mark opens with Jesus' appearance on the scene, already an adult, announcing the good news that the kingdom of God is at hand (Mark 1:14-15). It closes with the Easter proclamation, making sense of the death of Jesus (Mark 16:6).

Next in the development of the gospels were Matthew and Luke. They both depend upon Mark, but to the basic message of a crucified and risen Jesus, prefaced by a story of his ministry and teaching, Matthew and Luke both add infancy narratives and resurrection appearances. These additions to the story would have developed as the different churches faced differing pastoral situations, answering a variety of questions about Jesus: Was Jesus really human? How could he be Son of God? Did he really rise from among the dead? Where did he come from? In fact, as the early church moved more and more into a Gentile world, and began to preach Jesus and his message among people who were steeped in Hellenistic traditions, the question of *origins* became increasingly important. These questions, and many others that we cannot discuss here, caused our authors to write narratives about the beginnings of the life of Jesus. They did not simply invent their accounts, but based them upon certain ancient traditions, which would have been available to them. Of course, the fact that Matthew and Luke have different stories indicates that they worked from different traditions.

For the sake of completeness, it should be noticed that there is no hint of pre-existence in the infancy narratives. Jesus has his beginning when he is born of a woman. As far as both Matthew and Luke are concerned, the child is virginally conceived by a mysterious intervention of God, but from then on, he is born like any other child. It will take a few more decades, and the spreading of the early church into the wider Hellenistic world of Asia Minor, for the church to look farther back into the origins of Jesus, and to have the fourth evangelist proclaim:

> In the beginning was the Word, and the Word was turned in loving union towards God. What God was, the Word was. (John 1:1)[7]

From this indication of how the gospels grew, we can expand further on what we saw in more general terms in the first chapter of this book. While we naturally think of the life of Jesus, and tell the story of his life from pre-existence to infancy through to the death and resurrection of Jesus, the story itself grew *in the opposite direction*. This is best summarised by means of a diagram.

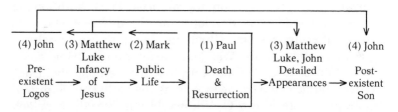

Thus, the infancy stories of Luke's Gospel, though their various parts may well have had their roots in ancient traditions, were developed and written *after* the story of the life and death of Jesus. Luke, therefore, was already well aware of the christology of the earlier traditions of the death and resurrection of Jesus, and of his life and teaching.[8] From this vantage point, he used a series of narratives concerning the infancy of John the Baptist and Jesus of Nazareth to present a synthesis of his christology and his theology in general, very similar in *function*, though not in *form*, to the Johannine prologue.

---

7. For this translation, see F. J. Moloney, *The Word Became Flesh*, Theology Today Series 14 (Dublin/Cork, Mercier Press, 1977), pp. 39–41.

8. This aspect of the infancy stories has been well caught in the title of R. E. Brown's little book: *An Adult Christ at Christmas. Essays on the Three Biblical Christmas Stories* (Collegeville, Liturgical Press, 1978).

The General Structure
and Message of Luke 1-2

A careful reading of the first two chapters of Luke's Gospel
indicates that, after a solemn introduction (1:1-4), there seems
to be a series of episodes that are associated with either John
the Baptist or Jesus of Nazareth:

1: 5-25	The annunciation of the birth of the Baptist.
26-38	The annunciation of the birth of Jesus.
39-56	The visit of Mary to Elizabeth.
57-80	The birth and circumcision of the Baptist.
2: 1-21	The birth and circumcision of Jesus.
22-40	The presentation of Jesus in the Temple.
41-52	The finding of the boy Jesus in the Temple.

Although there is considerable discussion among the
specialists concerning the exact relationship between each of
these parts, it is clear that we have an obvious telling of two
"stories": the story of John the Baptist and the story of Jesus.[9]
Even at this early stage of our analysis, one can begin to
sense that the narrative is the product of some very skilful
writing.

Such an appreciation is even further enhanced by another
feature of the narrative. The whole story seems to be studded
with a series of very similar short comments which come
from the hand of the evangelist:

(a) The theme of *departure:*

1:23	And when his time of service was ended, he went to his home.
38	And the angel departed from her.
56	And Mary remained with her about three months, and returned to her home.

9. There is a brief but very clear indication of the various suggestions that
have been made by different scholars in Brown, *The Birth of the Messiah*,
pp. 248–53. Laurentin's analysis (*Les Évangiles de l'Enfance*, pp. 25–135)
is exhaustive, but very complex. See also Fitzmyer, *The Gospel According
to Luke*, pp. 313–16.

2:20	And the shepherds returned, glorifying and praising God . . .
39	And when they had performed everything according to the law of the Lord, they returned into Galilee, to their own city, Nazareth.
51	And he went down with them and came to Nazareth . . .

(b) The theme of *growth*:

1:80	And the child grew and became strong in spirit . . .
2:40	And the child grew and became strong, filled with wisdom . . .
52	And Jesus increased in wisdom and in stature, and in favour with God and man.

(c) The theme of *treasuring in the heart*:

1:66	And all who heard them laid them up in their hearts . . .
2:19	But Mary kept all these things, pondering them in her heart.
51	And his mother kept all these things in her heart.

Luke 1-2 is a piece of extremely skilful writing, through which the evangelist wishes to communicate a unique point of view. The vehicle for his message is this narrative, which he has assembled from his traditions. He knits them together, edits them as he goes, and makes his own comments, so that the reader will not miss the issues at stake. This is quite clear from the two structural features that we have seen so far: the obvious pairing of the story of the birth and naming of John the Baptist with the story of the birth and the naming of Jesus, and the careful use of his own themes of departure, growth and treasuring.

We are now in a position to go one step farther, and discover in this carefully written narrative a beautifully balanced structure. Although one can never be absolutely certain of the themes and structures that were in the mind of our skilful evangelist, he seems to have told the story of the birth and infancy of Jesus in the following symmetrical fashion:

A. THE TWO ANNUNCIATIONS

1. *Annunciation of John's birth (1:5-25).*	2. *Annunciation of Jesus' birth (1:26-38).*
Introduction of the parents (vv. 5-7).	Introduction of the parents (vv. 26-27).
Apparition of the angel (vv. 8-11).	Entry of the angel (vv. 26-28).
Zechariah is troubled (v. 12).	Mary is troubled (v. 29).
Fear not . . . (v. 13a).	Fear not . . . (v. 29).
Annunciation of the birth (vv. 13b-17).	Annunciation of the birth (vv. 31-33).
Question: How shall I know this (v. 18)?	Question: How can this be (v. 34)?
Answer: A sign is given: dumbness (v. 19).	Answer: A sign is given: Elizabeth's pregnancy (vv. 35-37).
Constrained silence of Zechariah (vv. 20-22).	Spontaneous reply of Mary (v. 38).
Departure of Zechariah (v. 23).	Departure of the angel (v. 8).

B. THE PROTAGONISTS ARE BROUGHT TOGETHER

3. *The Visitation (1:39-56)*
Canticle: The Magnificat.
Conclusion: departure of Mary.

C. THE TWO BIRTHS

4. *The birth of John (1:57-80).*	5. *The birth of Jesus (2:1-21).*
The birth of John (vv. 57-58).	The birth of Jesus (vv. 1-7).
Joy at the birth (v. 58).	Joy at the birth (vv. 10-11).
Circumcision (vv. 59-66).	Circumcision (v. 21).
Canticle: the Benedictus (vv. 67-79).	Canticle: the Gloria (vv. 13-14).
Refrain of growth (v. 80).	Departure of the shepherds (v. 20).

D.   THE CHILD JESUS IS MANIFESTED AS SAVIOUR

6. *The presentation of Jesus in the Temple (2:22-40).*

The manifestation to Simeon (vv. 25-27, 33-35).

Canticle: the Nunc Dimittis (vv. 28-32).

The manifestation to Anna (vv. 36-38).

Departure to Nazareth: refrain of growth (vv. 39-40).

E.   BRIDGE TO THE PUBLIC MINISTRY

7. *The finding of the boy Jesus in the Temple (2:41-52).*

Theme: Jesus, Son of God, in the Temple, prepares to perform his father's task (v. 49).

Conclusion: refrain of growth (v. 52).

Luke tells his readers of the wonderful annunciation and birth of the Baptist in accounts full of the presence of God in his angel (1:11), in wonders (1:24-25, 60-64) and in spirit-filled praise (1:67-69). Yet, however extraordinary and awe-inspiring all this may be, it pales into insignificance when paralleled (and that is what Luke does) with the story of the annunciation and birth of Jesus of Nazareth. God is again present in his angel (1:26), but the wonder of the virgin conceiving (1:31-35) and the heavenly multitude announcing the birth (2:13-14) surpass the wonder of Elizabeth's conceiving in her old age and the mysteries surrounding the name "John". Now Elizabeth sings praise (1:42-45), Mary sings praise (1:46-55), shepherds glorify God (2:20), Simeon welcomes the arrival of the Saviour (2:28-32) and Anna thanks God for the redemption of Israel (2:38). There is no denying the greatness of John the Baptist, but how wonderful, then, is Jesus of Nazareth! The reasons for such greatness are clearly given, first in the annunciation to Mary:

> The Holy Spirit will come upon you, and the power of the most high will overshadow you; therefore the child to be born will be called holy, the Son of God. (1:35)

and then to the shepherds:

> . . . to you is born this day in the city of David a Saviour, who is Christ the Lord. (2:11).

Narrative has thus become proclamation. Jesus of Nazareth is announced, *at his birth*, as Saviour, Son of God, Messiah and Lord. These are the major terms used to speak about Jesus, and which are used through his ministry and then through his death, resurrection and ascension (Son of God — 3:22; 4:3, 9, 41; 8:28; 9:31; 22:70. Messiah — 3:15; 4:41; 9:20; 20:41; etc. Lord — 7:13, 19; 10:1, 39, 41; 12:42; etc.). They then become the heart of the message of the early church's preaching of Jesus, as it is reported in the Acts of the Apostles (Saviour — Acts 5:31; 13:23. Son of God — 9:20; 13:33. Messiah — 2:31, 36; 3:18, 20; 4:26; 5:42; 8:5; 9:22; etc. Lord — 1:21; 4:33; 5:14; 8:16; etc.). In this way, before Jesus has even uttered a word, we have already been presented with a powerful synthesis of his significance.[10]

Many other themes are initiated in the infancy narratives that later become central to the gospel story and The Acts of the Apostles. I will mention and outline a few of these, and then, given the centrality of Mary, the Mother of Jesus, in the Lucan infancy story I will devote a short section of this reflection to a further development of the figure of Mary, as she is presented at the birth of Jesus (Luke 2:1-21).

As we have already seen, there is a great interest in the fulfilment of the Old Testament in the transitional characters

10. See O'Toole, *The Unity of Luke's Theology*, pp. 97–187.

of Zechariah, Elizabeth, and especially Simeon and Anna. The choice of John the Baptist as a foil to Jesus is also vital for the later development of this favourite Lucan theme: "The law and the prophets were until John; since then the good news of the kingdom of God is preached" (16:16). All these figures, in one way or another, point away from their own achievements to the new age now being ushered in by this child (see also 1:41-45, 76-79; 2:27-35, 38).

In the beautiful portrait of Mary, the Mother of Jesus, we find a powerful presentation of a woman as the first and most wonderful of believers. Her openness to the word of God plays a major role in the history of salvation. In this way we have been given a fine prelude to the famous Lucan interest in the role of women in salvation history (see, for example, 7:11-17, 36-50; 8:1-3; 10:38-42; 13:10-17; 23:49-24:12).[11]

Again touching an issue that was studied at some length in our overall consideration of the Gospel of Luke, his central theme of a "journey" already begins in the infancy narratives. In Matthew's infancy account, the birth happens in Bethlehem, Joseph's village (see Matthew 1:18-25) and in his house (see 2:9). In Luke 2:1-20 Joseph and Mary are on a journey to Bethlehem, and on that journey "because there was no place for them in the lodgings" (2:7. AT).

The city of Jerusalem and its Temple loom large throughout the infancy narrative (1:5-23; 2:22-38, 41-50), as throughout the gospel (see the programmatic 9:51, the centrality of the Temple in 19:45-21, 37, and of Jerusalem in Luke 24 and Acts 1-5).[12] It is to the simple and poor shepherds that the infant is revealed; through an angel, heavenly acclamations, and the "sign" of the swaddling cloths and the manger (2:8-20).[13] The spirit of God is powerfully present in the infancy narrative (1:15, 17, 35, 41, 67, 80; 2:25, 26, 27), the beginning of a life that will be lived "in the spirit" (see, for example,

11. For a study of the women in the Gospel of Luke, see F. J. Moloney, *Woman: First Among the Faithful. A New Testament Study* (Melbourne, Dove Communications, 1985), pp. 40–64.

12. See above, pp. 89–90, and the bibliography given there.

13. See O'Toole, *The Unity of Luke's Theology*, pp. 109–48.

Luke 3:22; 4:1, 14), and which will close when Jesus goes to his Father so that he might send that spirit upon his followers (see 24:49; Acts 1:8; 2:1-4).[14]

The Birth
of Jesus (2:1-21)

Because of the unique nature of an infancy narrative within early Christian literature, we have described the origins and the form of Luke 1-2. I would now like to devote my attention to a more detailed analysis of one particular passage from the Lucan infancy narrative.

The account of the birth of Jesus opens with a typically Lucan indication of known people, places and times (2:1-7; see also 3:1-3). Luke is anxious to show that God's salvation history happens in the events of real people, living in our world and caught up in our time. His indication of known people, times and places is one of the techniques he uses to do this. However, there is more to it than just that. The account opens with a careful presentation, in what the world would call a *descending* order of importance, of three sets of characters:

(1) The Emperor Augustus, the most famous and respected of all the Roman Emperors. He it was who settled the internecine strife after the murder of Julius Caesar, and only during his time did the Roman Empire know any lasting peace within its borders. In fact, one speaks of the *Pax Augustiniana*: the Augustan peace. The whole of verse 1 is given to his decree that "all the world should be enrolled".

14. The classic work in English on this theme is still G. W. H. Lampe, "The Holy Spirit in the Writings of St Luke", in D. E. Nineham (ed.), *Studies in the Gospels. Essays in Memory of R. H. Lightfoot* (Oxford, Blackwell, 1955), pp. 159–200. Another fine analysis is to be found in the posthumously published study of one of the best contemporary Lucan scholars: A. George, "L'Esprit Saint dans l'oeuvre de Luc", *Revue Biblique* 85 (1978), pp. 500–42.

(2) Verses 2-3 are devoted to the Governor Quirinius, another Roman dignitary, who ruled over and established order in one of the regions of the Empire. It is a well-known problem that there was a Quirinius, and that he did see to a census, but the dates are impossible to fit exactly into the story of the birth of Jesus. That was not of great importance to Luke, as he looked back over the years to the beginnings of the Christ event, and was anxious to place a significant Roman dignitary, second only to the Emperor, at the head of the story of the birth of Jesus.[15]

(3) Last in this series of characters is Joseph, a son of David, on a journey from Galilee to Bethlehem, the City of David, bringing with him his wife who is with child. While they are still "on the journey", the child is born. However, there is no resting place for this child. He is born on a journey, laid in a manger and wrapped in swaddling cloths (verses 4-7).

Notice the apparently descending order of importance from the great ones of this world (the Emperor), through his envoy (Quirinius) to the "little ones" (Joseph, Mary and their son, born on a journey). Here two of Luke's favourite themes are already in evidence: the theme of a journey, and the theme of God's reversal of values, where the great ones are, in fact, the "little ones". Indeed, the Christian reader of this passage knows already that the real bringer of a lasting peace to all who are open to what he has come to offer is the child—not the author of the *Pax Augustiniana* (see especially 2:14).

I have already referred to the laying of this child in a manger, and to his being wrapped in swaddling cloths (see 2:7). The manger and the swaddling cloths appear to have particular significance; they are referred to as "signs" in the message to the shepherds: "And this will be a sign for you: you will find a babe wrapped in swaddling cloths and lying in a manger" (verse 12). When the shepherds go to find the

15. For a good discussion of this complicated question, see Brown, *The Birth of the Messiah*, pp. 547–56.

child, the reference to the manger reappears in verse 16. This "sign" must say something, and it appears possible that the background for these "signs" is the Old Testament.

In the Old Testament only one reference is made to swaddling cloths. They were linen bandages, wrapped around a newly born infant's limbs to ensure that they would grow straight. It is found in Wisdom 7:4-5, where the great Davidic king, Solomon (presented as the personification of the wise man in Wisdom 7-9), writes of his own birth: "I was carefully swaddled and nursed, for no king has any other way to begin at birth." By stressing the swaddling cloths as a "sign", Luke symbolises a newly born Davidic king, born in the city of David.

A similar Old Testament background can be found for the use of the manger. Readers will be well aware that the Christmas tradition has long used the imagery of a child in a manger, surrounded by the kneeling Mary and Joseph, shepherds (all of this from Luke's story) and kings (from Matthew 2:9-11). These images come from the narratives of Matthew and Luke; but generally our Christmas cribs also have an ass and an ox leaning over the child. Where does this come from? This is a fascinating question. The tradition reaches back into Christian antiquity and was made popular in the crib at Greccio by Francis of Assisi. Since then, it has become a regular part of our folklore.[16] The origins of this tradition are the same as the origins of Luke's use of the swaddling cloths as a "sign" of the new-born Messiah:

> I reared sons, I brought them up, but they have rebelled against me. *The ox* knows its owner, and *the ass* its *master's manger*. Israel knows nothing, my people understands nothing. (Isaiah 1:2-3. AT)

Luke takes this passage from the beginning of the prophecy of Isaiah. Jahweh laments the sinfulness of his people through

16. The background and development of this theme in Christian literary and artistic traditions is succinctly presented by Laurentin, *Les Évangiles de l'Enfance*, pp. 225–6. Laurentin does not believe that Isaiah 1:3 served as background for the Evangelist Luke, but that it was a later Christian development.

a parallel between the ox and the ass, who come to the manger to find their nourishment, and a hard-necked people, who refuse to do so. This newly born child offers Israel a new chance. The revelation of Jesus as the Saviour and the Christ (see 2:11) sees the reversal of Isaiah's lament, through the obedience of the shepherds who go to the manger.

The use of shepherds in 2:8-14 as the ones who are chosen to hear the proclamation of the good news from the heavenly hosts is again the deliberate and significant Lucan theme: the choice of the "little ones". Shepherds were not regarded very well by the religiously sound people of first-century Israel. There were always doubts about their honesty, as they were often involved in petty thieving. There was also considerable concern over the purity of their flocks, and of course, they were not loath to take their sheep into pastures not their own — an easy thing to do in a land without fences.

For the third time in Luke's infancy narrative there is an annunciation story (for the first two, more famous ones, see 1:5-24, 26-38).[17] An angel appears as a great revelation of God ("the glory of the Lord") and the shepherds are filled with fear (2:9). The angel calms their fears and announces the birth of a Davidic Messiah in Bethlehem, indicating that they will be able to identify him through the signs of the swaddling cloths and the manger. The scene ends with a further proclamation that this birth announces the God of peace to all who are blessed by the revelation which Jesus has come to bring (verse 14).

The shepherds come to find Mary and Joseph with the child (2:16). Their decision flows directly from their belief that what has been revealed to them comes from God. "Let us go over to Bethlehem and see this thing that has happened, which the Lord has made known to us" (verse 15). As so often in the Gospel of Luke, it is the little ones, the poor and the despised who have that basic openness to a new future. Such an attitude renders them receptive to the promise of

---

17. For the basic "form" of an Old Testament annunciation story (used by Luke and also by Matthew), see Brown, *The Birth of the Messiah*, pp. 292–8.

God's kingdom made to them in the word and person of Jesus Christ. In this way they come to Bethlehem, find the child in the manger and tell of the wonderful things that have been made known to them (verses 16-17). The powerful are too arrogant even to see the need (see especially 6:20-26).

Jesus is named in 2:21 as a conclusion to the whole account. The naming forms a close parallel with the birth and naming of John the Baptist in 1:67-80. Immediately before the naming, we find a subtle presentation of three possible reactions to the revelation of the mystery of God's ways through Jesus. In verses 18-20, in three very short remarks, we find the reactions of:

(1)   All who heard it (verse 18).
(2)   Mary (verse 19).
(3)   The shepherds (verse 20).

Notice how Luke has placed the reaction of Mary at the centre of this threefold structure. By doing this he wants to call the particular attention of the reader to her reaction, and to compare it to the reactions of the other protagonists in the story: "all who heard it", which precedes Mary's story, and "the shepherds", which follows it.

The reaction of "all who heard it" is one of astonishment: "and all who heard it wondered at what the shepherds told them" (2:18). There is no reference to faith, and there is no indication of any desire to go and see the child. At the wonders surrounding the birth of John the Baptist there was a similar reaction from all who heard and saw the wonderful things that were happening to this child (1:63). However, in the case of the Baptist's birth, there is a further reaction from this unnamed group of people: "and all who heard them laid them up in their hearts" (1:66). There is no such reaction from them at the birth of Jesus. Only Mary will be described as treasuring in her heart (2:19). This is an indication that "all who heard" have made a wrong choice!

The reaction of the shepherds is to go back to their flocks, and they play no further part in the story of Jesus. Nevertheless, they glorify and praise God, who has accomplished such wonderful things. Their departure from the scene was as necessary for Luke's story of Jesus' birth as it was necessary for the Evangelist Matthew to dismiss the Magi from his story by sending them home (see Matthew 2:12). Even though both Matthew and Luke present great figures of faith in their infancy stories, when they tell the story of Jesus' public ministry they remain true to "the story" as it came to them in their sources. Such figures had no place in the traditional story. The beginning of Jesus' public ministry is met with wonder and disbelief (see Mark 1:14-3:6). There are no Magi or shepherds who had followed the career of this remarkable young man from the cradle to the Jordan!

There is one person in the Lucan infancy story, however, who does play a role in the life of Jesus (see 8:19-21, 11:27-28), and who is still present at the beginning of Luke's story of the early church (see Acts 1:14): Mary, the Mother of Jesus. Her reaction to all that has happened through the remarkable events of the annunciation and the birth, where she was a central figure, is described in 2:19: "But Mary kept all these things, pondering them in her heart."

There is another moment in this narrative where the same expression is used to speak of the reaction of Mary. At the finding of Jesus in the Temple, after what can be understood only as a gentle reprimand, telling Mary and Joseph that what matters is that Jesus be about the affairs of his Father, we again read: "And they did not understand the saying which he spoke to them. . . . and his mother kept all these things in her heart" (2:50-51).

As is often the case with Luke's Gospel, a careful allusion to the Old Testament is the source of this expression. "To keep something in the heart", or the even better translation "to treasure something in the heart" is found quite regularly in the Old Testament, and it is found throughout the various books (see, for example, Genesis 37:11; I Samuel 2:13; Malachi 2:2). It appears that it was a particularly important expression for the authors of the Wisdom literature (see, for example, Sirach 39:1-3; Proverbs 31; Psalm 119:11) and the apocalyptic literature (see, for example, Daniel 1:8; 4:28; 7:28). This rich biblical tradition provides Luke with a notion that he then uses beautifully to speak of the Mother of Jesus.

The expression is generally found in contexts where a human being has had some sort of revelation from God. This is especially the case in the apocalyptic literature. These revelations, which have their origins in God, are quite beyond the understanding of the human recipient. There is obviously some mysterious meaning behind it, but it is well beyond the ken of a mere human. In such a situation, two reactions are possible. One can just "marvel", and then go one's way. This is obviously the decision taken by those who heard of the mysteries of the child at Bethlehem (Luke 2:18). However, according to the biblical tradition, those who treasure in their hearts do not reject the incomprehensible. The revelation is taken into the deepest recesses of one's being, treasured, guarded and pondered over. The faithful one simply awaits some time in God's future, a moment that will be determined by God's plan and God's history, when the whole truth will be received in all its fullness. This is an important concept for the Lucan theme of salvation history: a history of God's actions among the events of men and women, and it is used importantly to speak of the attitude of Mary, the Mother of Jesus.

Mary's situation is indeed an extraordinary one. She has been the recipient of a strange annunciation: a virginal conception of a son who will not only be the Messiah (1:32-33), but also the Holy One of God, the Son of God (1:35). Shepherds have come in from the fields, announcing visions of angels and messages from heavenly choirs. As she herself has said, in the midst of her confusion over the conception of her son: "How can this be?" (1:34). The same confusion is found as she discovers her son in the Temple of Jerusalem, after searching for him for three days, only to be rebuked (2:50-51). *Never* in these accounts is Mary presented as a woman in control of her own situation. *Always*, however, she is presented as someone who is totally open to God's ways in her life, as she "treasures" the revealed mysteries, and awaits the fullness of God's revelation, confident that they will come in God's time. The final gesture, which indicates this yet further, is the naming of her son Jesus, "the name given by the angel before he was conceived in the womb" (2:21). God and his word lead Mary in her decisions.

Thus, through the use of the expression "to treasure in one's heart", Luke has both placed Mary first among all believers, and at the same time he has shown, through her, the central importance of God's history of salvation. This history is not ours to determine. As Jesus said to his disciples at the beginning of Luke's story of the Church: "It is not for you to know times or seasons which the Father has fixed by his own authority" (Acts 1:71). Mary did not ask for "times and seasons"; she is thus the model for disciples of all ages.[18]

Conclusion

Luke 1-2 is a skilfully written and simple story. We read or hear of two wonderful annunciations and the recognition by Elizabeth of the wonder of Mary's child; two births and the recognition by the great Old Testament figures Simeon and Anna of the wonder of Mary's child. They joyfully proclaim the end of their era, although not without noticing that the following of Jesus will exact its price (see 2:34-35). The new era itself is opened in the final scene: the finding of the boy Jesus in the Temple, where the child of the earlier stories announces to his stunned and suffering mother (just as Simeon foretold, yet she believes, see verses 50-51) that he must be in his Father's house and about his Father's business (verse 49). A story that will reach "to the end of the earth" (Acts 1:8; 28:25-31) has been set in motion.

The Evangelist Luke wanted his own communities, Gentile churches far flung from the geography, culture, history and religious practices of Christian origins, to feel that they were

18. For an analysis of the Marian material in Luke–Acts, see Moloney, *Woman: First Among the Faithful*, pp. 40–56.

an intimate part of the "story". The journey that began with the annunciation scenes and led mother and child to Bethlehem did not cease there. The child was certainly the fulfilment of the hopes of Israel, their long-awaited Messiah (see especially 1:32-33), but he is more than that. He is also the Son of God (verse 35) and thus Lord and Saviour of all mankind (2:11).

Our own times are still farther away from "the story" of the historical beginnings of a mysteriously persevering reality, which we nowadays call "Christian life". Luke's infancy narratives can tell us that we too are caught up in an ongoing journey, a "never-ending story", which we go on hearing and treasuring in our hearts (see 2:19, 51). Like Luke's communities, we too are still being called to give witness to the wonder and joy that stands at the heart of his particular version of the birth of Jesus of Nazareth: Saviour, Son of God, Messiah and Lord. Luke's challenge is that we go on telling that "story", preaching it in Jesus' name to all nations (see 24:47-48).

PART IV
The Gospel
of Matthew

6.
Reading the Gospel of Matthew

It is quite clear from our reading of the Synoptic Gospels so far, that each evangelist "tells the story" of the public life of Jesus, which began in Galilee, of a journey to Jerusalem and of a death and resurrection in that city. As we shall see in the section devoted to the fourth gospel, John tells the story differently, and one of the major differences is a regular presence of Jesus in Jerusalem during his public ministry. However, restricting ourselves to Mark, Luke and Matthew, we have, in these gospels, the same basic story, told in different ways. I have attempted to single out the *uniqueness* of Mark's and Luke's point of view, so that we might appreciate the richness of our tradition concerning Jesus. God has shown his wisdom in revealing himself to us, through his Son, through the ages in this fourfold gospel tradition.

As with our study of Mark and Luke, we must now attempt to rediscover the uniqueness of Matthew's story of Jesus. Our reaching back over nearly two thousand years, to touch again the heart and the mind of an author must not be an exercise in ancient history or archeology.[1] If it is only that, then we find ourselves in touch with a dusty old text, written "way back then". Our approach to the Gospel of Matthew must be made with an important question in our minds. Is it possible that this ancient text can be a word of life for us in the 1980s?

A Starting Point:
Matthew 28:16-20

Strange as it may seem, scholars recognise that the most logical place to begin in any search for Matthew's mind and purpose is at the very end of his gospel.[2] Here we have the

1. A recent large-scale commentary on Matthew's Gospel is F. W. Beare, *The Gospel of Matthew* (Oxford, Blackwells, 1981). However, a simpler but much better commentary is J. P. Meier, *Matthew*, New Testament Message 3 (Wilmington, Michael Glazier, 1980). Further good commentaries are: E. Schweizer, *The Good News According to Matthew* (London, SPCK, 1975); D. Hill, *The Gospel of Matthew*, New Century Bible (London, Oliphants, 1972); H. Benedict Green, *The Gospel According to Matthew in the Revised Standard Version*, New Clarendon Bible (Oxford, Clarendon Press, 1975); J. Fenton, *Saint Matthew*, Pelican Gospel Commentaries (Harmondsworth, Penguin Books, 1963); D. Senior, *Invitation to Matthew: A Commentary on the Gospel of Matthew with the Complete Text from the Jerusalem Bible*, Image Books (New York, Doubleday, 1977). There is an excellent general introduction and "mini-commentary" (the expression is the author's) to the Gospel of Matthew in J. P. Meier, *The Vision of Matthew. Christ, Church and Morality in the First Gospel* (New York, Paulist Press, 1979). See also L. Doohan, *Matthew. Spirituality for the 80's and 90's* (Santa Fe, Bear & Co., 1985); R. A. Edwards, *Matthew's Story of Jesus* (Philadelphia, Fortress Press, 1985); D. Senior, *What are They Saying about the Gospel of Matthew?* (New York, Paulist Press, 1983); J. D. Kingsbury, *Matthew. A Commentary for Preachers and Others* (London, SPCK, 1978); P. F. Ellis, *Matthew: His Mind and His Message* (Collegeville, Liturgical Press, 1974); Neyrey, *Christ is Community*, pp. 81–104.

2. A most important study on this was first published in German in 1950. It is only now readily available in English: O. Michel, "The Conclusion of Matthew's Gospel. A Contribution to the Easter Message", in G. Stanton (ed.), *The Interpretation of Matthew* (London, SPCK, 1983), pp. 30–41. See also another important study, originally published in German in 1964, and only recently made available in English: G. Bornkamm, "The Risen

commission of the risen Jesus to his disciples. There can be no doubt that the Matthean community understood itself and its apostolic task in terms of the commission that the Lord had given them. It is so important that we will consider this text in some detail. This famous passage runs as follows:

> Now the eleven disciples went to Galilee, to the mountain to which Jesus had directed them. And when they saw him they worshipped him; but some doubted. And Jesus came and said to them, "All authority in heaven and on earth has been given to me. Go therefore and make disciples of all nations, baptizing them in the name of the Father and of the Son and of the Holy Spirit, teaching them to observe all that I have commanded you; and lo, I am with you always, to the close of the age." (Matthew 28:16-20)

This passage is more than encouraging and comforting words. If we situate these words of Jesus, which are crucial for an understanding of the Gospel of Matthew, in a largely Jewish-Christian community in the 80s of the first century (and that appears the best place for the original writing of this gospel), then they reflect a Christian community marked by an extraordinary new openness, in sharp contrast to the Jewish world where that community had its roots.[3]

After the Easter events (Matthew 28:1-15), the disciples return to Galilee, to the mountain indicated by Jesus (verse 16). Does this refer to the mountain where the new law was given to a new people of God by a new and perfect Messiah (5:1)? It is impossible to be certain, but as the situating of the giving of the new law on a mountain was important, so is it also important for the risen Lord's commissioning of his church. Both uses of a mountain, of course, have their origins in the importance of mountains, beginning with Sinai, in the biblical tradition. We are about to witness a significant communication of God's ways and God's teaching to the

Lord and the Earthly Jesus: Matthew 28:16-20", in G. Bornkamm, G. Barth and H. J. Held (eds), *Tradition and Interpretation in Matthew* (London, SCM Press, 1982), pp. 301–27.

3. See especially, R. E. Brown and J. P. Meier, *Antioch & Rome. New Testament Cradles of Catholic Christianity* (New York, Paulist Press, 1983), pp. 11–86.

disciples.[4] One senses in these indications a community well-versed and full of respect and appreciation for the traditional religious symbols of Israel. Yet, the commission of Jesus to his disciples appears to contradict that respect and appreciation.

The reaction of the disciples to the sight of Jesus is ambiguous. Some worship him. The Greek verb used here (*proskunein*) is used extensively in the Gospel of Matthew to show a correct understanding of who Jesus is and how one should relate to him (see, for example, Matthew 2:2, 8 [!], 11; 4:9-10; 8:2; 9:18; 14:33; 15:25; 18:26; 20:20; 28:9, 17). Despite the dramatic significance of this final scene, Matthew still reports: "but some doubted". This hesitation before the risen Lord, one of the hallmarks of all the synoptic resurrection accounts (see Mark 16:8, 9-11, 14, and Luke 24:10-11, 13-35, 36-37), is also an important part of Matthew's realistic theology of the Church. The disciples believe, yet they falter in their belief.

Jesus first makes a most significant declaration about himself, and then spells out the consequences for his disciples. The man whom they had known as Jesus of Nazareth claims that all authority on heaven and earth has been given to him. This is nothing less than to claim that Jesus has taken over the authority and dignity that traditional Israel allowed only to Jahweh. Passages that indicate this are innumerable (see, for a basic passage on the oneness of God and his complete

5. Some scholars are content to let this seeming contradiction stand as evidence of Matthew's use of different traditions: some in favour of a Gentile mission and some against. The gospel as a whole, however, indicates that these "contradictions" (which certainly do reflect different traditions) have been blended to form a particularly important theological contribution to the church's understanding of the mystery of Jesus and its relationship to him. I have been greatly influenced in this by J. P. Meier, *Law and History in Matthew's Gospel. A Redactional Study of Mt 5:17-48*, Analecta Biblica 71 (Rome, Biblical Institute Press, 1976); see especially pp. 25–40. His excellent commentary (see note 1, pages 1–118) is also based on this insight. See also idem, "Salvation-History in Matthew: In Search of a Starting Point", *Catholic Biblical Quarterly* 37 (1975) 203–15. See further, Senior, *What are They Saying about the Gospel of Matthew?*, pp. 28–36; J. D. Kingsbury, "The Structure of Matthew's Gospel and His Concept of Salvation History", *Catholic Biblical Quarterly* 35 (1973) 451–74.

authority, the famous Deuteronomy 6:1-4. There is probably also a very important reference to the ultimate giving of all authority to the "one like a son of man" in Daniel 7:14). Thus when Jesus on a mountain with his failed and failing disciples claims to have been given all the authority, this is a bold claim indeed. It certainly would not have been happily received by Rabbinic Judaism, struggling to establish its identity after the disastrous effects of the Jewish war of AD 70. It must be noticed that the Evangelist Matthew has a very exalted idea of Jesus. The profound understanding of Jesus reflected in Matthew 28:17 is paralleled only by some of the christological claims of the fourth gospel (see, for example, John 5:17-18; 10:30).

Flowing from the uniqueness and universality of his authority, the Matthean Jesus then breaks through three further basic elements in traditional Jewish belief and practice.

(1) He commands his disciples to "Go therefore and make disciples of *all nations*" (28:19a). This breaks through the belief in Israel's exclusive place among the nations of the world as God's chosen people. Once again this would have been hard for post-war Rabbinic Judaism to accept. Although there had been an openness to the idea of a universal salvation in the prophets (see, for example, Isaiah 2:1-4), it had always meant a movement from the Gentile world towards Zion. Here this is reversed: the foundation members of the new people of God, founded by Jesus of Nazareth, are to "go out" to make disciples of all nations.

(2) These disciples are further instructed to "baptise" in the name of the Father and of the Son and of the Holy Spirit (28:19b). A new initiation rite is introduced into the new people of God, setting out on its mission. It is to replace the centrally important Jewish rite of circumcision. The centrality of this rite can be sensed through a reading of Genesis 17:1-27, an early reflection on the relationship between circumcision and the Covenant, and I Maccabees 1:10-15, an indication of its enduring importance in the history of the Jewish people.

(3) As if what had been commanded so far was not

enough, the final command demolishes the very basis of traditional Jewish faith, built upon the teaching and the learning of the Torah. Even the Torah is replaced. Jesus uses words commonly found in passages on the importance of the Torah: "to teach", "to observe", "commandments" (see, for example, Deuteronomy 5-6, especially 6:1, where all these terms appear) to indicate a new teaching: "teaching them to observe all that I have commanded you" (28:20a).

His final words are not words of departure, but words assuring that he will always be with his disciples (28:20b). In our study of Luke I mentioned that only that evangelist develops the idea of an ascension into a pictorial image of Jesus actually leaving the earth and returning to his Father (see Luke 24:50-51; Acts 1:9-10). In Matthew there is no trace of any such event. In fact, one could say that the opposite is the case. Matthew's Gospel ends with Jesus' promise that he will never leave them. Of course, *theologically*, one can point out that Luke is saying exactly the same thing through his message of a return to the Father and his eventual sending of the Spirit. Such a concept is not found in Matthew or Mark. Yet the Lucan concept of the Holy Spirit alive in the church is very close to the Matthean Jesus' promise to be with his church always. This is an excellent and important example of the fact that the different evangelists can use *different narratives* to communicate the *same truths* about God's ways among women and men through Jesus Christ. Whether it is Jesus' spirit sent by the Father (Luke) or the abiding presence of Jesus who will never leave his church (Matthew), the message of God's purposes to found and sustain a holy people in and through Jesus rings true.

From these last few verses of the Gospel of Matthew (28:16-20), one could well argue that we are dealing with a gospel that is extremely hostile to the traditional ways of Judaism. They could be read as the charter of a Christian church that has broken definitively from its origins in Judaism. We are clearly in touch with a community being strongly exhorted to set out on a journey away from the confines of Israel into the new world of a universal church, where Jesus, his ways and his teachings are to be the measure of one's "belonging".

A Strange Contradiction

Yet to read only the conclusion of Matthew's Gospel and to draw one's conclusions from that passage alone would be to do our evangelist a serious disservice. It is a part of Christian tradition that Matthew's Gospel is the most Jewish of all our gospels. How can it be that he disregards all that is traditional and sacred to Judaism? This is an important matter. Is Matthew's Gospel concerned only with the new? What is his attitude to the old, the ways of God in the history of Israel?

Matthew 28:16-20 is found at the very end of the gospel. There is an equally important passage much nearer the beginning:

> Think not that I have come to abolish the law and the prophets; I have come not to abolish them, but to fulfil them. For truly, I say to you, till heaven and earth pass away, not an iota, not a dot, will pass from the law until all is accomplished. (Matthew 5:17-18)

In the light of 28:16-20 we seem to be faced with a strange contradiction. The matter becomes even more urgent when we begin to read through other parts of the gospel. There are two different occasions during the public ministry when Jesus speaks about the exclusiveness of his mission to Israel and he similarly limits his disciples' mission. They are very puzzling: "These twelve Jesus sent out, charging them: 'Go nowhere among the Gentiles, and enter no town of the Samaritans, but go rather to the lost sheep of the house of Israel'" (10:5-6). To the Canaanite woman's pleas, he replies sharply: "I was sent only to the lost sheep of the house of Israel" (15:24).

These important passages from the public ministry of the Matthean Jesus clearly limit the mission of Jesus and his disciples to Israel, and exhort the followers of Jesus to live and teach the traditional law of Israel. How can we reconcile this with the boldness of the thrust into the Gentile mission, which is at the heart of the risen Lord's mandate?[5]

It would appear, therefore, that the Gospel of Matthew is to be marked by two points of view. One is full of openness and enthusiasm about the newness of the Christian church along with the challenge of the Gentile mission; another presents Jesus speaking to his disciples and about himself in terms of a mission limited to Israel (10:5-6; 15:24), and a perfect living of the law (5:17-18).

Jesus among the Gentiles

The impression gained from our reflections thus far is only slightly weakened by the two miracles that Jesus performs for Gentiles during his public ministry. Both miracle stories come to Matthew from his sources.

In 8:5-13 Matthew reports the story of the healing of the Gentile centurion's servant, a story that he has in common with Luke (see Luke 7:1-10). However, this miracle is worked within the context of the lack of belief which Jesus finds in Israel, and is used ultimately as a "teaching" for Israel:

> Truly, I say to you, not even in Israel have I found such faith. I tell you, many will come from east and west and sit at table with Abraham, Isaac, and Jacob in the kingdom of heaven, while the sons of the kingdom will be thrown into the outer darkness; there men will weep and gnash their teeth. (Matthew 8:10-12)

This saying of Jesus was a part of the experience of the Matthean community. It was an important indication to this group of people, deeply respectful of their ancient Jewish traditions, but now inevitably involved in the Gentile mission. Despite Jesus' personal mission to Israel alone, he had already spoken of the later experience of the Matthean church itself: refused by "the sons of the kingdom", but sent on a mission to peoples "from east and west".

A similar point is made in Matthew 15:21-28, where the Marcan story of the Syrophoenician woman is rewritten (see

Mark 7:24-30; Matthew calls her a "Canaanite" woman). At the end of the encounter Matthew makes it very clear why this particular woman has gained her request: "O woman, great is your faith! Be it done for you as you desire" (verse 28). However, this point is not reached until the woman herself has placed her understanding of herself and her request within the context of Jesus' unique mission to Israel (see verses 23-27). The greatness of her faith has created an exception that proves the rule![6]

"Until heaven and earth pass away"

This apparent contradiction is, in fact, a key to an understanding of the situation of the Matthean community, of the evangelist's appreciation and presentation of Jesus, of his mission and of the mission of the Church. It is important to notice that all the passages that limit Jesus' and his disciples' activities are located in the public ministry of Jesus (5:17-18; 10:5-6; 15:24). Scholars have often thought that only the Gospel of Luke introduced the idea of a gradual and historical revelation of God's salvation through events of history. We can see here that it is also important to Matthew. There is also a "journey" in the gospel story as it is told by Matthew. Something happens both to Jesus and to the disciples, in the story as Matthew tells it, between Jesus' insistence on the mission to Israel during the course of his public ministry and his final commission as the risen Lord to the Matthean disciples to go out to the whole world. The event that stands as a sort of watershed between the ministry of Jesus and his final words is, of course, Easter. The paschal events seem to change the perspective of the story, as the words sending this

6. On these two miracle stories, see the apposite remarks of Meier, *Matthew*, p. 171: "Both stories indicate that, while Jesus' earthly ministry was restricted in principle to Israel, the church's mission after the death-resurrection will include Gentiles, who will have access to the Lord through faith and humility." See also Kingsbury, *Matthew*, p. 51. For a fine study of this whole issue, see D. Senior and C. Stuhmueller, *The Biblical Foundations for Mission* (New York, Orbis Books, 1983), pp. 235–54.

young church out to the whole world in the service of a new universal Lord, teaching his commandments, come from the lips of the risen Jesus.

Crucial for our understanding of Matthew are those words of Jesus, found in the Sermon on the Mount (5:17-18), which we quoted earlier. They need a closer examination.

> Think not that I have come to abolish the law and the prophets; I have come not to abolish them but to fulfil them. For truly, I say to you, *till heaven and earth pass away*, not an iota, not a dot, will pass from the law *until all is accomplished*.

You will notice that I have stressed two different expressions in the passage: they are both references to some future "time". There is the "now" of Jesus' preaching during his public ministry, but there is a moment "yet to come" when the present order of things will be changed. These expressions refer to a time in the future when the perfection of the law will be completed: "till heaven and earth pass away . . . until all is accomplished". We can again sense a "history of salvation" behind these words. God's salvation will be effected in and through the events of our history, touched by the saving presence in his Son, Jesus of Nazareth.

When might that future time be? In the light of our general understanding of Jesus' eschatological teaching (also present in Matthew; see chapter 24) we are immediately led to regard these words of Jesus as referring to the end of time. This position, however, would make Matthew 28:16-20 almost impossible to understand. The commission of the risen Lord to his disciples foresees a long period of missionary activity before the end of all time. Again, an understanding of the *uniqueness* of this particular gospel throws light on this problem.

There are two moments in the gospel story—in passages found *only* in Matthew—where there are descriptions that could be regarded as "heaven and earth passing away". The first of these moments is at the death of Jesus:

> Now from the sixth hour there was darkness over all the land until the ninth hour. . . . the curtain of the temple was torn in two, from top to bottom; and the earth shook, the rocks were split; the tombs also were opened, and the bodies of the saints who had fallen asleep were raised . . . (27:45, 51-53)

The second of these moments is found in the unique Matthean description of the events surrounding the resurrection of Jesus:

> And behold, there was a great earthquake, for an angel of the Lord descended from heaven and came and rolled back the stone, and sat upon it. His appearance was like lightning, his raiment white as snow. (28:2-3)

Heaven and earth are passing away! Matthew has taken some of the imagery that he uses here from the tradition concerning Jesus' death already used by Mark. That evangelist also reported the tearing of the veil and the darkness at the death of Jesus, along with the whiteness of the robe of the angel at the tomb, although he was a "young man", not an angel, in Mark 16:5. When the overall context is put together, however, it is obvious that Matthew has changed the scenario considerably. He has drawn upon some traditionally apocalyptic symbols from Jewish thought, but he has shifted their timing. The events described: darkening of the skies, splitting open of the rocks, earthquakes, lightning, the rising of the dead and the appearance of angels are events that were expected to happen at the end of time.[7] Matthew indicates that all these events not only *will happen* at the very end of history, as was believed by Jewish thinkers at the time of Matthew, they

7. On the use of this apocalytic imagery within the context of Matthew's story of Jesus' death and resurrection, see Hill, *Matthew*, p. 356; Meier, *Law and History*, pp. 33–5; and D. Senior, "The Death of Jesus and the Resurrection of the Holy Ones. Matthew 27:51-53", *Catholic Biblical Quarterly* 38 (1976) 312–29. See especially D. C. Allison, *The End of the Ages has Come. An Early Interpretation of the Passion and Resurrection of Jesus* (Philadelphia, Fortress Press, 1985). On Matthew, see pp. 40–50.

already *have happened* at the death and resurrection of Jesus. Only Matthew's story makes this point. Again we see the skilful use of narrative to make a profound theological point. This is Matthew's way of saying that the death and resurrection of Jesus from the turning-point of the ages. It is the paschal mystery of Jesus that alters everything. Yet, as we have seen from the gospel itself, Matthew is anxious to show that Jesus himself lived out the perfection of the old law (for example, read 3:13-17 in the light of what we have just uncovered), as well as becoming, through his death and resurrection, the foundational figure of the new law.

We would do Matthew a profound injustice if we did not see the great care he takes to show that Jesus does not abolish the old law. Rather, Jesus perfects the law, not only in what he does, but also in who he is. This is made particularly clear in Matthew 1-2. The events of the birth and infancy of Jesus, bridging the time between the former covenant into the days of Jesus, are a fulfilment of the promises of old. Almost every scene in the Matthean infancy narrative indicates that the events of Jesus' birth and infancy are to fulfil what was said by the prophet (see 1:22-23, 2:5-6, 15, 17-18, 23). The same theme also flows into the ministry of Jesus (see 3:3; 4:6-7, 14-16). The Evangelist Matthew was convinced that Jesus was the perfection of all the promises of the Old Testament.[8]

It is time to indicate just how these apparently disparate and contradictory elements in the Gospel of Matthew are really an indication of our evangelist's idea of salvation history. This gospel begins in the Old Testament, through the genealogy of Jesus (1:1-17), where God's providential handling of the history of a chosen people is already obvious. Nevertheless the promise of the Old Testament is fulfilled in the events of the birth and the public life of Jesus. Yet Jesus

8. For a brief analysis of this theme, see Neyrey, *Christ is Community*, pp. 85–8. A more complete study can be found in G. M. Soares Prabhu, *The Formula Quotations in the Infancy Narrative of Matthew*, Analecta Biblica 63 (Rome, Biblical Institute Press, 1976). Despite the title, this work considers the whole of the gospel and its use of the Old Testament. There are now several works on this theme. Full bibliographical details can be found in Soares Prabhu's study.

appears to be extremely anxious that his life and ministry be the *perfection* of the old law. He himself attempts to live the law perfectly, and he exhorts his followers to do the same.

However, after his death and resurrection, those same followers are instructed to reach out to the Gentile mission, commanded by a new Lord to teach a new law, to forge a new community with a new initiation rite. This is possible because the death and resurrection of Jesus are understood by the Gospel of Matthew as the turning-point of the ages.

The members of Matthew's church, therefore, are caught up in the Gentile mission. Nevertheless, they are still very aware that they are the product of the perfection of the old law in the person and teaching of Jesus. As this is the case, the evangelist can claim that it is his community, the followers of Jesus of Nazareth who can regard themselves as the "True Israel". This scheme of salvation history can be summarised by a diagram (see page 130).

The Experience
of the Matthean Community

From what we have seen so far, it is clear that Matthew and his fellow Christians came from a largely Jewish background. It was important for them to recognise the greatness of God's ways with his people of old. But it also seems to be important for them to somehow understand how they related to the chosen people of old. In fact, one could say that the crisis that produced the Gospel of Matthew could be called an identity crisis.

It is easy enough for us, today, to lose sight of just how much it would have cost the earliest Christians—mostly Jewish people—to walk away from their traditional faith and practice and to enter a Christian community, such as the one to which our evangelist belonged. This remained a most difficult journey for believing Jews to make, even though they may have come to believe that Jesus Christ was the Messiah. Their faith in Jesus of Nazareth as the Christ, the Son of the living God (see 16:16) was causing them great suffering, as

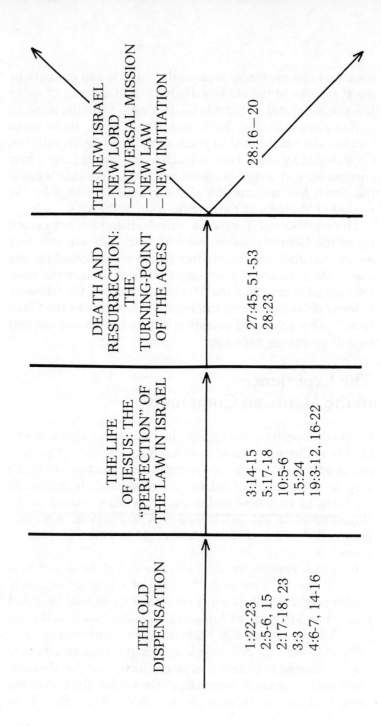

THE NEW ISRAEL
—NEW LORD
—UNIVERSAL MISSION
—NEW LAW
—NEW INITIATION

28:16—20

DEATH AND
RESURRECTION:
THE
TURNING-POINT
OF THE AGES

27:45, 51-53
28:23

THE LIFE
OF JESUS: THE
"PERFECTION" OF
THE LAW IN ISRAEL

3:14-15
5:17-18
10:5-6
15:24
19:3-12, 16-22

THE OLD
DISPENSATION

1:22-23
2:5-6, 15
2:17-18, 23
3:3
4:6-7, 14-16

their long-time friends from the synagogue in the town could no longer abide the presence of these renegades in their community. In fact, we know that their old friends now prayed every morning:

> For apostates may there be no hope and may the Nazarenes and the heretics suddenly perish. (Twelfth Blessing of the important synagogue prayer, the *Shemoneh Esreh*)[9]

To be thrown out of the synagogue meant that almost every aspect of their day-to-day life was changed. They were snubbed by their former friends from "the synagogue across the road";[10] they could no longer marry their sons and daughters within a community whose faith they shared and whose way of life they had always respected and also attempted to live. In a non-Jewish city (and Syrian Antioch looks like a good place for the birth of Matthew's Gospel), they were not even able to go into the confusion of the market place and buy their meat and bread from places where they had always been welcome, and where they knew that it had been prepared in the time-honoured and sacred ways.

Although these practical difficulties were many, they would have laboured under an even greater problem. They were now separated from what was the heart of the life of a good Jew in the time when Matthew was writing his gospel. They were excluded from the synagogue celebration of the Torah and its authoritative transmission by the rabbi, the teacher, the authentic interpreter of the greatest of all teachers: Moses.

Cut off from the world that they knew and loved so much,

---

9. On this so-called "blessing", see below, pp. 162–166. For a full discussion of the issues that created the blessing, and the effect that this would have had on the early church, see W. D. Davies, *The Setting of the Sermon on the Mount* (Cambridge, University Press, 1966), pp. 256–315.

10. This reference to "the synagogue over the road", which I have used several times, both here and later in my treatment of the fourth gospel, is taken from K. Stendahl, *The School of St Matthew and Its Use of the Old Testament*, Acta Seminarii Neotestamentici Upsaliensis XX (Lund, Gleerup, 1968), p. xi.

they had to find a new teacher and a new authority. If "the synagogue over the road" possessed Moses' law and its authentic interpreter in the rabbi (see, for example, 19:7 and 22:24), to whom could this struggling Jewish Christian church now turn? We have already seen that the last words of Matthew's Gospel tell us: the early church is commanded to teach all nations to observe all the things that Jesus had taught them (see 28:20). The theme of Jesus as the only authoritative teacher to a new chosen people is one of the major arguments of this gospel. It will serve us to see how the evangelist Matthew had used this theme as a basis for his careful structuring of his story of Jesus.

Jesus the Greatest of all Teachers

We have already seen in our chapter on Luke's infancy narrative how the evangelists came to use their infancy stories as authentic prologues to their gospels. So Matthew uses the infancy stories (Matthew 1-2) to prepare the ground for the theme of Jesus the new and perfect Moses, the great teacher and interpreter of God's ways. He presents the experience of the infant Jesus in close parallel to the experience of Moses.[11] As Jesus is born, there is a widespread slaying of innocent, male Hebrew children (2:16-18), just as Moses' birth was marked by violent murder of innocent Hebrew children (see Exodus 1:15-22). As Moses came out from Egypt, ahead of a people of God, so does Jesus. In fact, a very important passage from the prophet Hosea (11:1) — originally used to speak of the Exodus — is now taken up by Matthew and applied to Jesus' flight into Egypt:

> And he rose and took the child and his mother by night, and departed to Egypt, and remained there until the death of Herod. This was to fulfil what the Lord had spoken by the prophet, "Out of Egypt I have called my son". (Matthew 2:14-15).

11. For a full discussion of this theme, see Brown, *The Birth of the Messiah*, pp. 225-9.

After the prologue of the infancy stories, the whole of Matthew's Gospel is structured around five very long discourses, where Jesus teaches. On each occasion, the evangelist indicates that a great teacher has been at work.

(a) 5:1-7:29. The discourse of the Sermon on the Mount, dealing systematically with the new and higher righteousness, which will mark the "perfection" of the Christian life (see 5:48). This discourse concludes: "And when Jesus finished these sayings, the crowds were astonished at his *teaching*, for he taught them as one who had authority, *and not as their scribes*" (7:28-29).

(b) 10:1-11:1. The discourse on the mission of the disciples and of the whole church, unflinchingly preaching its challenge, and warning of the tensions and the difficulties of a ministry that must repeat the ministry of Jesus (see 10:40-42). This discourse also concludes: "And when Jesus had finished instructing his twelve disciples, he went on from there to *teach* and *preach* in their cities" (11:1).

(c) 13:2-53. After Israel's refusal of Jesus (see 11:2-12:50), he withdraws from them, and teaches his disciples through the enigmatic discourse of the parables, letting his disciples know that "many prophets and righteous men longed to see what you see, and did not see it, and to hear what you hear, and did not hear it" (13:17). They have been drawn into a privileged revelation, which Israel has refused to accept. Matthew concludes this discourse: "And when Jesus had finished these parables, he went away from there, and coming to his own country he *taught* them in the synagogue, so that they were astonished" (13:53-54).

(d) 18:1-35. The discourse from Jesus to his disciples on the way his church should live, insisting on a message of loving care for all, including the weak, as the measurement of their Christianity. Again Matthew concludes: "Now when Jesus had finished these sayings, he went away from Galilee" (19:1).

133

(e)   Chapters 24-25. The final discourse of the gospel,
        which deals with the Last Judgement. Again mutual
        love is a central argument, as a church is told that the
        sheep and the goats will be separated by means of a
        criterion of love for the lost ones (see especially 25:31-
        46). Matthew now rounds off all his five discourses
        and concludes solemnly: "When Jesus had finished *all
        these sayings*, he said to his disciples . . ." and the
        cross is announced (26:1-2).

This brief outline of the structural importance and the
message of the five great discourses in the Gospel of Matthew
indicates that our evangelist has deliberately constructed his
gospel around Jesus as the most perfect teacher of all history.
He is certainly a new and perfect Moses, but not just a
fulfilment of Moses. He is greater than Moses. This greatest
of all teachers communicates his message through five great
discourses, a repetition in the New Testament of the law of
ancient and modern Judaism: the five great books of Moses,
the fundamental teachings of the Old Testament People of
God.[12]

Matthew's portrait of Jesus as the teacher could be further
traced by looking in more detail at the many hints throughout
the gospel where this is made particularly clear. That would
take us beyond the limitations that we have in these few
general reflections on the theology and the structure of
Matthew. Perhaps it is sufficient for us to recall our earlier
study of the first of all the discourses, the famous Sermon on
the Mount (chapters 5-7).[13] We saw that a much shorter form

---

12. One must be careful not to absolutise this structure that I have just
outlined. There is no doubt that the five discourses, preceded by narrative
that in many ways introduces themes dealt with in the discourses, is an
important part of the structure of this gospel. However, it does not exhaust
all the subtle interplays that there are criss-crossing throughout the whole
gospel. See, on this, the remarks of Senior, *What are They Saying about
the Gospel of Matthew?*, pp. 16–27. For some idea of these subtleties, see
Ellis, *Matthew: His Mind and His Message.*

13. On the Sermon on the Mount, see the concise and most helpful work
of H. Hendrickx, *The Sermon on the Mount* (Manila, East Asian Pastoral

of this discourse is also found in Luke's Gospel, but there it is delivered "on a level place" (Luke 6:17-49)! Why did Matthew go to such trouble to indicate that the discourse was delivered most solemnly on a mountain, with Jesus seated and his disciples gathered at his feet (Matthew 5:1-2)? Matthew's readers are aware that Jesus is now the new and authoritative teacher of a new law. They are not surprised when the new teacher—like the old one, Moses, who went up on Sinai to receive the law from Jahweh—also goes on to *the* mountain" (Matthew 5,1). But there is a sharp difference between Moses and Jesus. While Moses *received* the law from Jahweh, Jesus *gives* the new law. He teaches his disciples (5:1) and "the crowds" (7:28) that they may have heard certain things from "the men of old", but he, by virtue of the authority of his own word ("but I say to you"), establishes a new law (see 5:21-22, 27-28, 31-32, 33-34, 38-39, 43-44). He sums this law up in his final command: "You, therefore, must be perfect, as your heavenly Father is perfect" (5:48).

Jesus of Nazareth perfects, fulfils and surpasses all that the old ways had treasured (see 5:17). The early Christian communities faced this problem: how were they to relate to the ways and the laws of Israel? Eventually, they had to cross the bridge that had been built by Jesus of Nazareth into a new and dangerous world, which they could not fully understand (see, for example, John 9:28: "You are his disciple, but we are disciples of Moses").

The problem of an authoritative "master" still remains. We are not faced with the same obvious difficulties that faced the Matthean Church: our difficulties are far more subtle. The contemporary world, and, even more urgently, the contemporary church, is quick to look to a variety of new and authoritative teachers, fathers and masters, searching for a security that has no place in the faith journey of a disciple

Institute, 1979). See, most recently, the valuable study of H.-D. Betz, *Essays on the Sermon on the Mount* (Philadelphia, Fortress Press, 1985). A most useful guide to the study of Matthew 5-7 can be found in W. S. Kissinger, *The Sermon on the Mount: A History of Interpretation and Bibliography* (Metuchen, Scarecrow Press, 1975).

who claims to be a follower of Jesus of Nazareth. There can be only one teacher and master of the church of all ages. Matthew's Gospel (and *only* Matthew's Gospel has this passage) has no hesitation in reporting some words of Jesus of Nazareth that will always warn against seeing Christ's church as a place where one carves out a career of honour and authority:

> But you are not to be called rabbi, for you have one teacher, and you are all brethren. And call no man your father on earth, for you have one Father, who is in heaven. Neither be called masters, for you have one master, the Christ. (23:8-10)

Disciples
and the Church

Our study so far has shown how Matthew constructed his gospel around five large discourses. Matthew 1-2 serves as a theological introduction to the whole book, and the passion and resurrection accounts (chapters 26-28) form an important conclusion, indicating therein the "turning-point of the ages". In the following chapter we will analyse Matthew's account of the death and resurrection of Jesus in a little more detail. Despite this obvious care in the construction of a gospel around five great discourses with an important introduction (chapters 1-2) and conclusion (chapters 26-28) our evangelist does not abandon the traditional story of the life of Jeus, as he found it in the Gospel of Mark. In fact, he uses nearly all of Mark's material, modifying it when needed to make that tradition speak very immediately to his own situation. What is more, the message that Matthew has left for his own church is a message of perennial importance.[14]

Like all the evangelists, Matthew was writing for a church. However, Matthew did not write only a gospel for a church, he more than any of the other evangelists also wrote *about* the church. Only in Matthew's Gospel do we find the Greek term *ekklesia*, a term that was very important for Paul, and

14. See my remarks above, p. 128, note 8.

for the subsequent theology of the church (including the Acts of the Apostles), to speak of the community of the Christian church. Matthew also devoted more space than the other evangelists to the role of the disciples, to the person of Peter—and to the failure of both![15]

Throughout his gospel, Matthew challenges his community and the church of all ages to take up and continue the ministry of Jesus of Nazareth. This is made particularly clear in the first half of the gospel. As the first days of Jesus' public ministry come to a close, the evangelist summarises his activity in 4:23-25:

> And he went about all Galilee, teaching in the synagogues and preaching the gospel of the kingdom and healing every disease and every infirmity among the people . . . and they brought to him all the sick, those afflicted with various diseases and pains, demoniacs, epileptics, and paralytics, and he healed them. And great crowds followed him . . .

This is followed by the Sermon on the Mount (chapters 5-7) and a long section devoted to Jesus' miraculous activity (chapters 8-9), which again closes with a comment from Matthew himself:

> And Jesus went about all the cities and villages, teaching in their synagogues and preaching the gospel of the kingdom, and healing every disease and every infirmity. (9:35)

Notice how the evangelist has concluded each section: a general description of Jesus' activity (2:1-4:22) concludes with reference to Jesus' preaching and healing (4:23-25); the report of the Sermon on the Mount and Jesus' miraculous activity (5:1-9:34) concludes in exactly the same way (9:35). This is obviously Matthew's way of summarising *Jesus'* ministry.

Towards the end of chapter 9, however, Matthew's message is taken one step farther. It is not only the ministry of Jesus

---

15. There are several important studies of the church in Matthew's Gospel. See D. Senior, *Matthew: A Gospel for the Church* (Chicago, Franciscan Herald Press, 1973); Doohan, *Matthew*, pp. 99–119.

that is described in this way. Such a ministry is about to be passed on to others. The passage (9:35-38) continues:

> When he saw the crowds, he had compassion on them, for they were harassed and helpless, like sheep without a shepherd. Then he said to his disciples, "The harvest is plentiful but the labourers are few; pray therefore the Lord of the harvest to send out labourers into his harvest." (9:36-38)

The gospel had reached an important moment. By means of the missionary discourse in chapter 10, the twelve disciples are associated with the task of Jesus. For Matthew, these disciples are both the foundation of the church and an image of what the church is called to be and to do.

> And he called to him his twelve disciples and gave them authority over unclean spirits, to cast them out, and to heal every disease and every infirmity. (10:1)

Through his careful and deliberate association of the disciples with the ministry of Jesus and then having them perform the tasks that Jesus did, Matthew has made it very clear that the church continues the ministry of Jesus. To ensure that the reader did not miss the point, the summary used by the evangelist to refer to Jesus' ministry (4:23-25; 9:35) is repeated—but it is applied to the ministry of the church (10:1). However, even though Matthew softens the theme of the failure of the disciples from Mark's portrait of them, he is also a realist, and very aware of the fragility of his community. He was aware that the church would always be marked by failure and fear.

Disciples: Men of little Faith

Matthew picks up the theme of the failure of the disciples in his major source, the Gospel of Mark, and it is most instructive to trace how Matthew has taken that theme, using it to address the problem of a believing yet fragile church.[16] In Mark, the disciples simply cannot or will not understand. Matthew rewrites his Marcan passages to show that they do understand, but that they are "men of little faith".

A fine example of this is found after the second miracle of the loaves and fishes. There Mark reports:

> "Take heed, beware of the leaven of the Pharisees and the leaven of Herod." And they discussed with one another. Saying, "We have no bread." And being aware of it, Jesus said to them, "Why do you discuss the fact that you have no bread? Do you not yet perceive or understand?" (Mark 8:15-17)

As is obvious, in the Marcan account the disciples simply do not understand. They are unable to see what is before their eyes. It is all too much for them. This is rewritten by Matthew as follows:

> "*O men of little faith*, why do you discuss among yourselves the fact that you have no bread? . . . How is it that you fail to perceive that I did not speak about bread? Beware of the leaven of the Pharisees and Sadducees." *Then they understood* that he did not tell them to beware of the leaven of bread, but of the teaching of the Pharisees and the Sadducees. (Matthew 16:8, 11-12).

I have stressed two of Matthew's important changes. What Jesus is saying is not beyond the ken of the disciples. There is understanding, but insufficient faith. The expression "O men of little faith" appears regularly as Jesus speaks to his disciples (see 6:30; 8:26; 14:31; 16:8). It is one of the indications used by Matthew to show the fragility of the

16. For further studies of the disciples in Matthew's Gospel, see G. Barth, "Matthew's Understanding of the Law", in Bornkamm, Barth and Held (eds), *Tradition and Interpretation in Matthew*, pp. 105–25; Kingsbury, *Matthew*, pp. 78–106; U. Luz, "The Disciples in the Gospel according to Matthew", in Stanton (ed.), *The Interpretation of Matthew*, pp. 98–128; Doohan, *Matthew*, pp. 121–39.

disciples, and the reason for it: lack of faith, not lack of understanding. This is an incredibly realistic appreciation of discipleship, which none of us should find difficult to understand. As we are all well aware, the church, called to continue the challenge of the ministry of Jesus of Nazareth, is made up of disciples "of little faith". Matthew's analysis of the situation is as true today as it was then.

Peter: his Primacy and his Failure

Among the disciples in the Gospel of Matthew, Peter is outstanding. He is the first to be called (4:18) and he is always the spokesman for "the church" of the disciples (15:15; 16:16, 22; 17:4; 18:21; 19:27). However, like the rest of the church, Peter is one who knows the truth, but attempts to sidestep its consequences.[17] The most famous of all Matthean Petrine texts (Matthew 16:13-23) shows this beautifully.

When the disciples are asked who they think the Son of Man might be, Peter makes his inspired confession of faith: "You are the Christ, the Son of the living God" (16:16). This confession receives a blessing from Jesus: Simon, son of Jonah, is blessed because he was open to this revelation. He thus becomes the Rock and the authoritative custodian of the Church and her mission (verses 17-19).

After the glory of the faith-filled confession and Jesus' blessing, Jesus indicates that this same Son of the Living God must go down the way of suffering and death, as he is also the Son of Man (16:21-22). Peter refuses to accept this (verse 22), and for his lack of faith he is reprimanded: "Get behind me, Satan! . . . you are not on the side of God" (verse 23). Peter understands who Jesus is, and he confesses his faith, but he is not prepared to accept the suffering way of Jesus. Therefore he is reprimanded, accused of being a

17. See, on this, R. E. Brown, K. P. Donfried and J. Reumann (eds), *Peter in the New Testament. A Collaborative Assessment by Protestant and Roman Catholic Scholars* (London, Geoffrey Chapman, 1973), pp. 75–107; J. D. Kingsbury, "The Figure of Peter in Matthew's Gospel as a Theological Problem", *Journal of Biblical Literature* 98 (1979), pp. 67–83.

stumbling block to the church. Peter is the rock of the church when he professes faith in the true revelation that he has received; he is the stumbling block in the church when he attempts to impose his conditions on the way of Jesus in the world: the loss of self in love and service.[18]

The Church—
A Boat in a Storm

The challenge of Jesus as the definitive teacher of the new law of God to a new people of God, met by a believing but faltering response, is beautifully encapsulated in Matthew's version of the miracle of Jesus' coming to his disciples across a stormy sea (14:22-33). In the darkness and terror of nature gone wild, Jesus calls out to his panic-stricken disciples: "Take heart, it is I; have no fear" (verse 27).

Peter, anxious to share with Jesus, is summoned, as his Lord calls to him: "Come." Peter, showing what the church *could* do, duplicates the power of his Lord as he too walks across the waves. However, being "of little faith", he begins to hesitate, and sinking he cries out: "Lord, save me." (verse 30). As always, Jesus identifies the problem: "O man of little faith, why did you doubt?" (verse 31). The boat is reached, Jesus is "with his church". He takes control, the furies are quelled, and all proclaim: "Truly you are the Son of God" (verse 33).

The church has always been a fragile boat in a threatening sea. Its leaders (Peter) and its people (the disciples in the boat) still find their faith choked by fear, doubt, and a desire to sit still in comfort, happy with the cherished ways and the old truths. Who would risk the journey across a hostile sea in an open boat? But that is where the barque of Peter is supposed to be.

18. This structure: a confession of faith in Jesus, the Son of Man as the Messiah and the Son of God, followed by a blessing; a second statement about the suffering Son of Man, followed by a curse, has been carefully constructed in this way—using both Mark and his own traditions—by our evangelist. See, on this, Meier, *Matthew*, pp. 178–86.

Conclusion

Matthew has told his "story of Jesus" to a community that has been forcibly separated from Judaism, and which probably has many members longing for the "old and trusted ways". He was very aware of the fragility of his own community, yet certain in his faith that God had broken into the history of humankind irrevocably in the birth, life, death and resurrection of Jesus. To bridge the gap between the old and the new, Matthew draws out of his story his central theme: during his life Jesus lived and asked for the "perfection" of the old ways, and then, through his death and resurrection the turning-point of the ages came to pass.

Matthew tells his largely Jewish community that despite the hostility and the ridicule of the "synagogue over the road", they have lost nothing. God's ways in the world have now been fulfilled, as the Old Testament has led to and been perfected in Jesus. The old ways are now perfected further in the universal presence of Jesus, through his church, to the whole world. For Matthew, the true Israel is not to be found in the post-war synagogue stoutly defending its traditions to maintain its identity, but in the Christian community, now irrevocably committed to the Gentile mission.

Many of the Jewish people in Matthew's community were wondering if perhaps they had lost their way by becoming Christians, but Matthew's message clears away that doubt. He builds a bridge between the old and the new, and that bridge is the person of Jesus. The puzzled members of Matthew's church are told that they now belong to the new and perfect Israel, which has been given its new and perfect law by a new Moses on a new Sinai (see Matthew 5:1-48).

Matthew never destroys the old; he has a deep respect for two thousand years of sacred history. In fact, he rewrites Mark 2:22, which spoke of the uselessness of the old wineskins, to show the permanent value of the old, side by side with the new:

> Neither is new wine put into old wineskins; if it is, the skins burst, and the wine is spilled, and the skins are destroyed; but new wine is put into fresh wineskins, and so *both are preserved*. (Matthew 9:17)

As he leads a traditional Jewish Christian community into the challenge of the Gentile mission he looks back to Jesus. He tells his "story" so that the community might see the perfection of the old, through the death and resurrection of Jesus, in the newness in which they are living.

Our post-conciliar church struggles to come to grips once again with the challenge of the risen Lord questioning us and leading us into our "Gentile mission". We too must face the strange new ways and cultures that stand in our future. In that situation Matthew's Gospel tells us that we must allow ourselves to be led into a future that only God can create. We are called to leave the securities of the old and safe ways. Yet we must always love and respect those ways. Such ways came into existence as the fruit of accumulated wisdom and experience. They are not to be simply discounted, as an appreciation of them prepares us for the newness of God's strange plans.

To want to hold fast to our old ways, or to dream that God can be found by a return to such ways is to be unfaithful to the Word of God, revealed to us in the Gospel of Matthew. Yet, to scoff at the ways of old, and to fail to see that we are what we are today because of the loyalty, love and sacrifice of the men and women who loved and served the old ways is also to be unfaithful to that same Word of God.

Little wonder that Matthew described himself—and consequently all dedicated Christians—in a tiny biographical insertion, which gives his secret away:

Therefore every scribe who has been trained for the kingdom of heaven is like a householder who brings out of his treasure what is new and what is old. (13:52)

7.
Reading
Matthew 27:32 to 28:20:
The Cross
and Resurrection

The selection of passages from the gospels, which I have used to exemplify the work of the evangelists, has also been made with an eye to the different "literary forms" that exist in the gospels.[1] Thus far we have seen the Marcan use of a variety of traditions and forms to communicate a powerful message on discipleship, and Luke's use of an infancy narrative to communicate his particular understanding of Jesus. There will be many forms we are unable to examine, for example some of the apocalyptic sections in the gospels (e.g. Mark 13). However, given the centrality of the story of the death and resurrection of Jesus in all four gospels, it is important that we devote part of this study to a consideration of a passion narrative.

1. See above, pp. 10–13.

The Origin and Function
of a Passion Narrative

It is obvious that the first problem that the earliest Christians had to face, both for themselves and for their converts, was the problem of the cross. It was simply incredible to think that the man they believed to be the Messiah, and the Son of God, had been nailed to a cross in a terrible death.[2] Apart from the violence and humiliation that such a death entailed, it placed Jesus under the curse of the law (see Deuteronomy 21:22-23 and Galatians 3:13). These facts made the preaching of the message of Christianity very difficult indeed. One of the earliest of all preachers was the apostle Paul, and he has stated the case well: "For Jews demand signs and Greeks seek wisdom, but we preach Christ crucified, a stumbling block to Jews and folly to Gentiles" (I Corinthians 1:22-23).

Despite this difficulty, the early church had no desire to steer clear of this issue. One of the great realities of the life of Jesus of Nazareth was the way in which it ended, and there could be no avoiding that. To do so would be to preach someone else—and not Jesus of Nazareth—as the Christ. The cross was preached boldly, because it formed an essential part of the last days of Jesus. However, it is important to see that it only formed *a part* of the last days of Jesus. As the earliest preachers of Christianity went forth to make fools of themselves by preaching a crucified Christ, they did so burning with conviction that Jesus was no longer among the dead (see Luke 24:5). Their preaching of the cross was dominated by the awareness of the living presence of the risen Lord (see Matthew 28:20). The church certainly had to preach the cross—but it was an empty cross!

The importance of the cross and resurrection stories in the earliest preaching is seen from two pieces of evidence, which we can glean from the New Testament itself. First, we have

2. See M. Dibelius, *From Tradition to Gospel* (Cambridge/London, James Clarke, 1971), pp. 178–217, for the classical presentation of this case. The original German of this book (one of the founding works for the form critical study of the gospels) was published in 1919.

already mentioned that Paul does not tell "the story of Jesus". His whole message is dominated by the "new creation". Paul preaches a new possibility, which is now ours, to become daughters and sons of God, the Father of Jesus, because of the death and resurrection of his Son (see, among many passages, Romans 3:21-26; 6:1-10; 8:9-17: II Corinthians 5:16-21; Galatians 4:1-7; 6:14-15).

In the second place, it appears that the "story" of the passion and resurrection of Jesus was the earliest piece of coherent story-telling that the early church used in its preaching. The four gospels differ in the order of the events in the life of Jesus, and have some pieces of material that are unique to each one of them. Yet, once they come to the account of the passion of Jesus, all four gospels converge to tell the same basic story. Naturally, each evangelist tells the story in his own way, but all four seem to be looking back to the same ancient tradition, enshrined in the earliest story-telling of the preaching church.[3]

Our general study of Matthew's Gospel showed that this evangelist used the story of the death and resurrection of Jesus as a major element in his concept of God's history of salvation. Although we have already mentioned the main themes, it will be useful, for the purposes of this book, to see how one of the evangelists tells the story of the death and resurrection. Going back to the authentic traditions alive in the church, Matthew faithfully reports the message of what happened to Jesus. But there is more at stake. His account of the crucifixion, death and resurrection of Jesus (Matthew 27:32-28:20) makes it very clear that in these events God

3. I have taken a moderate line in a widely debated question. For a review of the contemporary discussion of the history of the passion traditions, and their importance in the early preaching of the church, see J. Donahue, "From Passion Traditions to Passion Narrative", in W. Kelber (ed.), *The Passion in Mark* (Philadelphia, Fortress Press, 1976), pp. 1–20. For the position that I have adopted, see also Senior, *The Passion of Jesus in the Gospel of Mark*, pp. 9–11. See also R. E. Brown, *A Crucified Christ in Holy Week. Essays in the Four Gospel Passion Narratives* (Collegeville, Liturgical Press, 1986), pp. 9–20.

was acting, not only in the life of Jesus of Nazareth, but also in the affairs of women and men down the ages.[4]

The Perfection
of the Scriptures

The first section of Matthew's account of the actual passion (27:32-44, leaving aside Gethsemane and the trials) largely follows the Marcan story (Mark 15:22-32). However, Matthew uses that story to insinuate a theme that was very powerful in the infancy story, never far from the surface during the public ministry, and which returns strongly here: the fulfilment of the Scriptures in the events of the life of Jesus.

This time the background is Psalm 22.[5] The psalm itself is cited directly in two places (Matthew 27:35 and 43), and it is alluded to very clearly on one occasion (verse 39). The overall theme of Psalm 22 is the suffering—and also the hope—of

4. For a full-scale scholarly study of the passion in the Gospel of Matthew, see D. Senior, *The Passion Narrative according to Matthew. A Redactional Study*, Bibliotheca Ephemeridum Theologicarum Lovaniensium 39 (Duculot, Gembloux, 1975). Senior has now produced a most readable and fascinating study in a more popular style: *The Passion of Jesus in the Gospel of Matthew*, The Passion Series 1 (Wilmington, Michael Glazier, 1985). What follows has been strongly influenced by pp. 124–61 of that work, and also by Meier, *Matthew*, pp. 345–74. On Matthew's passion, see also the following: N. A. Dahl, "The Passion Narrative in Matthew", in Stanton, *The Interpretation of Matthew*, pp. 42–55; H.-R. Weber, *The Cross. Tradition and Interpretation* (London, SPCK, 1979); E. Trocmé, *The Passion as Liturgy. A Study of the Origin of the Passion Narratives in the Four Gospels* (London, SCM Press, 1983); C. Kruse, "The account of Jesus' passion and death in Matthew", in H. McGinlay (ed.), *The Year of Matthew*, pp. 10–17; L. Morris, *The Cross in the New Testament* (Grand Rapids, Wm Eerdmans, 1965), pp. 13–62; Brown, *A Crucified Christ*, pp. 34–46. See also the reflections of G. O'Collins, *The Calvary Christ* (London, SCM Press, 1977).

5. See, on this, J. Reumann, "Psalm 22 at the Cross", *Interpretation* 28 (1974), pp. 39–58; Senior, *The Passion of Jesus in the Gospel of Matthew*, pp. 129–30, 136–9; idem, "A Death Song", *The Bible Today* 14 (1974), pp 1457–75.

the righteous one who is drawn into suffering. Jesus is presented in that light. His crucifiers, who will return in a different light a little later (verse 35), nail him to a cross and divide his garments among themselves. Thus the Scriptures are fulfilled: "they divide my garments among them, and for my raiment they cast lots" (Psalm 22:18).

Jesus, the righteous one, is hung between two thieves (Matthew 27:38), and again the Scriptures are close at hand: "Yea, dogs are round about me; a company of evildoers encircle me" (Psalm 22:16).

Caught in this desperate situation—as far as his human judges can see—they jeer at him, mocking his earlier trust in God, in his claim to be Son of God (Matthew 27:43). The experience of the Old Testament righteous one is again perfected: "He committed his cause to the Lord; let him rescue him, let him rescue him, for he delights in him" (Psalm 22:8).

The very description of the attitude of the passers-by and the mockers (Matthew 27:39, 41, 44) is the fulfilment of what the Old Testament had said would happen to God's righteous one: "But I am a worm, and no man; scorned by men, and despised by the people. All who see me mock at me, they make mouths at me, they wag their heads" (Psalm 22:6-7).

These indications make it clear that a major Matthean theme is present here. As well as the references to Psalm 22, there are other, more veiled references, and another quite explicit reference to Psalm 69:21 in the offering of the wine and the gall (Matthew 27:34). This carefully constructed interweaving of the Old Testament and the events of the crucifixion of Jesus shows that the death of Jesus is not some terrible accident that fell upon Jesus. It is yet another moment in the fulfilment of God's plans for Jesus, and thus for men and women of all times.[6]

6. See, for a fine detailed study of the use of the lament psalms in the passion accounts (with special attention given to the use of Psalms 22 and 69 in Matthew 27), D. J. Moo, *The Old Testament in the Gospel Passion Narratives* (Sheffield, Almond Press, 1983), pp. 225–300.

This is made clear through another skilful use of narrative. Through all the insult and injury, Matthew ironically uses the abuse of the onlookers to proclaim the truth. Jesus is twice proclaimed "King of Israel" (verse 27:37 and 42) and finally "the Son of God" (verse 43). The very mouths of the mockers and the rough sign that they hammer on his cross indicate the message that Matthew wants his readers to hear.

Amid all the mocking (27:39-44), the truth is proclaimed: Jesus will rise in three days, he will save others, he is the King of Israel, he is the Son of God. The reader of the gospel is aware of the ultimate truth of what is being said in mockery. An angel has announced at his birth that he was "to save" people from their sins (1:21) and on two occasions during his public ministry, the disciples begged their "Lord" to "Save" them (8:25; 14:30). On two occasions a voice from heaven announced that Jesus is God's Son: at his baptism in the Jordan (3:17) and at the transfiguration (17:5). The disciples recognised this Sonship: in the boat (14:33) and at Caesarea Philippi (16:16). Strange as it may seem, in the end these very people, those who "sat down and kept watch over him" (verse 36) will come to recognise it themselves (see verse 54).

The Death of Jesus

All of the material used by Matthew thus far in his account came to him from the traditional story, largely as it had been told by Mark. We have seen, however, the skill of Matthew in picking up one of his major themes through the reference to the Old Testament, fulfilled in the crucifixion of Jesus. From Mark, and in agreement with Mark, he continues to develop his teaching about Jesus: Jesus as the innocent righteous one, the King of Israel, the Son of God who will rise after three days, and who will save others.

The scene of the death of Jesus introduces some surprising new elements, found only in Matthew, which go to prove that the ironical proclamation contained in the insult hurled at him by "all who passed by" and by the chief priests and the scribes is true. In fact, those who had crucified him, and who then "sat down and kept watch over him there" (27:36) will come to see the truth of the insults. Already, in the death of Jesus, Matthew hints loudly that "the turning-point of the ages" is upon us.

The death of Jesus is marked by a series of signs, which come from a Jewish understanding of the end of time. The prophet Amos had spoken of the day of the Lord (the end time), about which God said: "And on that day I will make the sun go down at noon, and darken the earth in broad daylight" (Amos 8:9). And so it is as Jesus dies: "Now from the sixth hour there was darkness over all the land until the ninth hour" (27:45). Matching the fearful darkness is Jesus' cry: "My God, my God, why hast thou forsaken me?" (verse 46). The just man abandons himself completely to God in a strange mixture of anguish and filial trust.[7] Misunderstanding "Eli" (my God) as "Elijah" (the prophet), the bystanders will not admit what Jesus has said or who he is. As they wait to see if Elijah will come to his aid, he cries out again "and yielded up his spirit".

Suddenly a further series of events begins:

And behold, the curtain of the temple was torn in two, from top to bottom; and the earth shook, and the rocks were split; the tombs also were opened, and many bodies of the saints who had fallen asleep were raised, and coming out of the tombs after his resurrection they went into the holy city and appeared to many. (27:51-53).

Somehow, the "end time" is happening now.

Why has Matthew rewritten Mark so severely at this all-

7. The cry from Psalm 22:1 calls into play the whole psalm. This implies not only the abandon that marks the opening of the psalm, but also the trust that is involved in the closing verses of this lament. See, on this, Senior, *The Passion of Jesus in the Gospel of Matthew*, pp. 136–42, especially pp. 136–7: "Even though shredded by anguish, Jesus, the Just One, prays a prayer of raw, unadorned faith in God. As he had from the beginning of the Gospel, Matthew presents Jesus as the embodiment of Israel's faith, as the one who suffers with God's people and yet remains faithful."

important stage of his story of Jesus? He is telling his readers that history has reached its turning-point with the death of Jesus. This is the meaning of the signs and wonders that God works as Jesus dies (27:51-54). The events that *only Matthew* associated with the death of Jesus belonged to a series of signs that came to Matthew from the apocalyptic symbolism of the Old Testament (see Psalm 114:7-8; Isaiah 48:21; Nahum 1:5-6; and especially Ezekiel 37:1-14 and Daniel 12:2). They were used in the Old Testament to describe the end of time and the ultimate power of God. However, the "end of time" in these Old Testament passages meant exactly that: when all history would come to an end. Matthew has taken traditional signs, which were used to refer to the end of time, the final "day of the Lord" and located them in time, in the story of Jesus. This is what he is doing when he introduces this strange series of events into the story of the death of Jesus: the darkening of the skies, the shaking of the earth and the splitting open of the rocks. Already at the death of Jesus we are told of the resurrection of the holy ones, in close association with the resurrection of Jesus himself: "coming out of their tombs after his resurrection they went into the holy city" (verse 53). This is Matthew's way of affirming that, with the death of Jesus, a new age has broken into the old. Judaism and its cult have come to an end (the Temple veil is torn apart) and thus the way to God is open to all.[8]

At the cross, while death and sin are conquered, Matthew again slightly rewrites Mark to make this point very clear. He shows that all the Old Testament restrictions of race, cult and law are thrown down. This is the point of Matthew's rewriting of 27:54. Picking up the indications of verse 36, in reference to those who had nailed him to a cross, abused him, and who sat about watching over him, Matthew now writes, after the events of the death of Jesus:

8. See especially Senior, *The Passion Narrative according to Matthew*, pp. 319–23, and *The Passion of Jesus in the Gospel of Matthew*, pp. 142–8. See also J. Grassi, "Ezekiel 37:1-14 and the New Testament", *New Testament Studies* 11 (1964–65), pp. 162–4.

> When the centurion and those who were with him, keeping watch over Jesus, saw the earthquake and what took place, they were filled with awe, and said, "Truly this was the Son of God !" (27:54)

Notice that in Matthew it is not only the centurion, but also those who are standing with him who are forced to a confession of the Sonship of Jesus in the light of the world-shattering events that have accompanied his death. These soldiers standing with the centurion were the very people who nailed Jesus to the cross, who divided his garments, and who mocked him. The gathering of "all nations" (see 28:19) into the church is foreshadowed here, as soldiers look upon the criminal they have crucified, and proclaim him as the Son of God.

Thus, in 27:40 the Jews mock Jesus on the cross wagging their heads and jeering: "If you are the Son of God, come down from the cross." Now, at 27:54, the non-Jews, soldiers and centurion, proclaim: "Truly this was the Son of God!" Profoundly important themes intermingle here. The request from the Jewish onlookers reflects a crisis facing any believer who would have Jesus' Sonship conform to human criteria. It would seem impossible that the crucified one could be the Son of God. Yet, that is God's way in his Son, Jesus of Nazareth, and to separate Jesus from the cross would be to deny his Sonship. He is Son of God because he did not "come down from the cross" (verse 40).[9] A new age has begun, and the first fruits of it are a Gentile centurion and his company. They see the signs of the new age—"the earthquake and what took place"—and they proclaim the crucified Jesus as the Son of God.

9. This is a critical issue in Marcan christology. See, on this, Kingsbury, *The Christology of Mark's Gospel*, pp. 47–155, and Senior, *The Passion of Jesus in the Gospel of Mark*, pp. 117–32. It is retained in Matthew, and is especially obvious here. See Senior, *The Passion of Jesus in the Gospel of Matthew*, p. 138.

The Resurrection
of Jesus

Matthew's skilful use of Mark and his own traditions carries on into his resurrection story.

A careful reading of the text indicates that it is divided into four episodes and a conclusion. The episodes alternate between Jesus' friends and his enemies, between the light of the truth and the darkness of untruth. It is important to see this careful presentation of the light and dark elements that surround the resurrection of Jesus in the Gospel of Matthew.

(1) *A glimmer of hope.* From 27:55-61 we read of the women who watch from afar (verses 55-56, 61), women who have been with Jesus from the beginning of his ministry, and who have not abandoned him at the cross (unlike the male disciples—see 26:56). We also hear of the courage of Joseph of Arimathea, who asks for the body of Jesus and buries it in a new tomb, with reverence and care (verses 57-60). The women watch. For the Christian reader, who knows and has had experience of the fruits of this waiting and watching, an air of expectancy prevails.

(2) *The Response of Fear and Mistrust.* The next section, 27:62-66, turns away from such hopes. Here we are faced with the darkness of the fear, lack of faith and consequent duplicity of the chief priests and the Pharisees as they present their case to Pilate (verse 62). They demand that the tomb be guarded, to prevent tales of a resurrection after three days. Who knows, the disciples might steal the body and say that their Master had risen! (verses 63-64). As earlier, in the trial scene, Pilate again "wipes his hands" of the affair (see verses 24-26). He forces the leaders of Israel to accept the responsibility asked for when they had cried out to him: "His blood be on us and on our children" (verse 25). They see to it: the sepulchre is sealed and a guard is set (verses 65-66).

(3) *The Blinding Light of the Truth.* In 28:1-10 the women

from our first scene return—and a great earthquake breaks into the story.

> And behold, there was a great earthquake; for an angel of the Lord descended from heaven and came and rolled back the stone, and sat upon it. His appearance was like lightning, and his raiment white as snow. (28:2-3)

As signs normally associated with the end time occur at the death of Jesus, so further such signs are found at his resurrection. Only Matthew, among all the evangelists, has some sort of description of what actually happened at the tomb. An earthquake, an angel descending from heaven, lightning-like appearances, the brilliant colour of white, and guards who fall to the ground like dead men are further signs that the "turning-point of the ages" is at hand (see Judges 5:4; II Samuel 22:8; Psalm 68:8; Psalm 104:32; Joel 4:14-17).[10] The angel of the Lord who has rolled back the stone passes on the Easter message to the women and concludes with a commission: "Then go quickly and tell his disciples that he has risen from the dead, and behold, he is going before you, to Galilee; there you will see him" (28:7).

"Full of fear and great joy" (notice *both* elements, always present in Matthew's church?), the women rush away to tell the rest of the disciples, but they meet the risen Lord himself. He repeats the angel's commission *almost* verbatim, adding one further element. The angel sent the women to "his disciples", but Jesus sends them to "my brethren". The message they are to announce is not just to a group of failed disciples, but to a group who may have failed, but who

10. Senior, *The Passion of Jesus in the Gospel of Matthew*, p. 157: "These details, most of them typical of Jewish descriptions of the endtime, give Matthew's account an electric charge and reinforce the impression that from the moment of Jesus' obedient death the new and decisive age of salvation has begun."

remain, in the midst of their failure, Jesus' *brethren*: "Go and tell *my brethren* to go to Galilee, and there they will see me" (28:10).

(4) *A Lie to Replace the Truth.* The dark side of the story returns in 28:11-15. The guards posted in 27:62-66 rush back to the city, to the chief priests, and report "all that had taken place". The reader is well aware of "all that had taken place": it is the joyful announcement of the central truth of Christian belief: Jesus of Nazareth has risen from the dead (verse 11). This truth simply cannot be allowed. Therefore a lie is constructed: the body has been stolen! (verses 12-13). The lie is further aggravated by the use of money to bribe the soldiers into silence, and the hint of further corruption. The soldiers need not fear the Governor—the priests will look to it (verse 14). The money is taken and a story has its origins—a story that was still abroad as Matthew wrote his gospel (verse 15).[11] In this way Matthew has moved from light and promise to darkness and lies as he tells his story of the resurrection. The members of his own community, irrevocably separated from the synagogue religion that they had loved so much, now find that they must live and proclaim their Easter faith in the midst of lies and denials.

Conclusion

The scene is now set for the all-important conclusion to this magnificent gospel. At the beginning of the story of Jesus there was a promise that every aspect of the law would have to be lived to perfection "till heaven and earth pass away" (5:18). Now, in the death and resurrection of Jesus, heaven and earth have passed away. Thus Matthew can move easily to his incredible conclusion, as Jesus again meets his disciples on a mountain in Galilee (remember 5:1), where all worship—

11. It is interesting, from a historical point of view, to notice that 28:15 presupposes a current Jewish story that the body of Jesus was stolen. Thus we find a Christian story of a resurrection countered by the story of a grave robbery. Behind *both* stories stands the problem of an empty tomb.

but some still doubt. Even at this most significant moment in Matthew's gospel story, his realistic understanding of the church and the disciples who form it is in evidence. The reaction of the disciple to the presence of the risen Lord is still as it had been during his ministry, a mixture of both faith and doubt.

As we have already seen, to such a fragile group of disciples he can say:

(a) that all authority in heaven and earth has been given to him, as he takes over the prerogatives that Israel would allow only to Jahweh, their one and only God (28:18);

(b) that they are to go out into the whole world to make disciples, thus ending all the traditional geographical and national limitations that post-war Judaism placed upon God's choice of a people (28:19a);

(c) that they are to baptise in the name of the Father, the Son and the Holy Spirit, thus ending all adherence to the culturally conditioned initiation rite of Jewish circumcision (28:19b);

(d) that they are to teach the observance of all the things he has taught them, thus ending all adherence to the strict observance of the letter of the Mosaic law (28:20a).

This stirring conclusion to Matthew's Gospel (28:16-20a) leads the church away from all that it knew, loved and respected, and sends it on its journey into a Gentile world.

"The old" has been perfected in Jesus of Nazareth. Now the task of the church is to go fearlessly into God's furture, carrying with it treasures both old and new. Matthew's message is as challenging today as it was in the 80s of the first century. However, to be stirred and challenged is not enough. One must overcome the fears that block us from accepting this challenge and all its consequences. The gospel ends by telling us that we are not alone (28:20b).

Readers will recall that, in Luke's Gospel, Jesus returns to the Father via an ascension (see Luke 24:51 and Acts 1:9). This does not happen in Matthew's Gospel. Jesus *never leaves* his community. In fact, he promises the church of all ages: "I am with you always, to the close of the age" (28:20a). This promise is a repetition of something that was said to Joseph at the beginning of our carefully written gospel. The promises of the visiting angel at the beginning of the gospel are recalled and have become fact through the life, death and resurrection of Jesus of Nazareth—the Emmanuel: "A virgin shall conceive and bear a son, and his name shall be called Emmanuel (which means, *God with us*)" (1:23).

The death and resurrection of Jesus, the turning-point of the ages, have brought to fulfilment the Emmanuel prophecy. In the abiding presence of the Risen Lord, God is with us till the close of the age.

PART V
The Gospel
of John

8.
Reading the Gospel of John

Our reflections so far have made it clear that each of the gospels generally called Synoptic Gospels has its own uniqueness and profound vision. One would expect this to be even more the case with the fourth gospel. Already in the second century it was being called "the spiritual Gospel" (Clement of Alexandria, reported by Eusebius, *Hist. Eccl.* VI, 14, 7), and by the fourth century the author was known as "John the Theologian".[1] It is important to try to trace the situation in the early church that occasioned this magnificent gospel. From there we shall be in a better position to appreciate its structure and theology.

1. There are many excellent commentaries on the fourth gospel. I must mention four "great" commentaries, even though they may be out of the reach of the readers of this book. They are Schnackenburg, *The Gospel according to St John*; R. E. Brown, *The Gospel according to John*, Anchor Bible 29–29a (New York, Doubleday, 2 vols, 1966–70); R. Bultmann, *The Gospel of John. A. Commentary* (Oxford, Basil Blackwell, 1971); C. K. Barrett, *The Gospel according to St John* (London, SPCK, 1978). Briefer, but accurate and helpful single volume commentaries are: B. Lindars, *The Gospel of John*, New Century Bible (London, Oliphants, 1972); J. Marsh, *Saint John*, Pelican New Testament Commentaries (Harmondsworth, Penguin Books, 1968); P. Perkins, *The Gospel of John* (Chicago, Franciscan Herald Press, 1976). R. H. Lightfoot and C. F. Evans (ed.), *St John's*

"And they cast him out of the synagogue"

In our study of Matthew's Gospel we already had occasion to mention that towards the end of the century, especially after the Jewish war of AD 70, a rift grew between the church and the synagogue, which eventually led to total separation. Until the Jewish war there had been a variety of ways of living and interpreting the Torah, which we could term "Judaism". The Jewish historian Josephus mentions the Sadducees, the Pharisees, the Essenes and the Zealots as major groups.[2] However, once Jerusalem had fallen, and the remnants of the resistance at Masada had committed suicide, an enormous task of restructuring and reforming the people of Israel had to be undertaken. It was headed by an outstanding rabbi, who had managed to escape from Jerusalem in the midst of the confusion of the siege, Johannan ben Zakkai. He fled, with other Pharisees, to a small town called Jamnia, near the coast of Palestine, south of our present-day Tel Aviv.

Gospel. A Commentary with the Revised Version Text (Oxford, University Press, 1956). A quite unique commentary, which always deserves consultation, is that of E. C. Hoskyns and F. N. Davey (eds), *The Fourth Gospel* (London, Faber & Faber, 1947). At times Hoskyns's commentary reads like the poetry he is interpreting! See also the further important and useful books: C. H. Dodd, *The Interpretation of the Fourth Gospel* (Cambridge, University Press, 1953); S. S. Smalley, *John: Evangelist and Interpreter* (Exeter, Paternoster Press, 1978); J. Painter, *John: Witness and Theologian* (London, SPCK, 1975): R. A. Culpepper, *Anatomy of the Fourth Gospel* (Philadelphia, Fortress Press, 1983); R. Kysar, *John, the Maverick Gospel* (Atlanta, John Knox Press, 1976); idem, *John's Story of Jesus* (Philadelphia, Fortress Press, 1984); C. K. Barrett, *The Gospel of John and Judaism* (London, SPCK, 1975); B. Lindars, *Behind the Fourth Gospel*, Studies in Creative Criticism 3 (London, SPCK, 1971); D. M. Smith, *John*, Proclamation Commentaries (Philadelphia, Fortress Press, 1976); Moloney, *The Word Became Flesh*.

2. On these sects before and during the Jewish war, see the excellent and very readable work of D. Rhoads, *Israel in Revolution 6-74 C.E. A Political History Based on the Writings of Josephus* (Philadelphia, Fortress Press, 1976), pp. 32–46, 97–110.

Gradually this group of Pharisee leaders began to gather a broken and confused people, but this was possible only through the creation of a very clear Jewish identity. The pluralism of pre-war Judaism disappeared, and gradually Jamnian Phariseeism became the norm. Now there was, officially, only one "Judaism". Johannan and his associates set up the "great synagogue" in Jamnia, and from there began to organise the Jewish people and the practice of their synagogue faith. In this situation the early Christians soon found that they were a problem for emerging post-war Judaism. In a synagogue practice that looked forward to the coming of the Messiah and the messianic times, the Christians would be somewhat "out of step" as they whispered to their neighbours: "But the Messiah has already come. Jesus of Nazareth is the Messiah."

It was the first successor of Johannan ben Zakkai who solved the problem by adding a further "blessing" to an ancient Jewish morning prayer, the *shemoneh esreh*. To this beautiful prayer of eighteen benedictions, Rabbi Gamaliel II added a nineteenth, and had it inserted as the twelfth benediction. It has come to be known as the *birkat ha-minim*: "the blessing of the heretics". This prayer was to be prayed aloud in the communal prayer service, and anyone who refused to pray the twelfth benediction was put out of the synagogue. The text of the twelfth benediction is hard to determine exactly, but scholars have reconstructed it as follows: "For apostates may there be no hope, and may the Nazarenes and the heretics suddenly perish". This probably happened after AD 85, but some period of time would have elapsed before it entered into force in the synagogues scattered throughout the Mediterranean basin.

The reader may well be asking: what has this to do with the fourth gospel? It is important to notice that there was a Greek term used to speak of that process whereby a non-desirable element was "cast out of the synagogue": *aposun-agōgos*. What is more important to notice is that only one book in the whole of the New Testament uses that term: the Gospel of John. We find that the fourth evangelist describes an experience of a person in the life of Jesus, the man born blind of John 9, which parallels exactly that of those late first-century Christians.[3]

A man who had been completely without the light all his life (9:1: "blind from birth") gradually grows towards true faith in Jesus. In 9:11 he refers to Jesus as "the man called Jesus", while in verse 17 he goes farther, claiming: "he is a prophet". After further interrogation from the Pharisees (verses 25-29), he steps out even more boldly and mocks his interrogators by saying: "If this man were not *from God*, he could do nothing" (verse 33). Having dared to go so far in his recognition of Jesus, there is only one thing that the Pharisees can do. They "cast him out" of the synagogue (verse 34). Jesus now encounters the man a second time, and he falls on his knees and confesses his complete faith in Jesus as the Son of Man (verses 35-38).[4]

However, while that faith "journey" is going on, the Pharisees become more and more determined to show that Jesus is a hoax. In an attempt to prove that there never was a miracle, they call the parents of the man born blind. Who better to witness to the falseness of his claims to have been *born* blind? However, they refuse to speak for their son. This passage highlights the whole situation of the expulsion from the synagogue, which took place after the edict from Gamaliel II:

"We know that this is our son, and that he was born blind; but how he now sees we do not know, nor do we know who opened his eyes. Ask him; he is of age, he will speak for himself." His parents said this because they feared the Jews, for the Jews had already agreed that if anyone should confess him to be Christ, he was to be put out of the synagogue [*aposunagōgos*]. (9:20-22).

3. For the seminal—and still fundamental—work on this, see J. L. Martyn, *History and Theology in the Fourth Gospel* (Nashville, Abingdon Press, 1979), pp. 24-62.

4. On the interpretation of John 9, see F. J. Moloney, *The Johannine Son of Man*, Biblioteca di Scienze Religiose 14 (Rome, LAS, 1978), pp. 142-59.

There are two further uses of the term *aposunagōgos*, which also link this gospel with the experience of a Christian community cut loose from its traditional religion, setting out into a strange new world:

> Nevertheless many even of the authorities believed in him, but for fear of the Pharisees they did not confess it, lest they should be put out of the synagogue [*aposunagōgos*]. (12:42)

> They will put you out of the synagogues [*aposunagōgos*]; indeed, the hour is coming when whoever kills you will think he is offering service to God. (16:2)

We have touched an important link between the history of the early church at the end of the first century, and the Gospel of John. It should be said that what we find here is one of many crucial moments in a long history of the development of the Johannine community.[5]

It is clear from a reading of the gospel itself that this community had its origins at the very beginnings of the Christian experience. From those early days till the last decade of the century, the community struggled with tensions and difficulties that would have inevitably arisen from both inside and outside its ranks. Under the inspiration and guidance of the Beloved Disciple, the living link with Jesus of

5. In this discussion of the break that took place between the Johannine community and the synagogue, it is important to mention the extremely negative Johannine use of the expression "the Jews". It is not the condemnation of a people. The expression is used in the fourth gospel to indicate a group (in fact, for the Johannine community *then*, people from the synagogue) who refused to accept that Jesus was the revelation of God's glory (see especially 12:42-43). The term does not refer to the *ethnic* origins of those who oppose the revelation of God in Jesus, but to a *religious* attitude. For a good discussion of this issue, see E. Schillebeeckx, *Christ. the Christian Experience in the Modern World* (London, SCM Press, 1980), pp. 331–40.

6. Whether the Beloved Disciple was the Son of Zebedee or not need not detain us here. On this issue, see Moloney, *The Word Became Flesh*, pp. 15–19. For the sake of clarity, I will still refer to the author as "John", whoever that may have been.

Nazareth, all these experiences helped the community to gradually develop a remarkable "story of Jesus".[6] The break with Judaism through the *birkat ha-minim* was the product of a long struggle *within* Judaism, and it was crucial in the history of the faith journey of the community. Nevertheless, the community's journey did not end there. The Johannine letters are an important indication of that.[7]

An Old Story
Told in a New Way

The fourth gospel is a clear testimony to the early church's willingness to tell the story of Jesus over and over again, as it faced new situations and new challenges. Cut off from Judaism, it now needed to preach the Gospel of Jesus Christ in a world lacking the categories that Jesus himself and the earliest church had worked with: those of Jewish messianism and the highest forms of Old Testament piety. Such categories are found in the fourth gospel, and a large part of the Johannine community still had its roots in that history and religious practice. However, it would have been pointless to go on preaching *only* that story, true and foundational as it may have been. Eventually that sort of gospel, preached in the strange new world of Asia Minor at the end of the first century (and Ephesus still looks like the best place for the final form of this gospel) would have only resulted in an ageing Jewish-Christian ghetto.

The story of Jesus as it is told in the fourth gospel transcends traditional early Jewish-Christian categories. It moves courageously into another world: a world that understood the

7. There is a growing literature on this. As well as Martyn's work (note 3, page 1–64, see idem, *The Gospel of John and Christian History. Essays for Interpreters* (New York, Paulist Press, 1979); R. E. Brown, *The Community of the Beloved Disciple* (London, Geoffrey Chapman, 1979); and idem, *The Epistles of John*, Anchor Bible 30 (New York, Doubleday, 1982), pp. 47–115. See also, O. Cullmann, *The Johannine Circle* (London, SCM Press, 1976). For a survey, see F. J. Moloney, "Revisiting John", *Scripture Bulletin XI* (Summer 1980), pp. 9–15.

ascent and descent of the Son of Man (see 3:13 and 6:62), the Logos (1:1, 14), the only begotten Son of God (1:18), an eternal life made possible through the "knowledge" of the God whom Jesus had come to make known (see 17:3). There are many other uniquely Johannine expressions providing a *terminology* that makes sense to a new audience. However, while the terminology is "new", the basic story is "old". It is still the story of a God who has loved us so much that he has saved us through the death and resurrection of his son, Jesus of Nazareth.

The fourth evangelist was telling an "old story" in a new way. Thus, the fourth gospel as we now have it is the result of the journey of faith of a particular Christian community in the second half of the first century. We have already seen how important the "journey" theme is for an understanding of Luke's Gospel. As we will see in our analysis of John 2:1-4:54, it also has its importance for this gospel. Over the years the scholars have argued whether the fourth gospel should be classified as Jewish or Greek. The answer has to be: neither, but both!

The experience of the Johannine community and the rich theological vision it has produced indicate that this particular early Christian community committed itself seriously to "the problem of relating the givenness of the past with the exhilarating experience of the present".[8]

The Structure and Theology of the Fourth Gospel

It has often been said that the fourth gospel is like a magic pool in which an infant can paddle and an elephant can swim. This is very true at many levels. A mere first reading can be a moving experience, but a long-time study of the text

8. M. D. Hooker, "In His own Image", in M. D. Hooker and C. Hickling (eds), *What about the New Testament? Essays in Honour of Christopher Evans* (London, SCM Press, 1975), p. 41.

takes one much farther. It is written in one of the simplest forms of Greek in the New Testament, and yet it carries one of its profoundest theologies. The same thing can be said about the structure of the gospel. It is externally simple, but internally profound.

Readers of the gospel will notice that there are three major sections of the work. It opens with a very profound theological prologue (1:1-18) without parallel in the whole of the New Testament. To this the evangelist then joins the traditional story of the public ministry of Jesus, starting with the days of the Baptist (1:19). However, from this point onwards there is little contact with the story-line of the Synoptic Gospels, even though there are many passages where the synoptic tradition seems to be close at hand; for example, the confession of Peter in 6:67-69 and a passage that has much in common with the Gethsemane scene in the Synoptic Gospels in 12:27. The account of the public life of Jesus reaches a critical moment when, in the midst of rejection, Jesus departs from the public eye, to hide himself (12:36b). This gives the evangelist space to conclude the second section of the gospel with two solemn concluding summaries (12:37-50). As the second part of the gospel is entirely devoted to Jesus' public life and to his manifestation of himself as the revelation of his Father through words and miracles, it is often given the title "The Book of Signs".

In 13:1 Jesus is with "his own", beginning the series of events that will show that he loves them "to the very end". Through the last discourse, the passion and resurrection (13:1-20:31), the theme of Jesus' departure and his glorification rings clear. In the discourse it is proclaimed and explained. The consequences for the disciples and the future church are also made clear, and the important Johannine Paraclete teaching is spelt out (see 14:15-17, 26; 15:26-27; 16:7-11, 12-14). Once the mystery of "the hour" of Jesus passing from this world to the Father (see 13:1) has been explained, it takes place through the cross and the resurrection. Given this overall message, the third section of the gospel is often called "The Book of Glory". The gospel as we now have it in our printed texts has a further chapter, added by the Johannine community itself to an already completed gospel (20:31). It was probably added to deal with some further issues of concern for the community, which had not been covered in the gospel, especially in terms of its understanding itself as part of the larger church.[9]

Yet, despite the simplicity of this overall structure, once we begin to delve into the gospel, a series of difficulties appears. There are some passages that seem not to follow logically from a geographical or chronological point of view. The most important of these is the confused geography in chapters 5 and 6, which would be perfectly understandable if the chapters were reversed, and a strange indication in 14:31 that Jesus and the disciples are about to rise and leave the upper room. This indication is followed by two more chapters of discourse (chapters 15 and 16) and a prayer (chapter 17), still in the upper room.

These are only a few of the difficulties that have puzzled scholars over the years. After decades of attempts to sort these difficulties out with rearrangement theories, or theories of a variety of editions of the gospel, contemporary scholars now see that this gospel has its own criteria. Once again we are faced with the fact that we have a special "literary form". This particular example of the gospel form is the end-product of a long journey of faith and experience of a Christian community. As one of the most significant contemporary commentators on the fourth gospel has written:

> No arrangement can solve all the geographical and chronological problems in John, and to rearrange on the basis of geography and chronology is to give undue emphasis to something that does not seem to have been of major importance to the evangelist.[10]

As this is the case, I would like to reflect upon my understanding of the divisions and subdivisions of the structure

9. For a recent contrary view, see P. S. Minear, "The Original Function of John 21", *Journal of Biblical Literature* 102 (1983), pp. 85–98.

10. Brown, *The Gospel according to John*, p. 236.

and the argument of the fourth gospel. I shall presuppose that the gospel as we have it now, the result of almost two thousand years of tradition, is still in the form in which it was written by the author. This is an important consideration for me, as I firmly believe that there is a close link between the developing theological argument of the gospel and the unfolding of the text itself, in its present form. In other words, it appears to me that the structure and the theology of the Gospel of John are closely entwined. In the pages that follow I will attempt to show the link, in order that this may facilitate a further, deeper reading of the text of the gospel itself.[11]

SECTION ONE.
The Prologue (1:1-18)

This passage is one of the best known and most widely used texts in the New Testament. It contains one of the most sublime christological presentations of Jesus of Nazareth produced by the earliest church.[12]

From it we learn of the pre-existence of the Logos, turned from all time in loving union towards God. Their union is so intense that what God was, the Word also was (1:1-2). Salvation is impossible without the Logos, as he is the light and life of mankind (verses 3-4). This is a biblical way of saying that only in the Logos can women and men find the ultimate explanation of all their hopes and deepest desires. However, there are powers of darkness opposed to the

---

11. It is one of my long-cherished hopes eventually to write a study of the relationship between the structure and the theology of the fourth gospel. At the moment such a project can only be a dream. The pages that follow, however, are a brief indication of my present thoughts on the subject.

12. Given the importance of the prologue, both for John's Gospel and for the understanding of the development of the early church's christology, there is much literature devoted to it, and there are many theories connected with it. For a survey, and for an explanation of the underlying assumptions to my own very brief outline of the message of the prologue that follows, see Moloney, *The Word Became Flesh*, pp. 27–53.

revelation of the Word of God, and they attempt to overcome the light that he has come to bring. They fail. Although only a hint at this stage, we already have the beginnings of a Johannine theology of the cross in this succinct statement: "The light shines in the darkness, and the darkness has not overcome it" (verse 5).

The argument thus far has been concerned with God and his Word. It now shifts decisively into the experience of women and men in history, through the intervention of John the Baptist. Suddenly we are in history, as the Baptist points away from himself towards the true light (6-8). The light that the Logos brings, however, is neither recognised nor accepted, but to those who do receive it, a unique salvation is possible: they will become the children of God (verses 9-13). The Word that men and women must hear and accept as the light and the truth to become children of God is not some abstract notion. The Word has become truly man, and has dwelt among us, in the historical person of Jesus Christ, the fullness of the gifts of God. We are now able to see the revelation of God himself (the biblical notion of "the glory of God") in this man, Jesus of Nazareth (verse 14).

Once again the Baptist enters, calling out in his own words that Jesus, who may have come after him in terms of *our* time, is greater than him because he has existed *before all time* (1:15, recalling verses 1-2). The prologue closes with a very important reflection for the Johannine community, in its journey from Judaism into the wider world. Israel regarded the gift of the law as the greatest of all gifts that God could give. Now the fourth evangelist shows that there is a greater gift. From the fullness of God we have all received a new gift, which takes the place of a former gift (verse 16). The gift of the law was given through Moses, and it was a great gift indeed. However, there is now the perfect gift: the gift of the revelation of the truth that is given to us through Jesus Christ (verse 17). Taking up one of the existential problems of men and women of all time, the evangelist reminds us that no one has ever seen God. In this way he leads his readers into the actual life-story of Jesus, which now follows. This "story" is not ultimately about Jesus himself. Jesus' story tells a story of what God has done for us in and through Jesus of Nazareth. Jesus' life will make God known (verse 18). The life-story of Jesus can now begin.

This is an incredible way to begin a story of Jesus. The fourth evangelist begins a gospel with a prologue that tells his readers that the man Jesus of Nazareth is the pre-existent Logos, the unique revelation of God. This is so because he is the only begotten Son of God, without whom there is no revelation, and thus no sense or direction for the hopes of humankind. He perfects the gifts of God by replacing the former gift of the law given through Moses.

In many ways the fourth gospel is like a detective novel written backwards. Normally one must wait for the last page before one comes to the solution of the mystery. In the fourth gospel the author gives the reader the answer on the very first page. Once we have read through and absorbed the prologue's presentation of Jesus, we already know the secret of the mystery of Jesus of Nazareth, whose story we are about to read. Why does John do this? This is a deliberate choice on the part of the evangelist to draw *the reader* into the events of the story itself. Through the story, as we will read it from 1:19 to 20:31, there are a variety of people who interact with Jesus of Nazareth: John the Baptist, the disciples, "the Jews", the great characters from this gospel (the Mother of Jesus, Nicodemus, the Samaritan woman, Martha and Mary, Mary Magdalene). It must be remembered that *they have not read the prologue.* Only the reader has read the prologue. The evangelist tells the reader the answer to the mystery of Jesus so that during the whole of the story, as Jesus' revelation of his Father is met by refusal and misunderstanding, the reader will react in the light of the knowledge already provided in the prologue.

This gospel is a call to decision. The *reader* is asked to make a decision as the story unfolds. Do you believe that the unique revelation of God is taking place through this story? Or, rather, are you on the side of the various people who simply cannot come to accept the revelation of God in Jesus in the story itself? In each event and in each discourse it is not ultimately the person in the narrative who is being called to a decision: it is the reader. The evangelist has given the answer, but asks whether his readers are prepared to commit themselves to that answer through the story of the life of this man. In the last verse of his work the evangelist tells us why he wrote this gospel. He makes it clear that it is not written to tell us a story from the past, but to call us (the readers) to faith and life: "these things are written that *you* may believe that Jesus is the Christ, the Son of God, and that believing *you* may have life in his name" (20:31).

SECTION TWO.
The Book of Signs (1:19-12:50)

This section of the gospel, devoted to the public revelation of God in the preaching and activity of Jesus throughout his public ministry, should be further divided into five sub-sections. As the evangelist changes key, and shifts into another direction, he generally gives very clear indications. I will try to draw the reader's attention to those indications as I pass through the text.

1.   The first days of Jesus (1:19-51)

Although our next chapter will be devoted to a more detailed study of John 1:19-4:54 the first two sub-sections of the Book of Signs must still be considered in some detail.

I have entitled this sub-section "the first days of Jesus" because of the indications of the text itself. It seems that there is a deliberate setting of this first section of the gospel within the context of days. This is shown by the use in 1:29, 35 and 43 of the expression "the next day". This appears to lead into 2:1, where we find the further indication of time: "on the third day". We can thus say that there are four days involved in the narrative from verse 19 through to verse 51, followed by the indication of "on the third day" for the first miracle at Cana.

It is important to point out that on the first day we find a series of guesses about who John the Baptist might be, framed in terms of titles and hopes that were linked to first-century Jewish messianic expectations:

"Who are you?" (verse 19)
"I am not the Christ." (verses 20, 25)
"Are you Elijah?" (verses 21, 25)
"Are you the prophet?" (verses 21, 25)
"What do you say about yourself?" (verse 22)

The second day (see 1:29) finds the Baptist giving witness (see verses 6-8, which is fulfilled here) to Jesus. This time the terms used transcend Jewish hopes. They are thoroughly Christian and thoroughly Johannine:

"Behold, the Lamb of God, who takes away the sin of the world!" (verse 29)
"After me comes a man who ranks before me, for he was before me." (verse 30, again recalling the prologue, verse 15)
"this is he who baptises with the Holy Spirit" (verse 33)
"this is the Son of God" (verse 34)

The third day (see 1:35) sees the Baptist pointing to Jesus of Nazareth as the Lamb of God, and the disciples of the Baptist set out to "follow" Jesus. However, from here to the end of this first sub-section of the Book of Signs, we find the ex-disciples of the Baptist guessing about the identity of Jesus in terms of first century Jewish messianic hopes:

"Rabbi" (verse 38)
"'We have found the Messiah' (which means Christ)." (verse 41)
"We have found him of whom Moses in the law and also the prophets wrote" (verse 45)

"Rabbi, you are the son of God! You are the King of Israel!" (verse 49)

Looking back over this list of titles from our perspective, we may think that the disciples have come to an excellent confession of faith, but Jesus does not appear to be happy with the conclusions of Nathanael. In 1:50-51 we read:

> Jesus answered him, "Because I said to you, I saw you under the fig tree, do you believe? You shall see greater things than these." And he said to him, "Truly, truly, I say to you, you will see heaven opened and the angels of God ascending and descending upon the Son of Man."

There is obviously something lacking in Nathanael's confession of faith, based on his wonder at Jesus' having seen him under the fig tree. Greater faith is required of him, and of all the disciples. They are promised, as a consequence of true faith, nothing less than the revelation of the divine in the man Jesus of Nazareth.[13]

What sort of faith is required if the faith expressed by Nathanael and his companions is insufficient? That question is tackled immediately, in the following sub-section of the Gospel.

2. From Cana to Cana, a journey of faith (2:1-4:54)

Again, although we will be studying this sub-section in our next chapter, it is important for the purposes of our present reflection to indicate its major theme, and to show how it has been developed by our evangelist in a brilliant combination of a structured narrative and theology.

This section moves clearly between two miracles at Cana: in 2:1-11 the water is changed into wine at Cana, and in 4:46-54 the royal official's son is healed at Cana. In the evangelist's use of two miracles that take place at Cana, we have a

---

13. For a detailed study of John 1:51 and its place in the logic of this first chapter of the Gospel of John, see Moloney, *The Johannine Son of Man*, pp. 23–41.

literary "frame" around a series of episodes that recount a variety of reactions to Jesus. We must keep in mind the question that 1:19-51 raised: what kind of faith is needed to commit oneself totally to all that Jesus has come to reveal? Once this question is seen to be at the centre of John's unfolding story, then we notice immediately that both the Mother of Jesus in 2:1-11 and the royal official in 4:46-54 trusted completely in the efficacy of the word of Jesus. Even though she is rebuked (see 2:4) she simply says to the attendants: "Do whatever he tells you" (2:5). Similarly, the royal official is rebuked (see 4:48), but as Jesus promises health to his son, "the man believed the word Jesus spoke to him and went his way" (4:50). An unconditional acceptance of the "word of Jesus" is evident in the two examples of faith that frame the narrative.

Between these two examples of perfect Johannine faith, there are six indications of possible reactions to the word of Jesus. As we will see in a later chapter, each reaction to Jesus makes several important points. However, all we can do at this stage is indicate the story line, and the use John makes of it.

(a) "The Jews" totally reject the "word of Jesus" (2:13-21). They are to be judged as in a situation of no faith.

(b) Nicodemus is prepared to admit that Jesus is a great teacher from God because he does great signs, but he is not prepared to let go of his categories when Jesus speaks of the need to be reborn from above (3:1-10). He is in a situation of partial faith. There is a commitment, but within controllable categories.

(c) John the Baptist is prepared to disappear totally from the scene, as he is only the friend of the bridegroom who listens for his voice (3:22-30). This is obviously a repetition of the complete commitment that we found in the "frame". Here we find true faith.

Once this cycle of a journey from no faith to partial faith to true faith is completed, we find that it starts again, in the experience of the Samaritan woman and the Samaritan villagers.

(a) In a first moment, the Samaritan woman is unable to go beyond her ideas of wells and water, and is completely incapable of grasping the words of Jesus as he promises a water that will give eternal life (4:1-15). In this first stage she has no faith.

(b) Once Jesus shifts the discussion onto something that she can understand (her marital situation), she comes to see that he is a "prophet", and suspects that he may even be the Messiah (4:16-26). She is still within her own categories, but she has moved into a situation of partial faith.

(c) Finally, the Samaritan villagers come to hear the word of Jesus himself, and on his word (not the woman's), they proclaim that "this is indeed the Saviour of the world" (4:39-42). Again, we have arrived at true faith.

This episode is immediately followed by the second Cana miracle, and thus we find that there have been two movements from no faith, through partial faith into complete faith: a real journey of faith. If the first days of Jesus closed with the reader wondering what kind of faith is called for by Jesus, we now have the answer: a complete and unconditional trust in the efficacy of the word of Jesus; that is, in his person and in everything that he has come to reveal.

It is important to recall what was said in our reflections on the prologue. This "journey" is not reported here to retell stories about past reactions to the revelation of Jesus. The characters who are used are typical of all the readers of the gospel. We, the readers, have read the prologue and have come to know the gospel's understanding of the mystery of Jesus. Now, as we read further into Jesus' life-story, the evangelist asks us: "What is your involvement in this mystery?"

3. The feasts of the Jews (5:1-10:42)

In this sub-section of the Book of Signs, the fourth evangelist addresses one of the great pastoral problems that his community was facing. Again we can draw a parallel with the experience of the Matthean community. Earlier we described its difficulty, as the Christians found themselves cut off forcibly from their traditional roots. We saw that Matthew's solution was to write a history of God's salvation showing that it was the Christian community that was the true Israel, not the synagogue that had cast them out.

John's problem was more specific, and his answer is found in his understanding of the person and role of Jesus Christ. The pastoral problem that John was facing was the loss of contact with the feasts of old. This may not mean a great deal to us, but "the feast" was something more than a chance to celebrate. As Israel celebrated its great feasts, it not only recalled the great moments of God's saving intervention in the history of his people, but it made that same God and that same intervention present to every community celebrating the feast. This ancient Hebrew notion, of course, stands at the basis of our Christian concept of the real presence of the sacrifice of Jesus in the celebration of the Eucharist.

In the Johannine community, this loss of contact with their living God—celebrated in the synagogues and families of their old friends who had now excluded them from their life—was a matter of serious concern. Although John uses this section of his gospel to develop further his major christological themes, and to show the mounting rift between Jesus and "the Jews", the general background of the feasts is an important key to help us in our reading of John 5-10. His technique is quite simple. He takes four of the major feasts of the Jews, situates the ministry of Jesus within the setting of those feasts, and develops a christology that indicates that the presence of the living God once celebrated in the feasts has now been incarnated in the person of Jesus.

178

I mentioned earlier that the fourth evangelist generally gives clear indications of a change of direction. We have already seen it in the use of "days" in 1:19-51 and the "frame" of the two Cana miracles in 2:1-4:54. The evangelist indicates a new section with its own theme in 5:1: "After this there was a feast of the Jews, and Jesus went up to Jerusalem."[14]

From this point on, the evangelist makes clear reference to a series of feasts:

> Now that day was the sabbath. (5:9b)
> Now the Passover, the feast of the Jews, was at hand. (6:4)
> Now the Jews' feast of Tabernacles was at hand. (7:2)
> It was the feast of the Dedication at Jerusalem. (10:32)[15]

We will now limit ourselves to a view of each of these feasts and trace the fourth evangelist's teaching about Jesus, showing that he both perfects and replaces the feasts of old.

John 5:1-47. After the introduction to the theme of the feasts in 5:1, the evangelist makes it clear that the setting for the whole of 5:1-47 is the Jewish feast of the Sabbath (see verses 9b-10, 26, 18). The miracle of the healing of the paralytic at Bethesda on the Sabbath (verses 2-9a) leads, via the healed man, to a conflict between "the Jews" and Jesus. The key to an interpretation of the whole chapter is found in the reply of Jesus to the accusation that he has committed an unlawful act by working on a Sabbath. He claims: "My Father is working still, and I am working" (verse 17).

The prohibition of work on the Sabbath, well founded in

14. There have been many attempts to decide just which feast is indicated here. The main point that the reader must pick up is not the exact feast referred to, but the "theme" of the feasts, which is about to begin. If one must attach this reference to a feast, then it would have to be the Sabbath, which forms the background for the whole of John 5 (see verses 9b, 16, 18).

15. Even in the English translation, one does not need a trained eye to notice the close link between all of these expressions and 5:1: "After this there was a feast of the Jews." These indications are the words of the evangelist himself, drawing his narrative together.

the Torah (see Genesis 2:2; Exodus 20:11; 31:17), led to a difficulty for the rabbinic theologians.[16] People died, and infants were born on the Sabbath; time and history, especially the history of God's people, took its course on a Sabbath. Somehow, God had to be working, even though the Torah said that he rested. Given these facts, the rabbis allowed *only* God to work on a Sabbath, and they indicated that the only work he did was to give life and to judge. He ceased from all other unnecessary activities. Once that is clear, we find "the Jews" *correctly* interpreting Jesus' claim to be working on the Sabbath, as his Father is working. This is the motivation for their seeking to kill him (5:18):

(a) He broke the Sabbath.
(b) He called God his Father.
(c) He made himself equal with God.

The following discourse applies this Sabbath-based theology of God to Jesus of Nazareth. As the Father could judge and give life on the Sabbath, so can the Son (see 5:19-30). The witness that Jesus bears to himself is not really his own witness, but the witness of the God of Israel and of Moses, the very person who gave them the Torah, which they are using in their condemnation of Jesus (verses 31-47).

It is not that the celebration of the Sabbath is finished; it is transformed. As the synagogue continued to celebrate its form of Sabbath worship, the presence of Jesus in the community makes all such celebrations a thing of the past. By the end of the discourse, those who accused Jesus in the name of God and Torah become the accused ones. The witness of the Father and of Moses are with Jesus, not with the Jewish Sabbath celebrations:

> Do not think that I shall accuse you to the Father; it is Moses who accuses you, on whom you set your hope. If you believed Moses, you would believe me, for he wrote of me. But if you do not believe his writings, how will you believe my words? (5:45-47)

16. For more detail of the rabbinic discussion, see Moloney, *The Johannine Son of Man*, pp. 69–70.

John 6:1-71. John 6 is dominated by themes and symbols taken from the Jewish feast of the Passover. After the indication that this feast was at hand (6:4), Jesus multiplies bread and fish, but he is misunderstood as the crowd attempts to make him king (see verses 14-15). He then comes to his disciples on the stormy sea and reveals himself to them as "I am he" (verses 16-21), but the crowds who ate the bread have not been privileged with such a revelation. They search for Jesus in confusion (verses 22-24). Once they find him at Capernaum, Jesus warns them to seek the only true food, which will be given to them through the gift of the Son of Man. They are to leave their false pursuits and seek only to believe in the one whom God has sent (verses 25-29).

This introduction leads "the Jews" into a question. They demand a sign from Jesus that will at least put him on a par with their fathers who ate manna in the wilderness. We are now at the centre of the Passover theme, especially as "the Jews" quote their scriptures to him: "as it is written, 'He gave them bread from heaven to eat'" (6:31). The text is a combination of Exodus 6:4 and 15, a passage used in the Jewish Passover liturgy. Provided with this Passover text, a whole new interpretation of it is developed around the discourse that follows.[17]

Through 6:32-51b the major theme is that of the gift of bread from heaven. Using the general background of Jewish Wisdom motifs, Jesus spells out that there is a new "bread from heaven", a new nourishment, which replaces the old gift from heaven: the revelation of the Father in his Son: "For this is the will of my Father, that everyone who sees the Son and believes in him should have eternal life" (verse 40). Such a claim is possible if one accepts that only Jesus who comes from the Father has seen him and thus can make him known. The section concludes with a restatement of the Johannine

17. Here I am following the suggestion made by P. Borgen, in an important scholarly work, *Bread from Heaven. An Exegetical Study in the Conception of Manna in the Gospel of John and the Writings of Philo*, Supplements to Novum Testamentum 10 (Leiden, E. J. Brill, 1965). See Moloney, *The Johannine Son of Man*, pp. 94-8.

theme of revelation, blended with the Passover themes as the second part of the Old Testament passage quoted in verse 31 ("to eat") comes into the discourse:

> Not that anyone has seen the Father except him who is from God; he has seen the Father. Truly, truly, I say to you, he who believes has eternal life. I am the bread of life. Your fathers ate the manna in the wilderness, and they died. This is the bread which comes down from heaven, that a man may eat of it and not die. I am the living bread which came down from heaven; if anyone eats of this bread, he will live for ever . . . (6: 46-51b).

In this way, the discourse is open for its final section (6:51c-58), which insists on the eating of the body and the drinking of the blood of the Son of Man. This clearly refers to the encounter that can be had with Jesus, the bread from heaven, in the celebration of the Eucharist.

The skill of our evangelist is again in evidence. Throughout the whole of the discourse Jesus has insisted that the days of the manna are finished, and that the experience of God's freeing presence through the Passover celebrated in Judaism has been replaced by the revelation of the Father in the Son. However, we must recall that the gospel was being read by people at the end of the first century. They would have been asking, as Christians from all subsequent generations might ask: "Where do I see the revelation of the Father in the Son? The events of the life of Jesus are no longer open to me." John answers such a query by pointing to the Eucharist. It is in the eating of the flesh and the drinking of the blood of the Son of Man—in the celebration of the Eucharist—that the Christian of all times can again meet the revelation of God in the love of a Son. His broken body and spilt blood are the supreme revelation of a God who is love (see also 13:1; 15:13; I John 4:8, 16).

The signs, symbols, biblical texts and the theology of the Jewish Passover have all been taken up and rendered irrelevant. They are replaced by the person and the revelation of the Father in Jesus.

John 7:1-10:21. The Feast of Tabernacles was one of the most spectacular feasts of the Jewish calendar. It was marked by two important rituals. The first was a great mounting of lights: four golden candelabra set in the centre of the Temple area in the Court of the Women. This was a significant symbol, and the Temple was claimed to be the light of all Jerusalem. The second major ritual was a solemn procession to the Pool of Siloam, where water was gathered, and then taken back to the Temple area, where copious baths and ritual washings were carried out.

With that ritual as background, the imagery used in John 7:1-10:21 takes on a special significance. Although Jesus claims that he will not go to the feast in Jerusalem (7:1-9), he eventually does arrive, only to be met with puzzlement and disbelief (verses 10-36). This is an important section of the gospel, as it deals with some of the key Johannine issues: the messiahship of Jesus and the crucial importance of the recognition of his origins for a correct recognition of him and all he has come to reveal. The hostility to Jesus mounts. Then, on the major day of the feast, Jesus stands up and proclaims:

> If any one thirst, let him come to me and drink. He who believes in me, as the scripture has said, "Out of his heart shall flow rivers of living water." (7:37-38)

To this, the evangelist adds his own interpreting comment:

> Now this he said about the Spirit, which those who believed in him were to receive; for as yet the Spirit had not been given, because Jesus was not yet glorified. (7:39)

The water that quenches all needs is not the ritual water of the feast, but the water that Jesus will give in his death and the gift of his spirit (see 19:30).

In 8:12 the other theme is taken up. The Temple may well have been the "light of Jerusalem", but Jesus spoke to them saying: "I am the light of the world; he who follows me will not walk in darkness, but will have the light of life." There is a mixed response to Jesus as the unique light and revelation of God for the whole of humankind (see also 8:24 and 28).

Some of "the Jews" believe in him (see verse 30), but others hint that Jesus' origins are in doubt, whereas theirs are so perfect that they have all the "truth" that they need. This question of origins leads to Jesus' remarkable claim: "before Abraham was, I am" (8:58), and they took up stones in order to kill him for such blasphemy. The reader, of course, who has read the prologue, knows that Jesus has the truth, and that his interlocutors and accusers are living in a false security.

The theme of Jesus as the light of the world is then acted out dramatically through the experience of the man born blind. Although we have already seen some of the themes of John 9, it is important to notice the use that is made of the Tabernacle themes once again. In 9:5 Jesus again proclaims, "I am the light of the world", and the miracle is effected through Jesus' sending the blind man to wash in the Pool of Siloam. However, the evangelist adds a note to explain that it is not really the waters of Siloam that effect the cure: it is Jesus, the Sent One: "'Go, wash in the pool of Siloam' (which means Sent). So he went and washed and came back seeing" (9:7).

Through all of this the leaders of Israel move farther and farther into the darkness, until at the end of John 9 they are accused of being blind with a blindness that refuses to accept Jesus. "The Jews" think that they have all the answers in what they know already (see 9:39-41). This leads Jesus directly into the parable of the Good Shepherd, taken from the Prophet Ezekiel, where it was used to accuse the false leaders of Israel (see Ezekiel 34:11-16). Against the falseness of the now "blind" leaders of Israel, Jesus is presented as the Good Shepherd, whose sheep know his voice, and who is prepared to lay down his life for his sheep (see 10:1-18).

The feast of light and the feast of water have also been superseded by the revelation of God in Jesus the light of the world, and the living water poured forth in his death, as he hands over the spirit (see 19:30-34). It is no longer the synagogue that is celebrating the true light and the living water, but the community of Jesus Christ, full of the spirit of life and living in the light.

John 10:22-42. In many ways the final feast, which forms the backdrop for 10:22-42, was a relatively minor feast. It had come into existence in remembrance of Judas Maccabeus' restoration of the Temple of Israel in 164 BC. The Feast of the Dedication, however, was more than a celebration of the restoration of the sticks and stones of a building. For Israel, the Temple was the very dwelling-place of God, the place where the "glory of God" dwelt among his people. For this reason the loss of the Temple meant the loss of that place where the loving presence of their saving God could be seen and visited in the heart of the nation. Its restoration was something of great significance.

As this is the case, the final encounter of Jesus with "the Jews" as they celebrate their feasts explains all that he has been claiming throughout the whole section dedicated to the feasts of Israel. During the Feast of the Dedication the Jews come to reject Jesus' claims to be the Son of God, and again attempt to take him and kill him (10:31 and 39). They do not belong to the good shepherd, as they do not respond to his voice, i.e. to the revelation he has come to bring (verses 22-29). They do not recognise the Sonship of Jesus, and thus do not realise their own chance to become sons (verses 31-39); see also 1:13). It is dramatic that this violent refusal of the Son's revelation and the new possibilities of such a revelation takes place at the feast that commemorated the gift of the visible presence of God in their midst. It is during that feast that Jesus can point to himself—eliminating all further need to look to a Temple—and claim: "I and the Father are one" (verse 30).

Because the fourth evangelist can argue that to look upon Jesus is to see the revelation of God and his ways, the solution to the pastoral problem that stood behind this section of the gospel was near at hand. The Christian community no longer needed to look to the signs and symbols of the Jewish rites.[18] It now had the person of Jesus Christ, who embodied all that these signs and symbols revealed. However, as we saw in our glance at John 6, the members of the Johannine community would have wondered where the fulfilment of the signs and symbols of Israel could be found, now that Jesus had returned to his Father. They were told that they could find it in their Eucharist (see 6:51c-58). Here we have the beginning of an understanding of the living presence of Christ in the Church beautifully summed up in a homily delivered some fifteen hundred years ago:

> Lord, you drew all things to yourself so that all nations everywhere in their dedication to you might celebrate in a full, clear sacramental rite what was done only in the Jewish Temple and in signs and shadows. (Leo the Great, *Sermon 8 on the Passion*, 6-8)

4. Jesus turns towards the cross (11:1-12:36)

A first reading of John 11-12 could leave the reader with the impression of a tensely written narrative of Jesus' last days. This would be a true impression: in rapid succession we read of the sickness, death and resurrection of Lazarus, accompanied by the support and affection of his sisters, Martha and Mary (11:1-44). This resurrection miracle leads to the final decision on the part of the Jewish authorities that Jesus must die (verses 45-57). In preparation for his death, and

18. One might ask why the fourth evangelist makes so much use of these signs and symbols, which were part of the Temple cult, when at the end of the century the Temple was no longer in existence. For a *mistaken* use of this argument, see J. A. T. Robinson, *Redating the New Testament* (London, SCM Press, 1976), pp. 275–8, and, most recently, idem, *The Priority of John* (London, SCM Press, 1985), pp. 70–2. It is very important to realise that as the problem created by the destruction of the first Temple had been overcome through the return from Babylon and the building of the second Temple, there were similar profound hopes that there would be a third Temple. These hopes would have been very alive at the end of the first century. Clear evidence of this is found in the fact that the foundational document of post-war Judaism, *The Mishnah*, finally written on the basis of traditions about AD 212, contains lengthy discussions of the structure of the Temple and its rituals.

amidst disapproval from his disciples, Mary anoints Jesus' feet (12:1-8), and then, amid further plotting, Jesus enters Jerusalem (verses 9-19). Once he has arrived in Jerusalem for his final Passover feast (see 11:55 and 12:1), some Greeks ask to see him. This leads Jesus to declare that the hour for the glorification of the Son of Man has come. He calls all who would follow him to understand that his way is the way of the grain of wheat that falls into the earth and dies before it bears fruit (12:20-26). Jesus then repeats his decisive statement about his "hour", and describes it as the final victory over the world. But he is both misunderstood, and in the end rejected. He urges his Jewish audience to walk in the light while they have the light. The public appearance of Jesus ends dramatically as the evangelist tells his readers: "When Jesus had said this, he departed and hid himself from them" (verse 36b).

There can be no doubt that this is a dramatic narrative, but there is more to it. By now we are aware that our evangelist will use this narrative to communicate more than the events of the life of Jesus. He will offer us an authoritative interpretation of those events. The overarching theme of this section is found in the title that I gave above: Jesus turns towards the cross.

Twice in the account of the miracle of Lazarus, the evangelist comments that the "glory of God" will shine forth through the miracle. However, on one occasion he says more than that: "This illness is not unto death; it is for the glory of God, so that the Son of God may be glorified by means of it" (11:4). There are two issues here. The glory of God certainly shines forth in the raising of Lazarus (see 11:40), but there is a further glorification of the Son of God, which will take place because of this event. This is a reference to "the hour of Jesus" set in motion by the Lazarus event.

Following the story-line traced above, this miracle leads to the decision that Jesus must die for the nation, and not for the nation only, but to gather into one the children of God who are scattered abroad (see 11:49-52). It is important to know that up to this point in the gospel, the death of Jesus has never been mentioned. There have been hints of it in the use of the term "to lift up" (see 3:14; 8:28) and the ominous references to "the hour" that had not yet come (see 2:4; 4:21, 23; 7:30; 8:20). However, the actual use of the verb "to die" (Greek: *apothnēskein*) appears for the first time in 11:16. From now on, as Jesus moves decisively through these events, from his public ministry into his "hour of glory" (chapters 13-20), such references multiply (11:16, 50, 51; 12:24, 33).

There is an important link between all the events that take place in the story of Jesus as it is told in chapters 11-12. After Jesus raises Lazarus, a decision is made by Caiaphas that he must die. However, the evangelist adds a note to a Caiaphas' prediction, explaining that the death of Jesus will also be a "gathering" of the children of God who are scattered abroad:

> But one of them, Caiaphas, who was high priest that year, said to them, "You know nothing at all; you do not understand that it is expedient for you that one man should die for the people, and that the whole nation should not perish." He did not say this of his own accord, but being high priest that year he prophesied that Jesus should die for the nation, and not for the nation only, but to gather into one the children of God who are scattered abroad. (11:49-52)

Lazarus is still present as his sister anoints Jesus, and Jesus' entrance into Jerusalem (12:12-16) leads to a decision that both Jesus and Lazarus must die (verses 9-11, 17-19). As this section of the account comes to a conclusion the Pharisees themselves declare: "look, the world has gone after him" (verse 19). The theme of the "gathering" around Jesus in his hour is unfolding further. In proof of this, some Greeks, representing those children of God who are scattered abroad, seek him (verses 20-22). Jesus can now announce that the hour for the glorification of the Son of Man has come (verse 23).

There is a growing link between the glorification, the hour and the death of Jesus. This is carried further in 12:31-33:

> Now is the judgment of this world, now shall the ruler of this world be cast out, and I, when I am lifted up from the earth, will draw all men to myself.

The themes that have emerged over these few chapters are now very clear. The hour of Jesus is at the one time his being lifted up to glory and his crucifixion; it is the end of the rule of the world. The cross of Jesus is the place where the glory of God will shine forth in a perfect way, gathering all to himself.

Chapters 11-12 provide the outline of a theology of the cross that both looks backwards and forwards in the gospel for further support. In 8:28 Jesus had told "the Jews": "When you have lifted up the Son of man, then you will know that I am he . . ." The very last verse of the scene describing the actual death of Jesus will point into the future role of this revelation of God on the cross: "They shall look on him whom they have pierced" (19:37).

5.   Conclusion to the public ministry (12:37-50)

These remaining verses of John 12 are used by the evangelist to raise two issues. First, in verses 37-43 he asks a question that plagued the early church (see, for example, Romans 9-11): why did Israel refuse the revelation of God in Jesus? There was a traditional answer to this question, which John also reports: the theory of the "divine hardening". For some strange reason the heart of Israel was "hardened", and this hardening was a part of God's plan so that the message might be preached to the Gentiles (verses 37-41). However, the uniquely Johannine reason is given in verses 42-43. Playing upon the double sense of the Greek word *doxa*, the evangelist argues that the leaders of Israel loved the *"doxa of men"* rather than the *"doxa of God"*. The secular meaning of the word is linked to praise, esteem and honour, while the Johannine meaning, as we have seen, refers to the living presence of a saving God in their midst, especially in the event of the cross. For John, there has been a failure on the part of Israel to abandon its total trust in the letter of the law (see 1:16-17), the teaching of Moses (see 9:29) and its attempts to understand Jesus within a world-view that it could control (see 1:19-51; 3:2; 6:15; etc.). Thus it has failed to acknowledge the living presence of their God in Jesus of Nazareth.

Finally Jesus' words are reported, and they are a summary of the whole of the message of the Book of Signs (12:44-50). Jesus has come into the world as the unique revelation of light and truth. He also brings a judgement, but it is a judgement that the believer brings upon himself or herself. Those who believe in Jesus and all that he has come to reveal will not remain in darkness; but those who refuse the light and the truth of Jesus will finally be judged by that very revelation that they have rejected.

SECTION III.
The Book of Glory (13:1-20:31)

1. The last discourse (13:1-17:26)

Some acquaintance with the fourth gospel would make a reader aware that it features a long discourse that Jesus delivers to his disciples in the upper room, apparently on the eve of his death. This discourse is generally referred to in glowing terms as a document of extraordinary beauty. However, few are aware of the complexities of these five chapters.

There is a great deal of repetition in the discourse. Some further investigation also shows that there are apparently notorious lapses. We have already mentioned the difficult ending of 14:31, and the same could be said for 16:33. Scholars also argue whether 13:1-30 (the footwashing) belongs to the discourse, and most would say that it does not. Perhaps one of the most outstanding problems is the presence of the many very close parallels that exist between 14:1-31 and 16:4-33.[19]

Yet, despite these difficulties, there can be no denying the beauty of the discourse. The argument is ultimately very simple. Set on the eve of his "hour of glory", Jesus goes to the

19. For an excellent synoptic chart of these parallels, see Brown, *John*, pp. 589-91.

cross to show the immensity of his love (see 13:1; 15:13). He speaks most clearly of his oncoming departure, of his return to the Father, but he insists that he will not leave his disciples orphans (see 14:1-5, 30-31; 16:4-11, 31-33). After his departure, they will suffer and be persecuted (15:18-21; 15:26-16:3), but they are to abide in him (15:1-11), enlightened, guided and instructed by the Paraclete, which he will send them (see 14:15-17; 15:26-27; 16:7-14). In this period there is a new way of life to be lived, a way modelled on his life. They must keep the commandments of Jesus, loving one another as he has loved them, and this will result in their being loved by both Jesus and the Father (see 13:34-35; 14:15-24; 15:5b-7, 12-17; 17:20-26).

Four powerful statements, situated at the beginning and end of chapters 13 and 17 respectively (13:1, 31-38; 17:1-5, 24-26) frame this discourse. They lay the basis for the whole argument as they claim that:

(a) Jesus has brought to perfection the work which his Father gave him to do (13:1; 17:1-5).
(b) He has glorified the Father on earth and now returns to the Father to be glorified with the glory which was his before the world was made (13:1; 17:1-5).
(c) All this has happened because of his total gift of himself in love, in complete obedience to the will of his Father (13:31-38; 17:24-26).
(d) Jesus now prays that his love will be continued in the lives of "his own", whom he leaves in the world (13:31-38; 17:24-26).

At the very centre of the discourse, both theologically and structurally, we find the new commandment of love: "This is my commandment, that you love one another as I have loved you. . . . This I command you, to love one another" (15:12, 17). This love, however, flows from Jesus' initiative: "You did not choose me, but I chose you and appointed you that you should go and bear fruit" (15:16).

There can be no doubt that the discourse has grown during the faith journey of the Johannine community. The most obvious indication of this is the statement of a central argument about the departure of Jesus and the means by which the suffering that will ensue can be overcome, in 14:1-31. The same argument is restated in a slightly more developed way in 16:4-33. It is probable that we have here evidence of two versions of the same discourse of Jesus. It can also be shown that the prayer of Jesus' hour in chapter 17 had its own history before it was eventually used in the fourth gospel as Jesus' final words, on the eve of his death. However, whatever the earlier history of the various "parts" of the discourse, it is clear that the evangelist has used his various traditions—the footwashing, the two forms of the discourse found in chapters 14 and 16, the special material in chapter 15 and the prayer of chapter 17—to form a beautifully constructed unit.

Given the main themes, and the unfolding of the argument, I will simply present the overall message and structure of 13:1-17:26 by means of a diagram (see p. 193). The reader will find, following this structured diagram, that the apparently complicated statement and restatement of themes is not a strange confusion of traditions, but a powerful discourse and prayer on the ultimate glorification found in the gift of self in love. Jesus is presented as the model, and he calls his disciples to follow him into the joy which is his.[20]

2. The passion, death and burial of Jesus (18:1-19:42)

The whole of the fourth gospel has pointed forward to the death of Jesus as the moment when the glory of God would shine forth in a unique way. As this is the case, we can understandably expect our evangelist to continue his skilful use of narrative to communicate his beliefs about Jesus. Indeed, here we find him blending the traditional account of the

20. For this structure I am very much indebted to the work of Y. Simoens, *La gloire d'aimer. Structures stylistiques et interprétatives dans le Discours de la Cène*, Analecta Biblica 90 (Rome, Biblical Institute Press, 1981), pp. 52–80. For his structure, which I have adapted slightly, see p. 77.

THE STRUCTURE OF THE LAST DISCOURSE: John 13:1-17:26

13:1-38	14:1-31	15:1-11	15:12-17	15:18-16:3	16:4-33	17:1-26
13:1. AGAPE: love. TELOS: accomplish "the hour".						17:1-5. DOXA: glory. TELOS: accomplish "the hour".
	14:1-5. Departure to a place. "Let your hearts not be troubled".				16:4-11. Departure Spirit.	
		15:1-5a. Abide in Jesus: the life-giving vine.		15:18-21. Hatred— persecution due to ignorance.		
13:18-20. Fulfil Scripture (v.18). I have chosen (v.18). Word of Jesus: "I tell you this now" (v. 19). Those sent (v.20).	14:15-24. Disciples to keep the commandments and to love Jesus, leading to being loved by both Jesus and the Father.	15:5b-7. Abide in Jesus (v.5b). Not to abide in Jesus (v.6). Abide in Jesus (v.7).	15:12-17. Mutual love (vv.12-14). have chosen you (vv.15-16). Mutual love (v.17).	15:22-25. Word of Jesus/Sin (v.22). To have Jesus and the Father (v.23). Works of Jesus/Sin (vv.24-25).	16:21-24. Sorrow leading to joy: the image of the woman in child-birth— sorrow to joy in the disciples.	17:12-19. Fulfil Scripture (v.12). Joy (v.13). Gift of the Word (v.14). Hatred (vv.14-16). Those sent (vv.17-19).
		15:8-11. Abide in the love of Jesus.		15:26-16:3. Exclusion– death due to ignorance.		
	14:30-31. Departure. Encouragement.				16:31-33. Departure "Be of good cheer"	
13:31-38. DOXA: glory. AGAPE: love.						17:24-26. DOXA: glory. AGAPE: love.

passion with his own extraordinary vision of the person and significance of Jesus of Nazareth.

In the following reflection I will limit my study to general themes and indications of the structures that carry these themes. The reader will then be able to turn to the text itself to discover its beauty.

The very words John uses in his passion narrative indicate his theme. Throughout the gospel, up to this point, the word "kingdom" has been used only twice, and both times in a traditional passage, referring to "the kingdom of God" (see 3:3, 5). In the passion account it appears three times (18:36). Thus far in the gospel the title "king" has been found four times (1:49; 6:15; 12:13, 15). Each one of these uses is found on the lips of people who would like to make Jesus a king in their way. These passages reflect false messianic hopes, which others are attempting to impose upon Jesus, and none of them is satisfactory. Throughout the passion narrative, however, the term appears ten times, as here the kingship of Jesus is proclaimed, he is crowned and dressed as king, and he acts out his role as king, "lifted up" from the earth. Thus, although the traditional story is told, it can be seen that there is a careful rewriting of that story. The passion account in the fourth gospel unfolds around five major scenes.

1. *In the Garden. Jesus and his Opponents* (18:1-11). Although this scene is often entitled "the arrest of Jesus" by the commentators, Jesus is not arrested at all. Here the darkness comes to seek him, the light, and his opponents must arm themselves with lanterns and torches (18:3). Jesus is the master of the situation from the beginning of the passion story. He asks them whom they seek, and he reveals himself to them as "I am he!". This remarkable use of the expression "I am he" (Greek: *Egō eimi*) reaches back to God's revelation of himself to Moses at Sinai (see Exodus 3:14) and especially to the prophets who spoke of Jahweh, the one and only true God among many false gods (see, for example, Isaiah 43:10; 45:18; 46:4; 48:12). Here, as throughout the gospel (see especially 6:26; 8:24, 28, 58; 13:19), Jesus applies the expression to himself! His opponents fall to the ground

impotent, but Jesus calls them to their feet and prevents any violence from Peter, because he has come to drink the cup that his Father asked him to drink (18:11; see also 4:34 and 12:27). This first scene of the passion account, Jesus in a garden surrounded by his enemies, will match the final scene of the account: Jesus in a garden surrounded by his friends (19:38-42; see below).

2. *The Jewish Trial* (18:12-27). Outside in the darkness, Peter denies Jesus, and draws near to the fire, set by those who had come with lanterns and torches to take Jesus (18:15-18). One who has lived with the light draws near to the false light, set by the darkness, which opposes and rejects Jesus. Meanwhile, Jesus is inside, being interrogated about his disciples and his teaching (verse 19). He refuses to answer, as his time of public manifestation and teaching is over. However, the message has been made known. It is now the epoch of the church, the time for the disciples to preach what they have heard (verses 20-21). A soldier's slap rejects this message, but its "rightness" cannot be questioned (verses 22-23). However, one of the disciples is outside, denying Jesus a second and a third time (verses 25-27). This first indication of the future mission of the church is a realistic understanding of just what the church is. Jesus is the great witness to the Truth, and the church has the task of continuing that witness. That the disciples, the bearers of that message, often deny such knowledge does not alter the situation. This first scene, which indicates the mission of a fragile church, will be matched by the scene at the cross. There the church will be founded in the new family of Jesus, created as Disciple is given to Mother and Mother to Disciple (19:25-27).

3. *The Trial before Pilate* (18:28-19:16). The garden scene and hints of the mission of the church are both paired with the scenes that follow. This is not the case with this third and central scene of the Johannine passion narrative. The trial before Pilate is a magnificently structured and argued piece of narrative, where Jesus is both proclaimed (see 18:33-38a,

38b-40; 19:13-15) and crowned as king (19:1-3). The evangelist constructs this trial through a series of changes of place. At times the trial goes on inside the praetorium with Pilate, and at other times Jesus is presented before the crowds and "the Jews" outside. There is only one scene without a change of place: the central scene, where Jesus is crowned (19:1-3). A more detailed outline of the structure of this passage will allow readers to savour the drama as John tells it. (see p. 197).

Now that Jesus has been ironically proclaimed and crowned as king, the cross scene can follow, where this kingship is enacted, especially in the founding of the church and in the gift of life to that church.

4. *The crucifixion and death of Jesus* (19:17-37). The actual crucifixion of Jesus is rapidly told (19:18), and then the evangelist continues to use the story of the cross of Jesus to tell his readers of his kingship. He is proclaimed as king with the cruel plaque nailed to the cross (verses 17-22) and his kingdom will never be torn apart, even in the hands of the enemy (the symbol of the robe that will not be torn apart: verses 23-26). The central scene indicates the nature of that kingdom. The first of all believers, the Mother of Jesus (see 2:1-11) and the Beloved Disciple (see 13:23; 20:2-10) are given to one another as Mother and Son. "And from that *hour*" they become one. The centre of the cross scene is the foundation of the church, the formation of a new family, which cuts through all bonds of flesh and blood, but which is based on faith and love. It is, however, important to notice that the term "mother" is mentioned five times in 19:25-27. The evangelist also wishes to make clear that the "Mother" of Jesus becomes the "Mother of the Church" at the cross of her son.[21]

As Jesus dies, he can finally claim that he has—at last—brought to perfection the task which he was given (see 4:34 and 17:4). Thus, he "pours down" his Spirit on the

21. For a further discussion of the Johannine Marian material, see Moloney, *Woman: First among the Faithful*, pp. 87–92.

JESUS BEFORE PILATE

Introduction 18:28.
The actors and the place:
Pilate, Jesus, Jews,
Praetorium.

Conclusion: 19:16.
"He handed him
over to them
to be crucified."

1st scene: 18:29-32.
"Pilate went out . . ."
The Jews accuse Jesus as
a malefactor and ask for
crucifixion.

7th scene: 19:13-15.
"Pilate brought
Jesus out . . ."
"Behold your King!"
"Away . . . crucify him!"

2nd scene: 18:33-38a.
"Pilate entered . . ."
Jesus shows that he is
King of Truth.

6th scene: 19:8-12.
"Pilate entered . . ."
Authority comes from above;
otherwise there is none.

3rd scene: 18:38b-40.
"Pilate went out . . ."
He declares Jesus innocent
and "King of the Jews"
They prefer Barabbas.

5th scene: 19:4-7.
"Pilate and Jesus came out . . ."
Jesus innocent.
"Behold the Man!"
They ask for the cross.

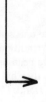

4th (central) scene: 19:1-3.
No change of place mentioned.
Jesus is crowned and dressed
as a king. He is proclaimed:
"Hail, King of the Jews!"
The revelation is rejected
by the slaps.

newly born Church (19:28-30). Finally the evangelist tells us of the blood and the water flowing from the side of the elevated Christ. Through this message he addresses his own community at the end of the century. This was no once-upon-a-time event in the past. It is happening daily among us all in the sacraments of Eucharist and Baptism. Thus the cross scene can challenge the church to look upon the crucified Jesus for the ultimate revelation of a God who is love: "They shall look on him whom they have pierced" (19:37). The church, presented as fragile during the trial before the Jewish authorities, is nevertheless challenged here to be church as Jesus asks, and to look to him for its direction and hope.

5. *In the Garden: Jesus and his Friends* (19:38-42). As the Johannine passion account began with a garden scene where Jesus met his enemies, it concludes with a further garden scene as Jesus is laid to rest by his friends. These friends are explicitly named as Joseph of Arimathea and Nicodemus. This gospel tells us that Nicodemus came to Jesus in secrecy (see 3:1-2), and we have also read that he tried, at one stage, to defend Jesus' rights (see 7:50-52), only to wilt under abuse. We know of Joseph of Arimathea from the synoptic tradition (see Mark 15:43; Matthew 27:57; Luke 28:51), and the fourth evangelist draws on the same traditions to couple these two men who move from secrecy into light as a result of the death of Jesus.[22] They bury Jesus with an enormous quantity of myrrh and aloes, a burial fit only for a king. He is buried in a new tomb, and the reader waits in eager expectancy for the proclamation of a new day.

Although Raymond Brown is writing only of the crucifixion

22. This is one example from the Gospel of John where one senses the close contact that John has with the same basic "Jesus traditions" that stood behind the Synoptic Gospels. However, as they have been used and reused over the faith journey of the Johannine community, they have taken on their own specific Johannine identity. On this, see C. H. Dodd, *Historical Tradition in the Fourth Gospel* (Cambridge, University Press, 1965).

scene, his words could well be applied to the whole of the Johannine passion narrative:

> The principal episodes of the crucifixion are concerned with the gifts that the enthroned king gives to those who accept his kingdom, for certainly these episodes have as a motif what Jesus does for the believer. The Johannine crucifixion scene is, in a certain way, less concerned with the fate of Jesus than with the significance of that fate for his followers.[23]

Equally true are the words of the opening chorus of J. S. Bach's *Johannespassion*:

> O Lord, our Ruler, whose glory
> is magnified in all lands,
> testify to us by thy passion,
> that thou, the true Son of God,
> hast at all times,
> even in time of deepest lowliness
> been glorified.

3. The resurrection and the appearances of Jesus (20:1-31)

Given the remarkable theology of the cross that is developed by this gospel, it is sometimes asked what point there is in having a resurrection story![24] As one reads through the Johannine account of the resurrection and the appearances of Jesus there are two things to notice. In the first place, John's basic resurrection story is in complete agreement with the tradition: an empty tomb discovered by women—here one woman: Mary Magdalene (20:1-2); an account of appearances (verses 11-18, 19-23, 24-29); and a final sending out of disciples on a mission (verses 21-23). Naturally, our evangelist

23. Brown, *John*, p. 912.

24. See, for example, C. H. Dodd, *The Interpretation of the Fourth Gospel*, p. 440: "For John the crucifixion itself is so truly Christ's exaltation and glory (in its meaning, that is to say), that the resurrection can hardly have for him precisely the same significance that it has for some other writers."

uses those traditional themes in his own way. However, three features of this resurrection account appear only here: the experience of Peter and the Beloved Disciple in their journey to the empty tomb (verses 2-10); the appearance to Mary Magdalene (verses 11-18); and the episode with doubting Thomas (verses 24-29).[25]

As this gospel opened with the indication of the possibility of a journey of faith, from no faith to complete faith, in the experiences recounted in the journey from Cana to Cana (2:1-4:54), so it ends with further indications of such a journey. This time, however, there is a difference. The original members of the Christian community, Peter and the Beloved Disciple, Mary Magdalene and Thomas all begin in a situation of unbelief (see 20:2-3, the disciples; 13-15, Mary; 24, Thomas). However, they are all led by the risen Lord, through their various experiences of little and partial faith (verses 9-10, the disciples; 16-17, Mary; 25, Thomas), into a final total commitment in faith (verses 19-22, disciples; 18, Mary; 28, Thomas).

Speaking to a Christian community at the end of the first century, our evangelist can point back to the foundational experience of the church. The encounter with the risen Jesus has led the very first believers to faith. That same Jesus blesses in a special way those who do not have the experience of seeing Jesus himself, but yet believe (verse 29). The evangelist then turns to those of his community and closes his gospel by telling them that they are to be the recipients of that blessing of the Lord. He has written the gospel story for that purpose:

> Now Jesus did many other signs in the presence of the disciples, which are not written in this book; but these are written that you may believe that Jesus is the Christ, the Son of God, and that believing you may have life in his name. (20:30-31)

---

25. For further detail, see F. J. Moloney, "John 20: A Journey Completed", *Australasian Catholic Record* 59 (1982), pp. 417–32. However, this should now be read in the light of the further suggestions of B. J. Byrne, "The Faith of the Beloved Disciple and the Community in John 20", *Journal for the Study of the New Testament* 23 (1985), pp. 83–97.

Conclusion

The fourth evangelist has brought his reader to a point of decision. His conclusion makes that clear, but it is equally clear in 3:16: "For God so loved the world that he gave his only Son, that whoever believes in him should not perish but have eternal life." Our evangelist knows no middle course, as he presents only two possibilities: to perish or to have eternal life. He seems to see humankind as inexorably caught between two cosmic forces. On the one side there is the darkness (blindness, evil, this world, the Prince of this world), and on the other is light (life, light, sight, the Spirit). To choose darkness means death, but the possibility of light and life has now been revealed in Jesus Christ. We judge ourselves by our own decision for or against the God revealed in and through Jesus Christ.

The fourth gospel has been written because of a passionate belief in the saving power of a decision for Christ. The appearance of Jesus in history is the irruption of light from the divine realm into the created order where darkness and evil are rampant. The struggle, however, is not fought out at a cosmic level (as in the gnostic myths), but in the historical events of the life of Jesus. This is why the fourth evangelist has written a gospel, a form of literature that tells the story of God's ways with the world through the story of his Son, Jesus of Nazareth. At the heart of the struggle that marked the life of Jesus, the cross is central. It is "the hour" (12:33; 13:31-32) when, at the level of human history, the powers of darkness appear to have brought their enemy down. Yet, with a telling irony so typical of this gospel, the reader learns that it is precisely in "the hour" that the Son of Man is glorified. He has revealed God so that men and women of all times—living in the presence and under the guidance of the Paraclete, sent by the glorified Jesus (14:16, 26; 15:26; 16:7, 13-15)—might gaze upon him and be saved (3:13-14; 8:28; 12:32; 19:37).

9.
Reading
John 1:19 to 4:54:
A Question of Faith

After the majesty of the prologue (1:1-18), the fourth gospel's narrative begins with two features that almost all commentators notice. First, there is a build-up of affirmations about the person of Jesus (see 1:20, 21, 23, 25, 26, 29, 33, 36, 38, 41, 45, 49, 51). Secondly, one finds an apparently deliberate presentation of this narrative within the framework of a series of "days" (see 1:29, 35, 43), which could lead into the expression "on the third day" in 2:1. At the beginning of the narrative dealing with the first Cana miracle, we read: "*On the third day* there was a marriage at Cana in Galilee . . ." While this continued use of "days" links the first Cana story to 1:19-51, there is yet another miracle at Cana in 4:46: "So he came again to Cana in Galilee, where he had made the water wine." The evangelist makes it clear that he wants his readers to see a link between the two Cana miracles in the final verse of this section: "This is now the second sign that Jesus did when he had come from Judea to Galilee" (4:54).

In any interpretation of a piece of literature, it is always important to pay a great deal of attention to the hints and indications of the text itself. Thus the interpretation that follows will depend largely upon these two features: the first "days" of Jesus, and a "journey" that runs from "Cana to Cana".

The First "Days" of Jesus (1:19-51)

A careful reading of these first moments of Jesus' public ministry shows that the whole dramatic movement towards Jesus' own proclamation of himself as "the Son of man" in 1:51 is set within a gradually unfolding scheme of days. Schematically presented, the first chapter of the fourth gospel can be seen in the following way:

FIRST DAY. The Religious authorities from Jerusalem ask John the Baptist about his messianic pretentions. He points away from himself. He is "the voice of one crying in the wilderness" (1:23): not the Christ, or Elijah, nor the prophet (verses 20-21; see also 25-27).

SECOND DAY ("The next day" [1:29]). The Baptist points decisively towards Jesus as "the Lamb of God, who takes away the sin of the world! . . . a man who ranks before me, for he was before me. . . . he who baptises with the Holy Spirit. . . . the Son of God" (verses 29, 30, 33, 34).

THIRD DAY ("The next day again" [1:35]). Two disciples of the Baptist are pointed towards Jesus as the Lamb of God. They "follow" him, stay with him, and come to confess their belief: "'We have found the Messiah' (which means the Christ!" (verse 41). Simon is brought to Jesus, and renamed Cephas (verse 42).

FOURTH DAY ("The next day" [1:43]). More disciples are called to "follow", and they proclaim their faith: "We have found him of whom Moses in the law and also the prophets wrote" (verse 45). Nathaniel's scepticism is overcome when Jesus tells him that he saw him under a fig tree (verse 46-48), and he too confesses his faith: "Rabbi, you are the son of God! You are the King of Israel!" (verse 49). As the section closes, Jesus promises a "sight" that will reach beyond all that the disciples have seen and believed so far: "you will see heaven opened, and the angels of God ascending and descending upon the Son of man" (verses 50-51).

As we have already noticed, the first Cana miracle begins with another indication of "days": "On the third day there was a marriage at Cana in Galilee" (2:1). It closes with a declaration from the evangelist that in the miracle the disciples saw the glory of Jesus for the first time, and consequently made their first steps in a journey of faith: "This, the first of his signs, Jesus did at Cana in Galilee, and manifested his glory; and his disciples believed in him" (2:11).

The "days" of the gift of the Law

This play on a series of "days" is not new in the biblical literature. As Israel prepared to receive the law on Sinai, Moses is instructed to speak the words of the Lord to the people:

> Go to the people and consecrate them today and tomorrow, and let them wash their garments, and be ready by the third day; for on the third day the Lord will come down upon Mount Sinai in the sight of all the people. (Exodus 19:10-11)

The theophany is then reported as taking place "on the morning of the third day" (19:16). A similar interest in "days" is found in Exodus 24.

As was most common in the development of Jewish thought, this suggestion of the days of preparation for the ultimate gift of the law on Sinai "on the third day" became the source of further reflection and development. Jewish rabbinic specu-lation drew on the original biblical use of these "days" of preparation, leading to a consummate revelation of God (through the theophany and the gift of the Law) "on the third day" (found in the Targums on Exodus, on Chronicles, the Mekilta and the Babylonian Talmud).[1]

---

1. For a full discussion of all the relevant Jewish literature and its importance for this section of the Fourth Gospel, see A. M. Serra, *Contributi dell'antica letteratura Giudaica per l'esegesi di Giovanni 2, 1-12 e 19,*

A careful study of the late Jewish speculation on the Sinai event indicates that there appeared to be a quite widely accepted idea that the law was given on Sinai in the following way:

FIRST DAY.   Preparation of the people.
SECOND DAY. Preparation of the people.
THIRD DAY.   Preparation of the people.
FOURTH DAY. Preparation of the people continues, but it now intensifies, as this "fourth day" is seen as the "first" of the all-important "three days" of Exodus 19:10-11, leading up to the manifestation of God's glory to his people "on the third day" (19:16).

Thus we come to the final three "days": the fourth, fifth and sixth day. On the "third" of these days the glory of God is seen by his people. A final, more intense preparation, which was to mark the final three days, began on the last of the first four days. "On the third day", the law was given.

The "days" of the gift of Jesus

It appears that this Jewish understanding of the gift of the law on Sinai, the revelation of the glory of God at this crucial moment in the history of his relationship with Israel (see Exodus 19:16-25), is fundamental to the fourth evangelist's narrative in John 1:19-51 and 2:1-11. There is a gradual "preparation" for the revelation of the glory of Jesus in the Cana miracle. The background for the narrative was the traditional days of preparation of God's people for his earlier decisive intervention among them at Sinai. Given this general

25–27, Scripta Pontificiae Facultatis Theologiae "Marianum" 31, Nova Series 3 (Rome, Herder, 1975), pp. 45–137. Similar suggestions had already been made by B. Olsson, *Structure and Meaning in the Fourth Gospel*, Coniectanea Biblica, New Testament Series 6 (Lund, Gleerup, 1974). See, however, the reservations of B. Lindars and P. Borgen, "The Place of the Old Testament in the Formation of New Testament Theology", *New Testament Studies* 23 (1977–78), pp. 59–75.

background, a closer analysis of the text indicates how our evangelist has used this background to arouse his reader's interest in two central issues: his unique understanding of who Jesus is, and the response of faith that is required from those who will commit themselves totally to his ways.

John the Baptist, the greatest of all "witnesses" to Jesus (see 1:6-8, 15), reponds to the messianic expectations of the religious authorities from Jerusalem by pointing away from himself (verses 19-23) towards the one who will come after him (verses 24-28). He makes it clear why his place in God's design is "lesser" (see also 3:25-30): Jesus is the Lamb *of God*, he "was" before the Baptist (see 1:1), he is full of the Holy Spirit, and he baptises with that Holy Spirit. In short, he is *the Son of God*! (verses 29-34). Here, as always with John the Baptist in the fourth gospel, the confession of Jesus is correct, and the Baptist places himself in a subordinate position.[2] Notice, however, that, even though the "preparation" of the future disciples has begun, Jesus himself has not yet appeared upon the scene in any active way.

This is changed as we move into the final two "days". Two disciples of the Baptist, having been told that Jesus was the Lamb of God, "follow" him (1:35-37). They are asked a question of major importance: "What do you seek?", but they trivialise it, and ask where Jesus is staying (verse 38). Again Jesus takes the initiative and issues the enormous challenge (in Johannine terms): "Come and see" (verse 39).[3] This

2. It is important to notice that the Baptist *always* shows the way in his expression of true faith in Jesus (see also 3:25-30). Since the turn of the century some scholars have argued that—given the evidence of a Baptist sect in the first century (see especially Acts 19:1-7)—the fourth evangelist "puts the Baptist in his place". This is an exaggeration. In the fourth gospel there is only one person (apart from Jesus) described as "a man sent from God": the Baptist. As in all the gospels, the Baptist is a truly great figure: but Jesus is so much greater. We have already seen this in our analysis of Luke 1-2. The same message is expressed, in a different way, by the fourth evangelist.

3. For an excellent "actualisation" of this invitation of the Johannine Jesus, see M. T. Winstanley, *Come and See. An Exploration into Christian Discipleship* (London, Darton, Longman & Todd, 1985).

experience eventually leads them to confess that Jesus is the Christ, as they attempt to bring Simon to him. Jesus "names" Simon with a new name, "Cephas (which means Peter)" (verses 41-42). The initiatives of Jesus are decisive and challenging, but one senses that all this is only "preparation", and that the confession of faith is still very much in terms that the newly called disciples can understand. This is made particularly clear in John's use of the expression: "*We have found*" (verse 41; see also verse 45). Faithful to Christian tradition, the fourth evangelist will always place the initiative for the discovery of God's ways in the world on the side of God and his Sent One. It is never the result of something which "we" succeed in doing (see also 9:24, 29, 31, where this point is particularly clear). Thus far the disciples (and indeed the religious authorities from Jerusalem) have either raised questions or made a confession about the identity of Jesus in terms that were perfectly comprehensible to their religious and cultural heritage. We will see that the encounter between Jesus and Nathanael on the fourth "day", the beginning of the more intensive period of preparation for the revelation of God in the traditional presentation of the Sinai event, will question all of this.

In 1:43-51 the evangelist goes into considerable detail to describe Nathanael's journey of faith. Jesus finds Philip, a compatriot of Andrew and Peter, who also follows him. Philip finds Nathanael, and a further confession of faith, again perfectly understandable in terms of first-century Jewish messianic expectations, is made by Philip: "*We have found* him of whom Moses in the law and also the prophets wrote, Jesus of Nazareth, the son of Joseph" (verse 45). In the light of Nathanael's subsequent scepticism, Philip invites him also to make that important Johannine journey: "Come and see" (verse 46).

However, it is Jesus who "sees" Nathanael first, describes him, and then tells a wondering Nathanael: "Before Philip called you, when you were under the fig tree, I saw you" (1:48). For Nathanael, this is an incredible statement. It would have been impossible for Jesus to have known that

Philip called him, or know that he was under the fig tree — yet he does. This is surely someone quite extraordinary. Thus we have yet another confession of faith in Jesus: "Rabbi, you are the Son of God! You are the King of Israel!" With Nathanael's confession we come to the culmination of a series of messianic confessions (or queries), which have been mounting throughout all these first "days".

But even Nathanael's confession can be understood in terms of first-century Jewish messianic expectations. While "Rabbi" is a term of honour, and "the King of Israel" is messianic, so also the title "the Son of God" is to be understood in terms of a Jewish title accorded to the expected Messiah, based on the use of such a term in II Samuel 7:14 and Psalm 2:7 to refer to the King of Israel.[4] Thus we must conclude that while the Baptist was able to point away from himself and towards Jesus as "Lamb of God", full of the Spirit of God and "the Son of God" in the fullest meaning of that last title, this is not the case with the first disciples.

One can only understand "who" Jesus is for the fourth evangelist in terms of his *origins*. For the Baptist, Jesus is "of God", but for these first disciples he is "of Joseph" (1:45), "from Nazareth" (verse 46), "of Israel" (verse 49). Such faith falls sadly short, and Jesus himself is not happy with the faith of Nathanael, based only on the slight event of the fig tree! Jesus' words conclude these "days" of preparation with a correction of Nathanael's faith, and a promise of a greater sight to all who will see with the eyes of a true faith:

> "Because I said to you I saw you under the fig tree, do you believe? You shall see greater things than these." And he said to him, "Truly, truly, I say to you, you will see heaven opened, and the angels of God ascending and descending upon the Son of man." (1:50-51)

True "sight" must go beyond the controllably miraculous, as it will enable the believer to see that in Jesus of Nazareth,

4. For a full discussion of this, with detailed analysis of the Jewish material, see B. J. Byrne, "*Sons of God — Seed of Abraham*", Analecta Biblica 83 (Rome, Biblical Institute Pres, 1979), pp. 9–78.

the Son of Man—a man among men and women—the heavenly and the earthly are one. Using language that comes from the apocalyptic tradition (heavens opening and angels appearing) and recalling the story of Jacob's dream of the ladder connecting heaven and earth at Bethel (see especially Genesis 28:12), these days of preparation call the reader to recognise that there is no earthly, culturally or historically conditioned religious category that can contain the mystery of Jesus of Nazareth. Many have tried throughout these days of preparation, but we can now see that true faith cannot be contained within such limits.

Within this context the first miracle of Cana takes place, with its reference to the revelation of the "glory" of Jesus. Thus, despite the limitations of the disciples' first days of preparation, "on the third day" (as in the days of the old covenant) the glory of Jesus shines forth and the disciples believe.

As this is the case, it is important to notice that, structurally, 2:1-11 forms both the closing section of the days of preparation, and the opening section of the journey of faith mapped out in 2:1-4:54: from Cana to Cana. The Sinai story tells that the "glory" of God is revealed in his law, given through Moses. This glory has now been prepared for and replaced by the "glory" of Jesus Christ. Such a point of view has already been a part of the message of the prologue. There (in verses 16-17) we were told that the new and perfect union between God and man has been achieved in the person of Jesus of Nazareth:

From his fullness we have all received, a gift to replace the former gift. For the law was given through Moses, but the gift which is the truth came through Jesus Christ. (1:16-17).[5]

5. For this translation, see F. J. Moloney, "The Fulness of a Gift which is Truth (Jn 1:14.16-17)", *Catholic Theological Review* 1 (1978), pp. 30–3.

From Cana to Cana
(John 2:1-4:54)

It must be admitted that Jesus' dissatisfaction with Nathanael's confession that he is Son of God and King of Israel (1:50) comes as somewhat of a surprise. Indeed, many scholars regard verse 49 as the original end of the encounter between Jesus and the ex-disciples of the Baptist. The remarks of Jesus in verse 50 and the promise of a further revelation are often seen as "a detached saying about the Son of Man".[6] Whatever the history of these last two verses may have been, before they became a part of John 1:19-51, they certainly belong where they are now.

Read as a whole, the message of the concluding section of these first days is that the disciples may have done well to arrive at this stage, but they will see more only if their faith is loosed from the absolutisation of their own cultural and historical conditioning. It must be remembered that all the confessions on the lips of the disciples so far (including that of Nathanael) are perfectly understandable in terms of first-century Jewish messianic hopes. The problem posed by Jesus as the section comes to an end indicates that this is not sufficient. What does the reader make of all this? One would think that "Son of God and King of Israel" were fitting titles for Jesus of Nazareth. It is vitally important that we understand the first days of Jesus' public revelation concluding in such a way that the *reader* must be asking a stunned question: if the faith expressed by Nathanael is insufficient, then what is required?

The answer is provided in the very next section of the gospel, 2:1 through to 4:54, a passage that runs from Cana (2:1-11) to Cana (4:46-54). While the structure and message that I shall draw out of this narrative in no way exhausts the riches of these passages, it appears that the theme of faith and the various "types of faith" are the issues that determine

---

6. Brown, *John*, p. 88. This opinion is also held by such important scholars as R. Schnackenburg, R. Fortna and M.-E. Boismard.

the whole passage. A problem is posed by "the first days" (1:19-51): it is answered in the journey from Cana to Cana (2:1-4:54).

I have already mentioned that we see here how John is quite happy to "overlap" his material. There is an obvious link between the first Cana miracle, clearly presented as the final revelation of God in Jesus, taking place "on the third day", and the preceding 1:19-51, also marked by a series of days. However, it is also clear that there is a deliberate use of two Cana miracles at the beginning and at the end of this next series of episodes from John's story of Jesus.[7]

There are very clear indications in the second Cana miracle that the evangelist wishes his reader to see the link between the two miracles. As he begins the account of the second miracle, he writes explicitly, "So he came *again* to Cana in Galilee" (4:46). As he concludes the account he pointedly adds the remark: "This was now the second sign that Jesus did when he had come from Judea to Galilee" (4:54). There is an obvious correspondence between two miracles that take place in Cana. Further study of what actually happens in the two accounts shows that both miracles are structured in the same fashion:

John 2:1-11
1. *Problem:* The wine failed (2:3).
2. *Request:* The mother of Jesus said to him, "They have no wine" (2:4).

John 4:46-54
1. *Problem:* An official whose son was ill (4:46).
2. *Request:* He went down and begged him to come and heal his son (4:47).

7. For a detailed and fully documented study, which has led me to the conclusions presented here in a more popular form, see F. J. Moloney, "From Cana to Cana (Jn 2,1-4,54) and the Fourth Evangelist's Concept of Correct (and Incorrect) Faith", in E. A. Livingston (ed.), *Studia Biblica II. Papers on the Gospels. Sixth International Congress on Biblical Studies. Oxford 3–7 April 1978* (Sheffield, JSOT Press, 1980), pp. 185–213. The article is also available in *Salesianum* 40 (1978), pp. 817–43.

3. *Sharp rebuke:* O woman what have you to do with me? (2:4).

4. *Reaction:* His mother said to the servants, "Do whatever *he tells you*" (2:5).

5. *Consequence:* A miracle that leads to the faith of others (the disciples) (2:6-10).

3. *Sharp rebuke:* Unless you see signs and wonders you will not believe (4:48).

4. *Reaction:* "Go; your son will live". The man believed *the word that Jesus spoke to him* (4:50).

5. *Consequence:* A miracle that leads to the faith of others (the household) (4:51-53).

These two Cana miracles form a frame around the section of the gospel that runs from 2:1-4:54, and the theme of this frame will be a sure indication to us of the major theme of the whole section. A major theme in these two Cana stories (among the many rich themes that are found here) is that of a radical faith in the efficacy of the "word" of Jesus. Despite the sharp rebuke (verse 4), the Mother of Jesus turns to the servants and believes unconditionally in the efficacy of *the word* of Jesus: "Do whatever he tells you" (verse 5). The Greek verb used here is *legein*, the verbal form of the noun *logos:* "word". The royal official is also rather unjustly rebuked (4:48), but "the man believed the word (*logos*) that Jesus spoke to him and went his way" (verse 50). His son is healed (verses 51-53).

The section of the gospel between the "frame" of two examples of complete faith is marked by the reactions of various individuals or groups to the revelation of Jesus, i.e. to the "word of Jesus". The expression must not be limited to something that Jesus "says". In the fourth gospel, Jesus himself is "the Word", and the term must be taken as referring to all that Jesus has come to reveal. It is not simply that one is called to give intellectual assent to all that he "says". It is a preparedness to risk oneself for the whole event of Jesus of Nazareth, as the unique once-and-for-all revealing Son of God.

Two most important reactions to Jesus' word are found in the examples of perfect faith found in the Mother of Jesus

(2:1-11) and the royal official (4:46-54). Between these examples of faith one finds six further "stories" of the various possible reactions of faith: "the Jews" (2:12-22), Nicodemus (3:1-21), John the Baptist (3:22-36), a first encounter with a Samaritan woman (4:1-15), a second encounter with the same woman (4:16-26), and the Samaritan villagers (4:27-30, 39-42). We have already glanced at these reactions in our previous chapter. For the sake of our argument here, however, we will see how our evangelist has continued to present his criterion of true faith as a radical openness to the Word of God in Jesus through these six episodes. The careful reader who has the Gospel text open will notice that these six episodes leave two sections of the passage unexplained: 2:23-25 and 4:31-38. I will return to those passages after my analysis of the six scenes.

(1) *"The Jews"* (2:12-22). The account of the purification of the Temple in the fourth gospel reaches its real point in its conclusion. "The Jews" ask for a sign that would legitimise such actions (verse 18), and Jesus gives them one. In direct speech, Jesus replies: "Destroy this temple and in three days I will raise it up" (verse 19). In a mocking refusal of what he says, they use *exactly the same words* as Jesus used: "It has taken forty-six years to build this temple, and will you raise it up in three days?" (verse 20). It is important to notice that the rejection of this "sign", which is ultimately the sign of his resurrection (see verse 21-22), takes place through the rejection of his very words. Unprepared to go outside what they have constructed and what they can control, they reject the word of Jesus, and thus are in a position of *no faith.*

(2) *Nicodemus* (3:1-10). We are still very much within the world of Judaism as a leader of the Jews comes to Jesus by night. He is moved towards Jesus because he believes that Jesus is a rabbi, a teacher from God, doing wonderful signs because God is with him (3:1-2). This is certainly a long way from the hostility of "the Jews" in the previous scene, but Nicodemus is still moving within a sphere of messianic hopes that he and his own cultural conditioning can control and understand. Jesus attempts to lead him away from this by

speaking of a rebirth from above, which can be had through water and the Spirit (verses 3 and 5). This is too much for Nicodemus at this stage. He can only think in terms of a physical rebirth (verse 4), and that makes no sense to him; and in the end he is reduced to total confusion: "How can this be?" (verse 9). Nicodemus still has a long way to go, and we can trace his journey through the gospel itself (see 7:50-52 and 19:38-42). However, at this stage the journey is only just beginning, and he must be judged as having a *partial faith*.

(3) *John the Baptist* (3:22-36). The final episode in this first set of three takes place around the Baptist. Again, the crux of the matter is found towards the end of the scene when, after a discussion about the Baptist's relationship to Jesus, the Baptist himself explains that he is not the Christ (verse 28). The Christ is the one who takes possession of the bride. Using the background of the customs of the wedding night, John describes himself as the "friend of the bride-groom", the one who stands by and listens for the voice of the bridegroom proclaiming his possession of his bride (verse 29). It has now taken place, and that voice has been heard in the voice of Jesus. It is this preparedness to "listen to the voice" that marks the Baptist as someone who displays *perfect faith*.

At this stage we should pause a moment and notice a further feature of the three examples of faith that the evangelist has used to make his point. All the characters found so far come from Judaism. It is very clear that for the fourth evangelist perfect faith was possible within Judaism. There will be no limitations of tribe or nation, but the criterion will always be the same: a radical acceptance of the word of God in Jesus. This becomes obvious once we notice that our following three examples of faith are from outside Judaism, in the experience of Samaritans.

(1a) *The Samaritan Woman* (4:1-15). There are two moments in the encounter between the Samaritan woman and Jesus. In this first moment a discussion is carried on at two levels. At one level Jesus is offering the woman a chance of life, but at another she is completely uncomprehending of what is offered. Again, like the refusal of "the Jews" in the first scene (although lacking the hostility), the woman refuses the actual words of Jesus. He promises her: "whoever drinks of the water that I shall give him will never thirst; the water that I shall give him will become in him a spring of water welling up to eternal life" (verse 14). The woman can only reply in terms of ordinary water, ordinary wells, and the need not to come back to carry water each day: "Sir, give me this water, that I may not thirst, nor come here to draw" (verse 15). At this stage she must be regarded as having *no faith*.

(2a) *The Samaritan Woman* (4:16-30). Jesus now carries the discussion into an area that she can understand: her marital situation. She now begins to move. This man is telling her things that he should not have known, and thus she begins to suspect: "Sir, I perceive that you are a prophet" (verse 19). The discussion on the place and manner of true worship (verses 20-24) leads to a moment of further understanding, as she suggests that he may even be the expected Messiah (verse 25). His ability to speak of wonderful things has brought her to this point of faith, but it is still a confession of faith that she can control and understand. It is a part of her heritage to believe that such a man would come. Jesus' reply to her goes beyond anything that she may have expected: "I am (*Egō Eimi*) is the one speaking to you" (verse 26).[8] As she rushes back to the village and asks: "Can this be the Christ?", we conclude that she has arrived at a stage of *partial faith*.

(3a) *The Samaritan Villagers* (4:39-42). In a first instance there is a movement from the villagers on the basis of the "word" of the woman (verses 39-40). However, Jesus' stay

8. This is a debated issue. The Revised Standard Version translates the expression in a way that has Jesus accepting her confession of him as the Messiah: "I who speak to you am he." However, given the Johannine technique of leading people through stages of faith, it appears to me that a more literal translation of the Greek is needed: "Egō eimi ho lalōn soi" is best rendered: "I AM is the one speaking to you." The original Jerusalem Bible in English translates it well: "I who am speaking to you", said Jesus, "I am he." The point is completely missed in the New Jerusalem Bible: "That is who I am, I who speak to you."

with them leads them into a different stage of faith, a faith based entirely on his word. The series ends with a clear statement of our theme, as the villagers say to the woman: "It is no longer because of your words that we believe, for we have *heard for ourselves*, and we know that this is indeed the Saviour of the world" (verse 42). Here we have our final example of *perfect faith*.

However, as the evangelist tells these "stories of faith", he pauses twice to comment. The six "stages of faith" receive further clarification in the two passages mentioned earlier: 2:23-25 and 4:31-38. In 2:23-25 he criticises a faith based on signs alone, but in 4:31-38 he comments on the all-important "work" or "task" of Jesus. There is one "sign" that remains at the basis of Christian faith: it is that sign that Jesus performed when, in the end, he brought to perfection the task that his Father had given him (4:34).

We have here a wonderful example of simple yet profound catechesis, as the evangelist forces the reader to make his or her own journey of faith, based on the experience of the journeys described and commented upon in this Cana to Cana section. The following (p. 218) schematic presentation of the structure and argument of John 2:1-4:54 is an indication of the skill and depth of this precious call to a total commitment to the word of Jesus.

For the fourth evangelist, true faith means a radical openness to the word of Jesus: to all that he has come to reveal. Anyone who will not accept this revelation (e.g. "the Jews" or the Samaritan woman in a first moment) has no faith. It is also important that the "signs" not be understood within the categories that men and women, history and culture can determine (neither Jewish: Nicodemus, nor non-Jewish: the Samaritan woman). Ultimately, it is taking the risk of accepting this revelation without condition (John the Baptist and the Samaritan villagers) that produces true faith. John himself explains that the high point of this revelation, which must be accepted, is not found in the externality of the "signs" (2:23-25). It is found in the event of the cross where, in his being "lifted up" (see 3:14; 8:28; 12:32) to reveal love to all those

From Cana to Cana (John 2:1-4:54)

2:1-11. The marriage feast at Cana. The example of the mother of Jesus: *complete faith* in a Jewish context.

a. 2:12-22. The expulsion of the vendors from the temple. The example of "the Jews": *no faith.*

(2:23-25. John comments, criticising a faith based on signs.)

b. 3:1-21. The encounter with one of the Pharisees, a ruler of the Jews. The example of Nicodemus: *partial faith.*

c. 3:22-36. The discussion with John the Baptist. The example of the Baptist: *complete faith.*

a¹ 4:1-15. The first discussion with the Samaritan woman, who refuses "living water". The example of the Samaritan woman: *no faith.*

b¹ 4:16-26. The second discussion with the Samaritan woman, who is now prepared to accept Jesus as a prophet and possibly as the Messiah. The example of the Samaritan woman: *partial faith.*

(4:31-38. John comments, through Jesus, recalling the essential "work".)

c¹ 4:27-30, 39-42. The advent of the Samaritan villagers who eventually believe because of the word of Jesus. The example of the Samaritan villagers: *complete faith.*

4:43-54. The official at Cana. The example of the official: *complete faith* in a non-Jewish context.

INCLUSION: Complete faith in a Jewish and in a non-Jewish context

The movement to faith in a Jewish context.

The movement to faith in a non-Jewish context.

that will look upon him (see 13:1; 15:13; 19:37), Jesus brings to perfection the task that the Father gave to him (4:31-48; see also 5:36; 13:1; 17:4; 19:28-30).

Conclusion

All four evangelists have used narrative to communicate a theological message, and we should not be surprised to see the same thing happening in the fourth gospel. It is sometimes asked whether such structures and levels of meaning are the work of the evangelists or the skill of the modern interpreter. There is always a risk that we will impose our own insights upon the gospel material. However, the skilful use of narrative to convey faith in Jesus of Nazareth, and to challenge readers to share that faith, is not an invention of modern scholars. There is sufficient "internal evidence" from the gospels themselves to show that they were written with that aim in view.

We have studied John 2:1-4:54 in some detail, but the same results could be found from a similar study of many other sections of the gospel. Hopefully, the chapter dedicated to the structure and message of the whole of the gospel is a good indication of that. These structures are not complicated. They are simple, and were part and parcel of the writing techniques of any first-century Hellenistic schoolboy.[9] What is surprising is the ever-challenging quality of the message contained in such structures.

The fourth gospel issues a challenge to take the risk of accepting that a God of love has been revealed through the Word of the cross. This message is always with us. The Cana to Cana story is not told so that we might be able to draw conclusions about the performance of any one of the actors in those scenes. On the contrary, it is told so that we may recognise where we are in our journey of faith away from our

9. See H. I. Marrou, *The History of Education in Antiquity* (London, Sheed & Ward, 1956), pp. 160–75, 194–205.

absolutes—through a multiplicity of "intermediate stages"—towards a total gift of ourselves into the mystery of God's ways.

PART VI
The
Living
Gospel

10.
"The Living Voice of the Gospel"
(*Dei Verbum* 8).

Some Reflections on the Dynamism of the Christian Tradition

I. Introduction

On 30 September 1965, only a month and a half before the final promulgation of the Dogmatic Constitution on Divine Revelation, Archbishop Florit of Florence, along with Archbishop van Dodewaard of Haarlem, made a final attempt to hold fast some hard-lost positions. Many of them had appeared as strong assertions of unquestionable dogmas in Sebastian Tromp's preconciliar scheme *De fontibus revelationis*, sent to the Council Fathers in the European summer of 1962. They were now in tatters. Only two years had passed, but what an incredible two years they had been. Correctly Archbishop

223

Florit wrote of the troubled passage of this extraordinary document:

> Because of its inner importance, as well as the many vicissitudes that it
> has undergone, the history of the draft of the Constitution on Divine
> Revelation has fused with the history of this Council into a kind of
> unity.[1]

It would be pointless for me to present yet another history of the Constitution on Divine Revelation, as there are many quite excellent such histories available.[2] I would like to take as my starting-point the indication of Archbishop Florit that there is an intimate link between the history of the Council itself and the history of this document.

I have already mentioned that the Constitution on Divine Revelation began as a rather traditional and aggressive restatement of what many simply accepted as the official teaching of the church, but which was, in fact, really the position of only one school of thought. It comprised five very defensive chapters on the sources of revelation. There was a heavy stress on the role of Tradition over against Scripture, a very verbal understanding of the phenomenon of inspiration, an extremely narrow interpretation of inerrancy and an understanding of the historicity of the gospels. Such an approach presupposed that historical-critical analysis, which had been employed by Catholic scholars since Pius XII's

---

1. For the original Latin text, see A. Favale (ed.), *La Costituzione Dogmatica sulla Divina Rivelazione*, Collana Magistero Conciliare (Torino, Elle di Ci, 1967), p. 487.

2. For a comprehensive and first-hand account, see U. Betti, "Storia della Costituzione dogmatica *Dei Verbum*", in Favale (ed.), *La Costituzione*, pp. 13–68. A briefer, but more theologically orientated description of the passage of this document can be found in J. Ratzinger, "Dogmatic Constitution on Divine Revelation. Origin and Background", in H. Vorgrimler (ed.), *Commentary on the Documents of Vatican II* (London, Burns & Oates, 1969), vol. 3, pp. 155–66. For an interesting popular presentation of the early days of this document at the Council's First Session, see P. Hebblethwaite, *John XXIII. Pope of the Council* (London, Geoffrey Chapman, 1984), pp. 452–8.

Encyclical *Divino Afflante Spiritu* in 1943, had never raised any serious problems to the traditional approach to these texts.

The Dogmatic Constitution that the council gave to the church on 18 November 1965 was a complete volte-face from such a position. If I may be so bold as to suggest the key to such a radical change of position, I would like to suggest that the document as we now have it shows (within the limits of a conciliar document) a deep sense of history, of the historicity of mankind, and therefore of the historicity of God's revelation to men and women. This is already evident in the choice of one of the key texts to the Constitution:

> In many and various ways God spoke of old to our fathers by the prophets; but in these last days he has spoken to us by a Son. (Hebrews 1:1-2; see *Dei Verbum*, 4 & 11).

The Council Fathers themselves had lived through the historic days of the council, and they were aware that God did indeed speak in various ways, and not only to the Old Testament prophets. It had been a part of their own experience, as the Dogmatic Constitution on Divine Revelation (*Dei Verbum*) developed under their eyes, as a result of the work of their own hands, even if such work was reduced (for many) to pushing a button to register *placet, non placet* or *iuxta modum*.[3] It is fitting that the very passage of the conciliar document on Revelation through its various stages of development reflects the dynamic action of the Spirit. We need to investigate this suggestion a little further by means of some analysis.

I. Some Evidence from the Constitution itself

My reflections on the conciliar document will be, of necessity, very limited. I propose to glance at section 7 of the Constitution

---

3. These were the three Latin terms used by the Council Fathers to register a positive vote (*placet*), a negative vote (*non placet*), or a vote that would be positive with amendments (*iuxta modum*).

on Divine Revelation, looking back to see its beginnings in the first draft of the Constitution (1962) for that paragraph. This will lead me to the briefest of glances at paragraph 8, where I found the expression I have used as a title for this reflection, and indeed for the whole of this book. This sort of study could be done—and has been done—for the whole document, and scholars are quite accustomed to uncovering the extraordinary developments that went on in conciliar circles between 1962 and 1965.[4]

Such research is much deeper than a simple comparison of documents. It has a theological importance in its own right. Most Catholics are not aware of the journey of the conciliar documents through their various preparatory stages. An appreciation of the dynamic presence of the Spirit, which can be sensed through such an analysis, may perhaps ease some of the tension and confusion felt by many believers. There is a widespread feeling among Catholics that one simply waits for Rome to speak. Once a document (conciliar or otherwise) has been published, then that word must be followed uncritically. There appears to be little or no awareness that such a "word" does not fall from the heavens, but is the result of a "dynamism" of its own, which eventually produces the texts that finally roll off the printing presses.[5] Thus I will pursue this short analysis both to make my immediate point

4. The best example of this method in the study of the council documents available in English is H. Vorgrimler (ed.), *Commentary on the Documents of Vatican II* (see note 2, page 224). This work was published in 5 volumes between 1967 and 1969.

5. This is an important pastoral concern, which does not seem to be addressed with sufficient seriousness. Bishops and clergy in general either regard their faithful as too ignorant or too busy to be interested in such matters, or they prefer to keep them at that level of "simple faith", which is much easier to administer. However, such a situation will not last, as this "simple faith" is now producing—especially among the young—an awareness of the rift that can open up between real life and the life of faith. For some interesting reflections on this, see the useful (but by no means definitive) analysis of J. Dominian, "Religion and the Young", *The Tablet* 239 (1985), pp. 899–901.

clear, and then to lead me into a further, more biblical, reflection on "the living voice of the Gospel".[6]

I have deliberately chosen to study a brief section of Chapter Two of the Constitution, dedicated to the transmission of Divine Revelation. This is a chapter vital to the whole argument of the Constitution, as here the Council Fathers found that they had to make up their minds about issues that had been either skirted or only partially handled in the ordinary Magisterium of the church up to this stage. Such matters as the historicity of the content of certain biblical material, the relationship between Scripture and Tradition, inerrancy, the development of Dogma and the possibility of the church teaching something that was not explicitly revealed in the Scriptures are all close to the surface.[7] It is not as if these matters were dealt with explicitly in our document, but the Council Fathers were well aware that positions taken here in a chapter dealing with the transmission of divine revelation would be crucial in any further study of these central issues.

In 1962 the preparatory document was able to assert, implicitly, and hopefully, laying to rest all the questions which I raised:

> Christ the Lord gave a mandate to the Apostles that they preach, as the source of saving truth and of discipline of life for every creature, his Gospel, which is all that he did and taught throughout his whole life. This indeed was what the Apostles did, both through Holy Spirit inspired writings and through orally passing down what they had received either

6. For an excellent synoptic presentation of the Latin original of the four major texts that the Council Fathers considered, see Favale (ed.), *La Costituzione*, pp. 86–127. The English text of the conciliar document reproduced here is from A. Flannery (ed.), *Vatican Council II. The Conciliar and Postconciliar Documents* (Dublin, Dominican Publications, 1981). The English of other texts are my own translations from the Latin found in Favale (ed.), *La Costituzione*.

7. For a careful and well-documented commentary on this chapter, where these deeper theological considerations are dealt with in full, see J. Ratzinger, "The Transmission of Divine Revelation", in H. Vorgrimler (ed.), *Commentary on the Documents of Vatican II*, pp. 181–98.

from the mouth of Christ or as dictated by the Holy Spirit. Thus, this written or handed-on word of God constitutes the one Deposit of Faith from which the Magisterium of the Church derives everything that she proposes as divinely revealed, to be received by divine faith. (*De Divinae Revelationis Transmissione*, 7).[8]

One can immediately notice a series of points basic to this statement, which would cause difficulty to a contemporary biblical and systematic theologian:

(a) Although it is not cited in the text, the formal "mandate" of Matthew 28:16-20 seems to be simply taken as historical and foundational.

(b) The "Gospel" is defined as all that Jesus did and taught.

(c) This very limited view of "Gospel", however, is presented as the solution to all questions of salvation and morals.

(d) One finds a static view of revelation, which sees the eternal truths as either coming to the disciples directly from the mouth of Christ or from the direct dictation of the Holy Spirit.

(e) This revelation, given to the Apostles, forms a ready-made "quarry" into which the Magisterium delves for its teachings.

It seems extraordinary—from the perspective of 1986— that such opinions could have had such a hold, despite the immense amount of work that had been done by both Protestant and Catholic scholars in these areas for more than a century. Almost on the very doorstep of the Gregorian University (where Tromp, the author of this document, was a Professor) scholars at the Biblical Institute and a little farther afield at the Ecole Biblique must have wondered who was reading their work. Even the introductory chapters of the 1953 edition of *La Bible de Jérusalem*, which had been accorded all the necessary ecclesiastical approvals before

8. Latin text found in Favale (ed.), *La Costituzione*, p. 96. The literal English translation is mine.

publication, would not have been able to meet all the strictures of such a document.[9]

Fortunately, such opinions were not allowed to hold the day. Two years and four texts later, the promulgated text showed a complete change in perspective.

> God graciously arranged that the things he had once revealed for the salvation of all peoples should remain in their entirety, throughout the ages, and be transmitted to all generations. Therefore, Christ the Lord, in whom the entire Revelation of the most high God is summed up (cf. 2 Corinthians 1:20; 3:16-4:6) commanded the apostles to preach the Gospel, which had been promised beforehand by the prophets, and which he fulfilled in his own person and promulgated with his own lips. In preaching the Gospel they were to communicate the gifts of God to all men. This Gospel was to be the source of all saving truth and moral discipline. This was faithfully done: it was done by the apostles who handed on, by the spoken word of their preaching, by the example they gave, by the institutions they established, what they themselves had received—whether from the lips of Christ, from his way of life and his works, or whether they had learnt it at the prompting of the Holy Spirit; it was done by these apostles and other men associated with the apostles who, under the association of the same Holy Spirit, committed the message of salvation to writing. (*Dei Verbum* 7a)

Through this carefully considered and painstakingly elaborated rewriting of a most difficult text, over a troubled (but certainly Spirit-filled) two-year passage of time, the

9. Behind the scenes these were difficult days for biblical scholars in Rome. Two outstanding Jesuit Scripture scholars, Stanislaus Lyonnet and Maximilian Zerwick, came under incredible fire from other "Roman school" scholars. They were eventually forbidden to teach at the Pontifical Biblical Institute by express order of Pope John XXIII. Although these two men were only using contemporary critical methods and presuppositions, with great care and with great loyalty to the Magisterium, it was obvious to many other Roman scholars that such an approach would have to be nipped in the bud. Pope Paul VI and *Dei Verbum* saw to the reinstatement of both scholars. For more detail on this unhappy moment in Roman ecclesiastical politics, see J. A. Fitzmyer, "A Recent Scriptural Controversy", *Theological Studies* 22 (1961), pp. 426–44. See also his further essay, "The Biblical Commission's Instruction on the Historical Truth of the Gospels", *Theological Studies* 25 (1964), pp. 386–402, especially pp. 398–402.

Council Fathers had made some significant advances, not only on their 1962 schema, but especially in terms of the general position of the Magisterium on these matters. In the section of *Dei Verbum* 7 I have cited, there are two important areas where a change of direction can be observed:

(1) There is a broader base of reference given to the origins of revealed truths. In the conciliar document we now find reference to the teaching of Jesus Christ, his life-style, and whatever may have been the fruit of further promptings of the Spirit.

(2) There is also a wider view of those responsible for the transmission of revelation. The apostles, and all those who wrote under the guidance of the Spirit are included. This is important, as through this gentler widening of the view of the Magisterium, "the Gospel" has been freed from the "leg-rope" that held it to "all that Jesus did and taught throughout his life" (*Divinae Revelationis Transmissione* 7). A new dynamism has been introduced, as the "good news" is communicated by Christ, by his disciples, and by the various institutions that flow from these origins.[10]

As a consequence of *Dei Verbum* 7a, the Fathers were able to rewrite completely the concept of the "quarry" where the Magisterium found its teachings in the following fashion:

---

10. It is most interesting to see a recent Roman document apply these principles. The Pontifical Commission for Religious Relations with the Jews has recently published (June 1985) an important document: *The Common Bond. Christians and Jews. Notes for Preaching and Teaching.* In paragraph 21 of this document one reads: "Here it cannot be ruled out that some references hostile or less than favourable to the Jews have their historical context in conflicts between the nascent Church and the Jewish community. Certain controversies reflect Christian-Jewish relations long after the time of Jesus. . . . This fact, accentuated as the Christian mission developed, especially among the pagans, led inevitably to a rupture between Judaism and the young Church now irreducibly separated and divergent in faith, and this state of affairs is reflected in the text of the New Testament and particularly in the Gospels." (English Translation published by the Catholic Media Office, Godalming, Surrey, 1985, p. 11.)

This sacred Tradition, then, and the Sacred Scripture of both Testaments, are like a mirror, in which the Church, during its pilgrim journey here on earth, contemplates God, from whom she received everything, until such time as she is brought to see him face to face as he really is. (*Dei Verbum* 7b).

Here we find a wonderful openness to the mystery of our God and of his ways, a mystery we are privileged to share (see Mark 4:11-12), but whose ultimate significance we shall come to see and understand only in God's good time (see I Corinthians 13:8-12). In the meantime, directed, enlightened and encouraged by his Spirit-filled Church, we wend our pilgrim way (see John 14:16-17; 16:12-15).

In the following paragraph of the Constitution there is a further, and equally balanced expression of the relationship that must exist between Scripture and Tradition. Again, the 1962 document simply states that the relationship exists, that the two sources of revelation have the same origins, and that both should be accorded equal honour.[11] The promulgated Constitution goes much further. It correctly points out that there would be no canon of Scripture if there had not first been Tradition, and that it is this dynamic interrelation of Scripture and Tradition that will go on unfolding the mysteries of God and his ways, now as it did in those formative days. A Gospel that tells us of God's past interventions can only lead us into history and archeology. A dynamic and ever-developing Tradition, in continual interaction with the givenness of God's Word in the Sacred Scriptures leads to "the living voice of the Gospel ringing out in the Church—and through her in the world".

The sayings of the Holy Fathers are a witness to the life-giving presence of this Tradition, showing how its riches are poured out in the practice and life of the Church, in her belief and in her prayer. By means of the same tradition the full canon of the sacred books is known to the Church and the Holy Scriptures themselves are more thoroughly understood and constantly actualized in the Church. Thus God, who spoke in the past, continues to converse with the spouse of his beloved Son. And the Holy

11. For this text, see Favale (ed.), *La Costituzione*, p. 98.

Spirit, through whom the living voice of the Gospel rings out in the Church—and through her in the world—leads believers to the full truth, and makes the Word of Christ dwell in them in all its richness. (*Dei Verbum* 8c)

Why is it that such a statement rings so true? Despite the obvious difficulty that some of the Council Fathers had, and indeed some of the polarisation that has taken place over these matters since the Council, it must be admitted that most of us thrill to hear such a resounding, confident and healthy understanding of the sources of our faith. Here, as happens so often in the conciliar documents, we are in close contact with the genuine renewal that was Pope John XXIII's programme for the Second Vatican Council: the appreciation and illumination of our precious Christian heritage, and its further expression in a language that would make sense to our contemporary world.[12]

The dynamic growth of concepts and their expression in these few numbers from the document on Revelation simply reflects the way things have always been, and how they will always be in the Christian tradition. A Christian church that firmly believes that it is guided by the spirit of Jesus must admit this as one of its foundational principles (see John 14:26; 15:26-27; 16:13). This appears to me *essential* to a correct understanding of Christian Revelation, no matter how "static" some of our more accepted positions in the preconciliar period may have been. Such positions were faulty, and urgently needed the correction that took place at the Second Vatican Council. The Dogmatic Constitution on Divine Revelation provided exactly that, in a quite inspired and inspiring fashion.

I have insisted that we understand Christian revelation as something of an open book, continually relating the givenness of the past with the exciting experience of the present. In so

12. For Pope John XXIII's opening speech, see W. M. Abbott (ed.), *The Documents of Vatican II in a New and Definitive Translation* (London, Geoffrey Chapman, 1966), pp. 710–19. Especially important for the point I have just made are pp. 713–15.

many ways, it is precisely this profoundly "Catholic" understanding of an interdependence of Scripture and Tradition
that makes this possible. In fact, one of the great gains of the
ecumenical movement has been the widespread recognition
that Scripture without Tradition sinks into archeology and
history, while Tradition without Scripture can lead to the
rigid imposition of one particular theological system.

II. Some Evidence
from the New Testament

I would like to devote this third section of our final chapter to
some examples, taken from the New Testament, that show
how the interplay of Scripture and Tradition led to a dynamic
growth in the early church's thought, and its articulation of
that thought. Hopefully, the reader will sense that here I am
drawing together some final conclusions, which follow logically
from all that we have seen together throughout the whole of
this book.

We have seen that the development of the conciliar document
Dei Verbum indicates that there is an inner dynamism at
work in the church's growing understanding of itself and its
mission. But such a dynamism in understanding and
presenting our traditions is not new. From what I have
written, it should be obvious that the church of Jesus Christ,
filled with his spirit, has approached its traditions in this way
from the very beginnings of its existence.[13] By way of
conclusion to our study of the gospels, and to highlight the
point just made, I would now like to examine two gospel
presentations of important Christian traditions: Jesus as
Messiah and Mary as Mother.

(a) Jesus of Nazareth

In all three Synoptic Gospels, the confession of Peter comes
at a critical moment. In fact, as we have already seen in some

13. For an excellent survey of contemporary methods in approaching the
New Testament's presentation of Jesus Christ, and its relatedness to the
teachings of *Dei Verbum*, see Neyrey, *Christ is Community*, pp. 7–26.

detail, for Mark's Gospel it is the watershed around which the whole of the argument of the gospel appears to unfold. However, it often comes as a surprise that these three gospels report Peter's understanding of just who Jesus is in three quite different ways.

In Mark's Gospel Jesus' words and works have led to this crucial question: "Who do you say that I am?" Peter replies: "You are the Christ" (Mark 8:29). At this stage of our journey through the gospels together, it does not come as a surprise to us that Peter's reply is so brief. We have looked at this passage in Mark's Gospel on two occasions. However, it must be admitted that we would generally say that "the Gospel" has Peter making a much longer confession. It is important, however, that we ask: "Which gospel?" Such a confession is not found in Mark. In fact, this gospel has Jesus insist that the disciples are not to tell anyone about him (verse 30). It appears that Peter's confession that Jesus is the Christ may not be the whole story. Jesus then proceeds:

> And he began to teach them that the Son of man must suffer many things, and be rejected by the elders and the chief priests and the scribes, and be killed, and after three days rise again. (8:31)

Notice that Jesus is not speaking of the normally expected Messiah figure, but of something quite different: a suffering figure. Mark then goes on to add: "And he said this plainly" (verse 32). The evangelist Mark has Peter confess his faith in Jesus as the Messiah, but this confession needs clarification. The messiahship of Jesus can be understood only in terms of his being a suffering Son of Man. This is what has to be proclaimed plainly.[14]

Turning to Matthew's version of this famous scene at Caesarea Philippi, we find that Jesus poses the question a little differently, as the Son of Man title is present from the

14. For more detail on this issue, see above, pp. 48–52, and especially Kingsbury, *The Christology of Mark's Gospel*, pp. 91–102. Kingsbury's further consideration of Mark's use of "the Son of man" is most helpful. See, on this, ibid., pp. 157–79.

very start. When asking of the opinion of "men", Jesus asks: "Who do men say the Son of man is?" (Matthew 16:13). After receiving an answer that fails because it is purely in terms of precursor figures, he poses the question to Peter, as did Mark's Jesus: "But who do you say that I am?" (verse 15). This time there is no shadow in Peter's answer. We have one of the most complete confessions of faith that can be found in the Synoptic Gospels: "You are the Christ, the Son of the living God" (verse 16). In this way, the evangelist Matthew has gone farther than his source, Mark, and here we find a series of christological titles gathered together: the Son of Man, the Christ, the Son of God. Little wonder that this confession is then followed by Jesus' blessing of Simon bar Jonah, who has been open to such a revelation from heaven (verses 17-19). It is important to notice, however, that this blessing, and Simon's installation as Peter, the rock, is *only found in Matthew*. We have already seen that there is no trace of it in Mark. Thus, we find in Matthew's Gospel that Peter answers with a full and blessed understanding of Jesus.

However, Jesus then proceeds to tell of his oncoming passion, in terms taken from Mark 8:21 (Matthew 16:31). As in Mark, Peter refuses to accept this, and is cursed as a hindrance (verses 22-23). Matthew has taken his Marcan account, and rewritten it to make Peter's confession a complete confession of the messiahship and divine sonship of Jesus, but he still shows that Peter hesitates when faced with the further element in Jesus' destiny: suffering.[15]

In Luke's Gospel there is no mention of Caesarea Philippi. There is an important indication that Jesus was at prayer and that his disciples were with him (Luke 9:18). The setting of the scene within the context of the praying Jesus is significantly

15. As I have already indicated above (see note 18, p. 141), this structure: a confession, followed by a blessing—a further statement about the person of Jesus, followed by a curse, is the work of a skilful evangelist. See, on this, J. P. Meier, *Matthew*, New Testament Message 3 (Wilmington, Michael Glazier, 1980), pp. 178–86. We have already seen (see above pp. 136–141) that Peter's response to Jesus embodies the hesitant faith that is a mark of the disciples in the Gospel of Matthew.

Lucan, as most major moments in Luke's Gospel are surrounded by prayer.[16] The reader is thus advised of the significance of the moment that follows, as Jesus questions his disciples: "Who do you say that I am? And Peter answered, "The Christ of God" (verse 20). As in Mark, this confession is followed by Jesus' prophecy of the need for the Son of Man to suffer (verse 22), but Peter does not object in any way. In fact, the narrative moves on, strongly insisting upon the need for a disciple to go down the way of the Son of Man (verses 23-27), leading into the transfiguration, where the sonship of Jesus is so clearly announced (9:35). After the descent from the mountain, Jesus heals the epileptic boy, and the section ends: "And all were astonished at the majesty of God" (verse 43). It is obvious that this section of Luke's Gospel is marked by a deliberate teaching of the full significance of Jesus: The Christ of God, the Son of Man, the chosen Son of God, the revelation of God's power, the one who calls others to follow him down his way. By this stage of the gospel, there is a clear indication to the disciples just who it is they were following, as in 9:51 a dramatic turn takes place in the narrative: "When the days drew near for him to be received up, he set his face to go to Jerusalem". The disciples find this very puzzling, but they are not shown as failing, as they are in Mark's Gospel. Luke is more gentle and easier in his dealing with the disciples' failure.[17]

What has been the point of this exercise? What *Dei Verbum* referred to as something that Jesus did and taught is at the source of all three versions of this famous confession scene. Yet, how differently each evangelist has used it. Already at the very beginnings of our Christian tradition there was a

16. On this, see especially the fine work of L. Monloublou, *La Prière selon Saint Luc. Recherche d'une Structure*, Lectio Divina 89 (Paris, Editions du Cef, 1976). See also S. S. Smalley, "Spirit, Kingdom and Prayer in Luke–Acts", *Novum Testamentum* 15 (1973), pp. 59–71.

17. Again, these are themes that we have already discovered in our study of Luke's Gospel: see above, pp. 82–84. See further the concise but accurate description of Edwards, *Luke's Story of Jesus*, pp. 48–53. See further, Schweizer, *The Good News According to Luke*, pp. 155–64.

deeply felt presence of a guiding, teaching Spirit (see John 16:12-15). It is this dynamic, Spirit-filled growth of the *tradition* that has given us a fourfold Gospel. The gradual growth of the church's own experience, and the growing needs of the church's preaching caused the earliest church to look back continually to its foundational event: the experience of Jesus. They saw, however, that this had to be told and retold, "in many and various ways". These many and varied ways in which the story is told and retold were concerned not only with minor details, such as geography or chronology, but touched the central issue of Christianity itself: "Who do you say that I am?"

The fourth gospel does not have a scene at Caesarea Philippi. However, after the multiplication of the bread and fishes (6:1-15), Jesus' revelation of himself on the waters to his disciples as "I am he" (verses 16-21) and the discourse on the true bread from heaven (verses 22-59), a critical moment in John's story of Jesus occurs.[18] "Many of his disciples" (verse 60), despite the special revelation that only they had had in verses 16-21, leave Jesus because of the difficulty of his "word", his revelation. Jesus then asks if his immediate disciples, the Twelve, will also leave him. This is a dramatic moment for the story, and also an important issue for the theological argument of the fourth gospel. For the first time in the gospel a "decision" is made about the revelation of Jesus. No doubt reaching back to the same tradition that stands behind Mark, Matthew and Luke, Peter replies:

Lord, to whom shall we go? You have the words of eternal life; and we have believed, and have come to know, that you are the Holy One of God. (John 6:68-69)

We saw earlier that the Council Fathers themselves experienced a remarkable growth of understanding and a

18. This is not the place to delve into the complexities of the structure and theology of this section of the fourth gospel. For some indications, see above, pp. 181–182. For a full discussion of John 6, the various theories of composition, its structure and meaning, see Moloney, *The Johannine Son of Man*, pp. 87–123.

similarly remarkable development in their expression of this renewed understanding through their long and tedious work on the conciliar document on Revelation. Our brief analysis of the confession of Peter in the gospel traditions shows us that they were treading a well-used path. Some of the most central confessions of faith in Jesus of Nazareth as Messiah, Son of Man and Son of God were forged in the early church. The various communities of faith had a similar experience to the Council Fathers. They too looked back to the word and person of Jesus of Nazareth, through the light of his resurrection and guided by the presence of his Spirit, they sought to speak and write of the mystery of his person. Here, of course, we find the common element in both experiences: a Spirit-directed use of traditions to forge an authentic word of God; in the Scriptures and in the magisterial teaching of an ecumenical council.

Of course, to plot a passage through the discussions and difficulties that dogged the ancient church until we reach Chalcedon would show us that the journey went a lot farther; well beyond the confession placed on Peter's lips at Capernaum in the fourth gospel.[19] It would appear self-evident that the dynamism that is the result of the life of the Spirit did not desert the Lord's church at the Council of Chalcedon in 451.

(b) Mary of Nazareth

It is well known that the Pauline literature devotes very little time and attention to the "life of Jesus", as the Pauline Gospel is so strongly centred upon his death and resurrection. We do learn, however, that Jesus was "born of a woman, born under the law" (Galatians 4:4). Similarly, the Gospel of Mark, which has no infancy narrative, tells that Jesus was the son of Mary (Mark 6:3). Naturally, there are various interpretations among scholars of the importance of these brief references,

19. For an accurate and very readable survey of this period, see F. Young, *From Nicaea to Chalcedon. A Guide to the Literature and its Background* (London, SCM Press, 1983). See also J. N. D. Kelly, *Early Christian Doctrines* (London, A. & C. Black, 1968).

but we can claim with certainty that our earliest written traditions assert *the fact* that Mary was the mother of Jesus.[20]

The next development in the growth of the church's written tradition were the gospels of Matthew and Luke. They both have stories of the infancy of Jesus, although they have very different stories. It is obvious that the Lucan story is full of joy and peace, dominated by the figure of a Virgin Mother, while in Matthew 1-2 she never appears in the first person.[21] Matthew's Gospel also carries the seemingly negative Marcan passage about Mary, the mother of Jesus (Matthew 13:55; see Mark 3:31-35), and many have argued that there is no development of the early church's Marian thought in Matthew. I would personally suggest that the use of the women figures in the Matthean genealogy of Jesus (Matthew 1:1-17) is deliberately employed to indicate women who had fearlessly accepted God's ways in his salvation history, no matter what it may have cost them (Tamar, Rahab, Ruth and Bathsheba). This list of courageous women comes to its climax in Mary, "of whom Jesus was born, who is called Christ".[22]

Mary plays a central role in the whole of the Lucan story. In the infancy narrative she is the perfect *anawim* figure: totally open to the strangeness of God's ways, despite a lack of understanding, yet singing God's praises for doing such wonderful things for her. But the story of Mary is carried further in Luke's Gospel. Twice during the public ministry of

---

20. For an attempt to gain a great deal of Mariological material for this section, see M. Miguens, *The Virgin Birth. An Evaluation of the Scriptural Evidence* (Westminster, Christian Classics, 1975), pp. 6–37. For a less optimistic view, see R. E. Brown and others (eds), *Mary in the New Testament* (London, Geoffrey Chapman, 1978), pp. 33–72.

21. For a brief discussion of the two narratives, and the importance of their differences, see Moloney, "The Infancy Narratives. Another View of Raymond Brown's *The Birth of the Messiah*", pp. 161–6. See also the general introduction to the infancy narratives above, pp. 93–98. For a further study of the Matthean infancy story, see my study, "The infancy narrative in Matthew", in H. McGinlay (ed.), *The Year of Matthew*, pp. 1–9.

22. On this, see Moloney, *Woman: First Among the Faithful*, pp. 33–9.

Jesus she is presented as the model of the perfect disciple who hears the word of God and lives by it, just as she had done at the annunciation and at the birth of Jesus (see Luke 8:19-21 and 11:27-28). At the beginning of the story of the church, as Luke tells it in his second volume (known to us as the Acts of the Apostles), we find that this place of honour in the order of faith and discipleship is further developed. As the earliest church gathered in prayer, awaiting "the promise of the Father" (Acts 1:4), Luke records: "All these with one accord devoted themselves to prayer, together with the women, and Mary the mother of Jesus, and with his brothers" (1:14). This may be a hint of a theme that is fully developed in the fourth gospel: Mary as the mother of the disciple, and thus as Mother of the church.[23]

In the fourth gospel the mother of Jesus is never called "Mary". She is "woman" and "mother". As we have seen both in our general study of the fourth gospel, and in our analysis of the Cana to Cana section of this gospel, the Mother of Jesus initiates the public ministry of Jesus at the first Cana miracle (John 2:1-11), and associates both her son and herself with "the hour", which has not yet come (2:4). The same themes emerge in 19:25-27 at the cross where, according to the Johannine view of things, "the hour" takes place (see 12:23; 13:1; 17:1).[24]

There is another scene in the fourth gospel where "a mother" plays an important role. In 16:21-24 the fourth evangelist uses the image of a woman, who, through her receptivity, suffers the pains of childbirth *now*, but who, through the coming of a man into the world, *afterwards* comes to great joy. This image is used as Jesus instructs his disciples how they must suffer the pain of his departure *now*, to eventually come to a joy that nobody can take away from them *afterwards* (verse 22). Themes present in the scenes of

23. For a fuller discussion of the Lucan Marian material, see Moloney, *Woman: First Among the Faithful*, pp. 40–56.

24. See, on the theme of "the hour", Moloney, *The Word Became Flesh*, pp. 101–11.

Cana and of the cross of Jesus reappear: "the hour", "woman", disciples and the theme of motherhood, even though the actual term "mother" does not appear. Perhaps John is leading his reader from the hour that has not yet come in 2:4 to the consummation of the hour in 19:27.[25]

At the cross, the "mother" of Jesus becomes the "mother" of the disciple. No doubt the main theme of the scene is ecclesial: the union between the believer (the Mother of Jesus) and the disciple (the Beloved Disciple). Yet in three verses the term "mother" appears five times. The relationship that once existed between Jesus and this woman (2:1-11, the Mother of Jesus) now exists between the disciple and this woman (19:27a, "Behold your Mother"). This is the point of 19:27b, "And from that hour the disciple took her to his own home." In a cross scene dominated by a theology of the newly born church, the Mother of Jesus is clearly being presented as the Mother of the church.[26]

It should now be amply clear that there is a wonderful growth of understanding—within the pages of the New

25. For the sake of completeness, it should be noted that there is a small number of scholars who would claim that John 1:13 should read in the singular: "He who was born, not of the will of the flesh . . ." As such this would be a further Johannine Marian passage. It was the text produced in the original Jerusalem Bible, but has now been changed to the more probable plural in the New Jerusalem Bible. The case has been recently argued with much vigour on textual, structural and theological grounds by I. de la Potterie, "La Mère de Jesus et al conception verginale du Fils de Dieu", *Marianum* 40 (1978), pp. 41–90, and idem "Il parto verginale del Verbo incarnato: 'Non ex sanguinibus . . . sed ex Deo natus est' (Gv 1,13)", *Marianum* 45 (1983), pp. 127–74. One of the strong thrusts of de la Potterie's contribution has been his contention that the fourth evangelist's insistence on the term "mother" is closely connected with the Johannine theology of the incarnation. While this may be a part of it, it appears to me that the theme of "mother" may reach wider. My suspicions about the use of "the woman" in John 16:21-24 would indicate this. They come to me from the suggestions of Y. Simoens, *La gloire d'aimer*, pp. 163–7.

26. See, on this, the fine reflections of E. C. Hoskyns and F. N. Davey (eds), *The Fourth Gospel*, pp. 526–37. For a fuller discussion of the Johannine Marian material, see Moloney, *Woman: First Among the Faithful*, pp. 87–92.

Testament itself—of who the Mother of Jesus was in God's plan of salvation. From the earliest recognition that Mary was Jesus' mother through to the fully developed theological idea of Mary as Mother of the church, a complete understanding was not always available to the people who lived with her or who later looked back in memory of her. Eventually the dynamism of the tradition came closer and closer to the truth: a part of that journey is witnessed to in the New Testament.

As with Jesus, so also with Mary, the discussions and the growing consciousness of the person and place of Mary in the Divine economy went on apace, until some crucial decisions were made at Ephesus in 431.[27] Naturally, Ephesus was not the end of that story either, as the Second Vatican Council again demonstrates. *Lumen Gentium*, 52-69 is the most copious Marian statement ever to be made by an ecumenical council.[28]

III. Conclusion

I have attempted to show that the experience of the Council Fathers has beautifully matched the experience of the early church, as *both* attempted to blend Scripture and tradition to express the inexpressible. Many contemporary Christians find this exciting, but not all appreciate the dynamism that is so much a part of the Christian tradition. Thus, a certain polarisation has taken place over these issues since the council.

The document sent to the bishops of the world in preparation for the special synod on the council in 1985 seemed to show an awareness of the crucial importance of this matter. After

27. For a good general survey of the development of Marian doctrine, see H. Graef, *Mary: A History of Doctrine and Devotion* (London, Sheed & Ward, 2 vols, 1963).

28. For a fine survey of contemporary Mariology, see A. J. Tambasco, *What are they saying about Mary?* (New York, Paulist Press, 1984).

some general observations and questions, the preparatory commission for the synod asked some specific questions. The very first "specific question" asked was: "In what way has the Constitution *Dei Verbum* been understood and applied?" From the richness of the conciliar and biblical reflections that we have shared, it is obvious that the challenge of the council still has to be met.

The experience of the Spirit, which can be sensed so powerfully through the dynamic growth of our Christian tradition in the formative days of the apostolic church, has led the church through the highways and the byways that took it to a Second Vatican Council. That same Spirit has led beyond the council to the special Synod of 1985. It is important that the church as a whole comes to appreciate, in our own time, the dynamic growth in our understanding and explanation of the mystery of God's ways among us which is the result of the interplay between lived tradition and written word.

It is our openness to the ever new and ever strange ways of our God that we can all play our part to ensure that the authentic teaching of an Ecumenical Council will not go astray:

> God, who spoke in the past, continues to converse with the spouse of his beloved Son. And the Holy Spirit, through whom the living voice of the Gospel rings out in the Church—and through her in the world—leads believers to the full truth, and makes the Word of Christ dwell in them in all its richness. (*Dei Verbum* 8).

Index
of Biblical
References

MATTHEW	PAGE
1-2	128
1-2	132
1-2	136
1-2	136
1-2	239
1:1-17	74
1:1-17	128
1:1-17	239
1:18-25	93
1:18-25	104
1:21	150
1:22-23	128
1:22-23	130
1:23	158
2:1-12	72
2:1-12	93
2:1-4:22	137
2:2	120
2:5-6	128
2:5-6, 15	130
2:8	120
2:9	104
2:9-11	107
2:11	120
2:12	110
2:13-15	7
2:13-23	93
2:14-15	132
2:15	7
2:15, 17-18, 23	128
2:16-18	132
2:17-18, 23	130
3:3	128
3:3	130

3:13-17	128
3:14-15	130
3:17	150
4:6-7, 14-16	128
4:6-7, 14-16	130
4:9-10	120
4:18	140
4:23-25	137
4:23-25	138
5-7	134
5-7	135
5-7	137
5:1	119
5:1-2	4
5:1-2	135
5:1-48	142
5:1-7:28	4
5:1-7:28	5
5:1-7:28	7
5:1-7:28	67
5:1-7:29	133
5:1-9:34	137
5:17	135
5:17-18	123
5:17-18	124
5:17-18	125
5:17-18	126
5:17-18	130
5:17-48	8
5:18	156
5:21-22	135
5:27-28	135
5:31-32	135
5:33-34	135
5:38-39	135

5:43-44	135
5:48	5
5:48	133
5:48	135
6:30	139
7:28	4
7:28	135
7:28-29	133
8-9	137
8:2	120
8:5-13	124
8:10-12	124
8:25	150
8:26	139
9	137
9:17	142
9:18	120
9:35	137
9:35	138
9:35-38	138
9:36-38	138
10	138
10:1	138
10:1-11:1	133
10:5-6	123
10:5-6	124
10:5-6	125
10:5-6	130
10:40-42	133
11:2-12:50	133
13:2-53	133
13:27	133
13:52	143
13:53-54	133
13:55	239

Ref	Page	Ref	Page	Ref	Page
14:22-33	141	27:54	150	3:13-14	32
14:30	150	27:54	152	3:13-14	37
14:31	139	27:54	153	3:13-14	53
14:33	120	27:55-61	154	3:13-19	31
14:33	150	27:55-56, 61	154	3:13-19	57
15:15	140	27:57	198	3:14	31
15:21-28	124	27:62-66	154	3:19	31
15:24	123	27:62-66	156	3:19	48
15:24	124	28:1-10	154	3:20-22	30
15:24	125	28:1-15	119	3:20-25	30
15:24	130	28:2-3	127	3:21	31
15:25	120	28:2-3	155	3:22	31
16:5-39	48	28:7	155	3:22-30	31
16:8	139	28:9	120	3:29	31
16:8, 11-12	139	28:11-15	156	3:31	31
16:13	235	28:15	156	3:31-35	30-31
16:13-20	58	28:16-20a	118-123	3:31-35	78
16:13-23	140	28:16-20a	157	3:31-35	239
16:15	235	28:16-20	118	3:35	31
16:16	129	28:16-20	122	4:1-25	78
16:16	140	28:16-20	126	4:1-34	31
16:16	150	28:16-20	130	4:11-12	231
16:16	235	28:17	120	4:35-5:43	31
16:16, 22	140	28:17	121	4:41	29
16:17-19	140	28:18	157	4:41	32
16:17-19	235	28:19a	121	4:41	49
16:21-22	140	28:19a	157	5:1-20	28
16:31	235	28:19b	121	5:1-43	78
17:4	140	28:19b	157	5:7	28
17:5	150	28:19	153	5:21-43	28
18:1-35	133	28:20a	157	6:1-6	75
18:21	140	28:20a	158	6:2	31
18:26	120	28:20b	157	6:3	238
19:1	133	28:20	122	6:4-6	31
19:3-12, 16-22	130	28:20	132	6:6-13	32
19:7	132	28:20	146	6:6-13	78
19:16	58	28:23	130	6:14-29	32
19-20	70			6:30	32
19:27	140			6:30	49
20:20	120			6:31-44	32
22:24	132	**MARK**	**PAGE**	6:31-44	33
23:8-10	136	1:1	6	7:1-5	33
24-25	134	1:1	18	7:6-23	33
25:31-46	134	1:1	28	7:21-8:10	38
26-28	136	1:1-13	28	7:24-30	125
26:1	134	1:1-13	71	7:27-28	33
26:56	154	1:1-13	94	7:28	125
27:24-26	154	1:13	28	7:31	32
27:32-44	148	1:14-15	97	7:31-37	32
27:32-28:20	147	1:14-3:6	110	7:37	32
27:32-28:20	145	1:15	28	8	13-18
27:34	149	1:16-20	28	8	96
27:35	149	1:16-20	31	8:1	14
27:35, 43	148	1:16-20	51	8:1-10	32
27:36	150	1:16-20	60	8:1-10	33
27:36	151	1:16-20	77	8:1-10	44
27:37, 42	150	1:16-3:6	77	8:6	14
27:38	149	1:21-28	28	8:11-13	44
27:39	148	1:24	28	8:14	14
27:39-44	150	1:27	29	8:15	14
27:39, 41, 44	149	1:29-31	28	8:15-17	14
27:40	153	1:32-34	28	8:16-17	139
27:43	149	1:40-45	28	8:17	45
27:43	150	2:1-3:6	29-30	8:17	62
27:45	151	2:13-14	31	8:18	13
27:45, 51-53	127	2:13-17	57	8:18	14
27:45, 51-53	130	2:20	29	8:21	235
27:46	151	2:21-22	30	8:22	15
27:51-53	127	2:22	142	8:22	48
27:51-54	152	3:6	29	8:22-23	235

Reference	Page
8:22-26	16
8:22-26	33
8:22-26	44
8:22-26	45
8:22-26	48
8:22-26	62
8:22-10:52	17
8:22-10:52	33-34
8:22-10:52	43-63
8:22-10:52	45-46
8:23	48
8:24	14
8:24	15
8:24	48
8:25	15
8:25	48
8:26	48
8:27-26	49
8:27-29	15
8:27-33	49
8:27-33	53
8:27-33	60
8:27-9:22	48-52
8:27-10:45	62
8:28	15
8:29	15
8:29	49
8:29	234
8:30	15
8:30	49
8:30	234
8:31	34
8:31	43
8:31	51
8:31	234
8:31-32	50
8:32	16
8:32	234
8:32-33	40
8:33	51
8:33	61
8:34	18
8:34	34
8:34	47
8:34	51
8:34-9:1	16
8:34-9:1	51
8:34-9:1	61
8:37-38	18
8:41	15
8:46-52	33
9:1	9
9:1	51
9:2	14
9:2-8	17
9:2-8	18
9:2-8	52
9:6	52
9:7	17
9:7	52
9:8	52
9:9-13	52
9:10	52
9:24	52
9:29	52
9:30	52
9:30-32	39
9:30-37	79
9:30-10:31	52-61
9:31	34

Reference	Page
9:31	43
9:31	44
9:31	53
9:32	53
9:33-50	54
9:34	40
9:34	53
9:35	34
9:35	53
9:35-37	47
9:37	54
9:38-41	54
9:38-48	54-55
9:42	54
9:45	53
10	70
10:1	55
10:1-31	55-57
10:2	55
10:3-4	55
10:5-8	55
10:9	55
10:13	84
10:13-16	56
10:16	56
10:16-21	57
10:17	58
10:17-22	56
10:21	57
10:22	58
10:23	58
10:25	59
10:26-27	59
10:29-30	59
10:31	59
10:32	39
10:32	60
10:32	43
10:32-33	44
10:32-33	34
10:32-34	59-62
10:33-34	60
10:35-36	61
10:35-37	34
10:35-37	40
10:37	60
10:38	34
10:38-39	61
10:41	34
10:41	61
10:42	34
10:45	47
10:45	62
10:46	62
10:46-52	44
10:46-52	46
10:46-52	62-63
10:47	62
10:49	62
10:52	63
11:9-10	35
11:11	35
11:11	85
11:12-26	35
11:15	85
11:27	85
11:27-12:43	29
12:1-12	30
12:1-12	35
12:13-17	35

Reference	Page
12:18-27	35
12:28-34	35
12:35-37	36
12:38-44	36
12:43	36
13	9
13	11
13	145
13:1-23	36
13:10	36
13:13	36
13:24-37	36
13:32	36
13:33	36
13:37	36
14:17-21	37
14:22-26	36
14:27-31	37
14:28	41
14:34	38
14:36	39
14:36	61
14:37	38
14:38-39	38
14:50	37
14:50	38
14:50	39
14:50	40
14:50-52	16
14:51-52	37
14:51-52	39
14:53-16:8	44
14:58	35
14:58	38
14:61-65	38
14:66-72	40
15:1-20	38
15:22-32	148
15:29	35
15:40-41	38
15:43	198
15:66-72	37
16:5	127
16:6	39
16:6	97
16:7	39
16:7	40
16:7	41
16:7	88
16:8	39-40
16:8	120
16:9-11	120
16:9-20	40
16:14	120
16:23	51

LUKE	PAGE
1-2	71
1-2	93-113
1-2	112
1-2	207
1:5-23	104
1:5-24	108
1:5-25	90
1:5-25	99
1:5-25	101
1:11	102
1:15	104

Reference	Page
1:17	104
1:23	99
1:24-25	102
1:26	102
1:26-38	99
1:26-38	101
1:26-38	108
1:31-35	102
1:32-33	111
1:32-33	113
1:34	111
1:35	103
1:35	104
1:35	111
1:38	99
1:39-56	99
1:39-56	101
1:41	104
1:41-45	104
1:42-45	102
1:46-55	102
1:56	99
1:57-80	99
1:57-80	101
1:60-64	102
1:63	109
1:66	100
1:66	109
1:67	104
1:67-69	102
1:67-80	109
1:76-79	104
1:80	104
1:80	100
2:1	105
2:1-5	72
2:1-7	71
2:1-7	105
2:1-20	104
2:1-21	99
2:1-21	101
2:1-21	103
2:1-21	105
2:2-3	106
2:4-7	106
2:7	104
2:7	106
2:8-14	108
2:8-20	104
2:9	108
2:11	113
2:12	106
2:13-14	102
2:14	106
2:14	108
2:15	108
2:16	107
2:16	108
2:16-17	109
2:18	109
2:18	111
2:18-20	109-111
2:19	100
2:19	113
2:20	102
2:21	109
2:21	112
2:22	100
2:22-38	104
2:22-40	99
2:22-40	102
2:25	104
2:26	104
2:27	104
2:27-35	102
2:28-32	72
2:29-32	112
2:34-35	103
2:38	104
2:38	100
2:39	100
2:40	104
2:41-50	99
2:41-52	102
2:41-52	112
2:49	110
2:50-51	111
2:50-51	112
2:50-51	100
2:51	113
2:51	100
2:52	105
3:1-3	103
3:15	74
3:20	103
3:22	105
3:22	74
3:23-38	105
4:1	74
4:1-13	74
4:3	103
4:9	103
4:14	105
4:14-15	75
4:16	76
4:16-30	75-77
4:17-21	75
4:22	76
4:23	76
4:23-24	74
4:25-30	75
4:25-30	76
4:30	77
4:31-41	76
4:31-44	103
4:41	76
4:44	57-58
5:1-11	77
5:1-11	77
5:4-8	77
5:10	77
5:12-26	77
5:33-6:11	5
6:13-16	78
6:17	9
6:17-19	5
6:17-49	67
6:17-49	135
6:17-49	78
6:20	109
6:20-26	78
6:20-49	78
7:1-10	124
7:1-10	78
7:11-17	104
7:11-17	103
7:13	103
7:19	78
7:21-23	78
7:24-30	78
7:36-50	78
7:36-50	104
8:1-3	78
8:1-3	88
8:1-3	104
8:1-3	78
8:14-18	78
8:19-21	110
8:19-21	240
8:19-21	78
8:22-36	103
8:28	78
9:1-6	79
9:7-9	48
9:10-27	235
9:18	79
9:20	87
9:20	103
9:20	236
9:20	79
9:21-27	236
9:22	236
9:23-27	103
9:31	79
9:35	87
9:35	236
9:35	79
9:37-43	236
9:43	79
9:43-45	44
9:44	79
9:46-48	79
9:49-50	69
9:51	80
9:51	90
9:51	104
9:51	236
9:51-14:35	81
9:51-19:44	82
9:51-19:45	70
9:51-19:48	80
9:52-10:20	83
9:57	69
10:1	103
10:13-15	81
10:25-37	84
10:38	69
10:38-42	84
10:38-42	104
10:39	103
10:41	103
11:1-13	83
11:1-13	84
11:13	83
11:27-28	110
11:27-28	240
11:37-52	82
12:1-12	83
12:22-34	83
12:33-40	83
12:41-48	83
12:42	103
12:51-53	83
12:51-13:9	82
13:10-17	104
13:22	69
13:23-25	82
13:31-33	81
13:34-35	81
14:16-24	82

Reference	Page	Reference	Page	Reference	Page
14:26-33	83	24:19	89	1:19-51	203
15	81	24:20	89	1:19-51	204-210
15:1-7	84	24:21	89	1:19-51	206
15:8-10	84	24:22-23	89	1:19-51	212
15:11-32	84	24:23	89	1:19-12:50	173-190
16:1-13	83	24:25-27	89	1:19-4:54	173
16:1-19:44	81	24:28-29	88	1:19-4:54	203-220
16:16	8	24:29-32	89	1:20	203
16:16	72	24:33	88	1:20-21	204
16:16	104	24:33	89	1:20, 25	174
17:11	69	24:36	88	1:21	203
17:22-18:9	83	24:36-37	120	1:21, 25	174
18:15	84	24:36-42	90	1:22	174
18:18	58	24:44-48	90	1:23	203
18:28-30	83	24:44-49	83	1:23	204
18:31	69	24:45-46	82	1:24-28	207
19:1-10	84	24:45-49	73	1:25	203
19:11	69	24:46-47	87	1:25-27	204
19:11-27	83	24:47-48	113	1:26	203
19:11-27	84	24:49	90	1:29	173
19:28	69	24:49	105	1:29	174
19:28-34	85	24:50	88	1:29	203
19:36-40	85	24:50-51	90	1:29	204
19:37	104	24:50-51	122	1:29-34	207
19:41	69	24:50-52	82	1:30	174
19:41-44	85	24:51	157	1:30	204
19:45	69	28:51	198	1:33	174
19:45-21	104			1:33	203
19:45-48	85			1:33	204
20:1-21:4	85			1:34	174
20:41	103	**JOHN**	**PAGE**	1:34	204
21:5-38	85	1:1	98	1:35	173
21:25-27	84	1:1	167	1:35	203
22:4-5	86	1:1	207	1:35	204
22:22-30	86	1:1-2	170	1:35-37	207
22:31-38	86	1:1-2	171	1:36	203
22:39-46	86	1:1-18	71	1:38	174
22:67	86	1:1-18	94	1:38	203
22:69	86	1:1-18	168	1:38	207
22:70	86	1:1-18	170-173	1:39	207
22:70	103	1:1-18	203	1:41	174
23:3-4	86	1:3-4	170	1:41	203
23:9-11	86	1:5	171	1:41-42	208
23:12	87	1:6-8	171	1:42	204
23:13-16	87	1:6-8	207	1:43	173
23:17-19	87	1:6-29	174	1:43	203
23:22	87	1:9-13	171	1:43	204
23:23-25	87	1:10-51	211	1:43-51	208
23:26	87	1:13	185	1:45	174
23:27-31	87	1:14	23	1:45	203
23:33	87	1:14	167	1:45	204
23:34	87	1:14	171	1:45	208
23:35	77	1:14, 16-17	210	1:45	209
23:35	87	1:15	171	1:46	208
23:37	87	1:15	174	1:46	209
23:38	87	1:15	207	1:46-48	204
23:39-41	87	1:16	171	1:48	208
23:42-43	87	1:16-17	189	1:49	175
23:44-45	87	1:16-17	210	1:49	194
23:46	87	1:17	171	1:49	203
23:47	87-88	1:18	167	1:49	204
23:49-24:12	104	1:18	172	1:49	209
23:50-56	88	1:19	168	1:49	211
24	104	1:19	172	1:50-51	175
24:1	88	1:19	174	1:50-51	205
24:4-8	88	1:19-23	207	1:50-51	209
24:5	146	1:19-51	173	1:51	175
24:10-11	120	1:19-51	176	1:51	203
24:13	88	1:19-51	179	1:51	204
24:13-35	120	1:19-51	189	1:54	211

249

Reference	Page	Reference	Page	Reference	Page
2:1	205	4:34	197	7:37-38	183
2:1	211	4:34	217	7:39	183
2:1-11	175	4:39-42	177	7:50-52	198
2:1-11	176	4:39-42	214	7:50-52	215
2:1-11	197	4:39-42	216	8:12	18
2:1-11	206	4:42	217	8:12	183
2:1-11	210	4:46	203	8:20	188
2:1-11	211	4:46	212	8:24	183
2:1-11	212	4:46-54	175	8:24, 28, 58	194
2:1-11	214	4:46-54	176	8:28	183
2:1-11	240	4:46-54	211	8:28	188
2:1-11	241	4:46-54	212	8:28	189
2:1-4:54	167	4:46-54	214	8:28	201
2:1-4:54	175-178	4:46:54	176	8:28	217
2:1-4:54	179	4:48	213	8:30	184
2:1-4:54	200	4:48	213	8:58	184
2:1-4:54	210	4:50	203	9	164
2:1-4:54	211-219	4:50	211	9	184
2:1-4:54	212	4:51-53	212	9:5	18
2:1-4:54	217	4:54	178	9:5	184
2:1-4:54	218	4:54	179	9:7	184
2:1-4:54	219	5-10	179	9:11	164
2:4	176	5:1	179-180	9:17	164
2:4	188	5:1-47	178-186	9:20-22	164
2:4	213	5:1-47	179	9:24	208
2:4	240	5:1-10:42	179	9:25-29	164
2:4	241	5:2-9a	179	9:28	135
2:4-4:54	213	5:9b	179	9:29	208
2:5	176	5:9b-10	121	9:29	289
2:5	213	5:16	179	9:31	208
2:6-10	213	5:17	179	9:33	164
2:11	205	5:17-18	180	9:34	164
2:12-22	214	5:18	180	9:35-38	164
2:13-21	176	5:18	179	9:39-41	184
2:23-25	214	5:19-30	180	10:1-18	184
2:23-25	217	5:26	219	10:22-29	185
3:1-2	198	5:31-47	180	10:22-42	185-186
3:1-2	214	5:36	186	10:30	121
3:1-10	176	5:45-47	237	10:30	185
3:1-10	214-215	6	181-182	10:31-39	185
3:1-21	214	6:1-15	179	10:31, 39	185
3:2	189	6:1-71	181	10:32	179
3:3, 5	194	6:4	181	11-12	188
3:3, 5	215	6:4	189	11-12	189
3:4	215	6:14-15	194	11:1-44	186
3:9	215	6:15	181	11:1-12:36	186-189
3:13	167	6:15	237	11:4	187
3:13-14	201	6:16-21	181	11:16, 50, 51	188
3:14	188	6:16-21	237	11:40	187
3:14	217	6:22-24	181	11:45-57	186
3:16	201	6:22-59	194	11:49-52	188
3:22-30	176	6:25-29	181	11:49-52	187
3:22-36	214	6:26	182	11:55	187
3:22-36	215	6:31	181	12	189
3:25-30	207	6:31	182	12:1	187
4:1-15	177	6:32-51b	186	12:1-8	187
4:1-15	214	6:40	237	12:9-11	188
4:1-15	215	6:46-51b	167	12:9-19	187
4:14	216	6:51c-58	168	12:12-16	188
4:15	216	6:51c-58	237	12:13, 15	194
4:16-26	177	6:60	183	12:17-19	188
4:16-26	214	6:62	182-185	12:19	188
4:16-30	216	6:67-69	183	12:20-22	188
4:21	188	6:68-69	179	12:20-26	187
4:23	188	7:1-9	183	12:23	188
4:27-30	214	7:1-10:21	182-185	12:23	240
4:31-38	214	7:1-10:21	183	12:24, 33	188
4:31-38	217	7:2	179	12:27	168
4:31-48	219	7:10-36	183	12:27	195
4:34	195	7:30	188	12:31-33	188

12:32	201	15:26	201	19:28-30	198
12:32	217	15:26-27	168	19:28-30	219
12:33	201	15:26-27	191	19:30	183
12:36b	168	15:26-27	232	19:30-34	184
12:36b	187	15:26-16:3	191	19:37	189
12:37-41	189	15:26-16:3	193	19:37	198
12:37-43	189	16	169	19:37	201
12:37-50	168	16:2	165	19:37	219
12:37-50	189-190	16:4-11	193	19:38-42	195
12:42	165	16:4-33	190	19:38-42	198-199
12:42-43	165	16:4-33	192	19:38-42	215
12:42-43	189	16:4-11, 31-33	191	20	200
12:44-50	190	16:7	201	20:1-2	199
13	37	16:7-11	168	20:1-31	199-200
13:1	168	16:7-14	191	20:2-3	200
13:1	182	16:12-14	168	20:2-10	197
13:1	191	16:12-15	231	20:2-10	200
13:1	193	16:12-15	237	20:11-18	200
13:1	219	16:13	232	20:11-18	199
13:1	240	16:13-15	201	20:13-15	200
13:1-30	190	16:21-24	193	20:16-17	200
13:1-38	37	16:21-24	240	20:17	82
13:1-17:26	82	16:22	240	20:18	200
13:1-17:26	190	16:31-33	193	20:19-22	200
13:1-17:26	192	16:33	190	20:19-23	199
13:1-17:26	193	17	169	20:21-23	199
13:1-20:31	168	17	192	20:24	199
13:1-20:31	190-200	17:1	240	20:24-29	199
13:18-20	193	17:1-5	191	20:24-29	200
13:19	37	17:1-5	193	20:25	200
13:19	194	17:1-5, 24-26	191	20:28	200
13-20	188	17:3	167	20:29	200
13:23	197	17:4	197	20:30-31	197
13:31-32	201	17:4	219	20:31	169
13:31-38	191	17:5	82	20:31	172
13:31-38	193	17:12-19	193	20:31	173
13:34-35	191	17:13	82	21	57
14:1-5	193	17:20-26	191	21	167
14:1-31	190	17:24-26	191	21:1-14	57-58
14:1-31	192	17:24-26	193	21:15-19	58
14:1-5, 30-31	191	18:1-11	194-195		
14:6	18	18:1-19:42	192-199		
14:15-17	191	18:3	194		
14:15-24	191	18:11	195		
14:15-24	193	18:12-27	195		
14:15-17, 26	168	18:15	195		
14:16-17	231	18:28	196		
14:16, 26	201	18:28-19:16	195-197		
14:26	232	18:29-32	196		
14:30-31	193	18:33-38a	196		
14:31	169	18:33-38a	195		
14:31	190	18:36	194		
15	169	18:38b-40	196		
15	192	19:1-3	196		
15:1-5a	193	19:1-3	197		
15:1-11	191	19:4-7	196		
15:5b-7	191	19:8-12	196		
15:8-11	193	19:13-15	196		
15:12, 17	191	19:16	196		
15:12-17	191	19:16	205		
15:12-17	193	19:17-22	197		
15:13	37	19:17-37	197-198		
15:13	182	19:18	197-198		
15:13	191	19:23-26	197		
15:13	219	19:25-27	195		
15:15b-7	193	19:25-27	197		
15:16	191	19:25-27	240		
15:18-21	191	19:27b	241		
15:18-21	193	19:27a	241		
15:22-25	193	19:27	241		

Francis J. Moloney was born in Melbourne, Australia, in 1940. Educated by the Sion Sisters, the Christian Brothers and at the University of Melbourne, he joined the Salesians of Don Bosco in 1960. From 1966-72 he studied in Rome, at the Salesian Pontifical University and at the Pontifical Biblical Institute, and was awarded a Licence in Sacred Theology and a Licence in Sacred Scripture. From 1972 to 1975 he carried out research at the University of Oxford, and was granted the degree of Doctor of Philosophy from that University in 1976. Since then he has taught Scripture at the Catholic Theological College in Melbourne, where he is head of the Biblical Studies Department, and at the Salesian Pontifical University, the Gregorian University and the Pontifical Institute 'Regina Mundi', as a visiting Professor. He is the author of numerous articles in *Salesianum*, *The Downside Review*, *New Testament Studies*, *The Journal for the Study of the New Testament*, *Biblical Theology Bulletin*, *The Australian Biblical Review*, *The Australasian Catholic Record*, *Compass* and is the author of a number of further books: *The Johannine Son of Man*, *The Word Became Flesh: A Study of Jesus in the Fourth Gospel*, *Disciples and Prophets: A Biblical Model for the Religious Life*, *Free to Love: Poverty-Chastity-Obedience*, *A Life of Promise*, and *Woman: First Among the Faithful: A New Testament Study*. He is also the translator and editor of a major study by Eugenio Corsini, *The Apocalypse: The Perennial Revelation of Jesus Christ*. In June 1986 he was appointed by Pope John Paul II to the International Theological Commission to the Holy See.